BELIEF AND RULE COMPLIANCE

Related titles

Managerial Decision-Making for Behavioral Economics

Market Insanity

A Fast and Frugal Finance

The Cognitive Basis of Institutions, 9780128120231

Smart Economic Decision-Making in a Complex World, 9780128114612

Decision-Making Management

Neuroscience of Preferences and Choice 2nd edition, 9780123814319

A Behavioral Approach to Asset Pricing, 9780123743565

Handbook of Reward and Decision Making, 9780123746207

Perspectives on Behavioral Economics and Economics of Behavior

BELIEF AND RULE COMPLIANCE

An Experimental Comparison of Muslim and Non-Muslim Economic Behavior

HAZIK MOHAMED

ABBAS MIRAKHOR

S. NURI ERBAŞ

ELSEVIER

ACADEMIC PRESS

An imprint of Elsevier

Academic Press is an imprint of Elsevier
125 London Wall, London EC2Y 5AS, United Kingdom
525 B Street, Suite 1650, San Diego, CA 92101, United States
50 Hampshire Street, 5th Floor, Cambridge, MA 02139, United States
The Boulevard, Langford Lane, Kidlington, Oxford OX5 1GB, United Kingdom

Library of Congress Cataloging-in-Publication Data
A catalog record for this book is available from the Library of Congress

British Library Cataloguing-in-Publication Data
A catalogue record for this book is available from the British Library

ISBN 978-0-12-813809-0

Publisher: Candice Janco
Acquisition Editor: J. Scott Bentley
Editorial Project Manager: Katerina Zaliva
Production Project Manager: Sojan P. Pazhayattil
Cover Designer: Mark Rogers

Typeset by SPi Global, India

CONTENTS

CHAPTER 1
Introduction

It is thus that man, who can subsist only in society, was fitted by nature to that situation for which he was made. All the members of human society stand in need of each other's assistance, and are likewise exposed to mutual injuries. Where the necessary assistance is reciprocally afforded from love, from gratitude, from friendship, and esteem, the society flourishes and is happy. All the different members of it are bound together by the agreeable bands of love and affection, and are, as it were, drawn to one common centre of mutual good offices.

Adam Smith in The Theory of Moral Sentiments II.ii.3.1 (1759)

1.1 BACKGROUND

In order to be prosperous, societies must be able to deal with 'social dilemma situations', where appropriate behaviour would be beneficial for everyone but where exploiting others can create even higher individual payoffs. Under such conditions, maximizing one's own utility can easily erode trust and deplete resources, leading to the 'tragedy of the commons' and free-rider problem that can be attributed to ill-defined property rights and imperfect information. Well-known examples that can arise out of poorly defined property rights are overfarming and overfishing. Free-riding (e.g. tax evasion) results from imperfect information, and environmental pollution and global warming seem to be a combination of the tragedy of commons and free-rider problems. Furthermore, weakly enforced property rights can also result in the tragedy of the commons, for example, the poorly policed territorial waters of Somalia resulting in overfishing and piracy. The breakdown of trust and cooperation and the failure of institutions to govern effectively can be seen as one of the critical causes of the global financial meltdown (de Larosière Group, 2009). As such, in order to achieve the vision of prosperity and progress for nations, mechanisms for ensuring trust, honesty, and cooperation are required. Cooperation and trust are important in reducing costs, inefficiencies, and waste of shared exhaustible resources.

Belief and Rule Compliance
https://doi.org/10.1016/B978-0-12-813809-0.00001-1

Social norms, including religious rules like Islamic tenets on property rights and preferred behaviour in uncertainty, provide a core to build around and self-enforce such mechanisms.

Modern economics, including neoclassical economics, however, in its attempt to instill ethics into economics as preferences or constraints relies on its own conceptions of reason and rationality, removing revelation as an authentic source for consideration. This part is missing in contemporary economics, where all economic goals are directed to the happiness of human beings in this world. A rational individual (in the neoclassical sense) is free to maximize his utility as much as possible without any moral, social, or religious commitment that involves a 'hereafter' reward and punishment of the consequences of economic choices and decisions made. Those aspects, instead, are constraints that will restrict an individual to maximize his utility. Islamic economics, on the other hand, utilizes and integrates both reason with revelation in choice selection and economic value application.

Mirakhor (2009) believes that, from an institutional perspective, "the ideal economy is composed of a collection of institutions – rules of conduct and their enforcement characteristics – designed by the Law Giver, prescribed in the metaframework (specified in the Qur'ān), and operationalized by the archetype model (the way the Messenger understood and implemented the rules) to deal with allocation of resources, production and exchange of goods and services, and distribution-redistribution of resulting income and wealth". He believes that the objective of these institutions is to achieve social justice (*qist*). Institutions specify rules that indicate what kind of conduct is most appropriate to achieving just results when individuals face alternative choices and must take action. Institutional development would mean moral, spiritual, and material development of the individual and society leading to maximum socio-economic welfare and the ultimate good of mankind. Hence, the legal, economic, and political institutions are the required infrastructure for continual balanced development. The impact of these rules of behaviour on growth and development can be analysed in terms of their effects on income and wealth distribution, resource allocation, savings, investment, and monetary stability within a society and its economic system.

In the recent past decades, our world has changed more quickly than ever. Globalization and technological leaps have made the world smaller with many systemic interdependencies, rapid connectedness, and much complexity. The nature and intensities of many 21st century problems are an immediate consequence of these realities. However, we lack a systematic framework to understand the world we have created, and many of our institutions are conceptually outdated. Despite (or possibly because of) all our great advances in science, technology, and financial innovations, many societies today are struggling with a shift in our new way of life. The presumptuous idea of an 'invisible hand' that was supposed to coordinate individual interests by self-organization and optimally self-regarding behaviour, as assumed by the standard microeconomic paradigm of the *economic man*, would create maximum social welfare. However, under many realistic conditions, at least one of the assumptions is not satisfied so that the welfare-optimal outcome is not guaranteed. This is, for example, the case if individuals interact in networks rather than through one homogeneous market or if externalities or transaction costs matter (Coase, 1960; Roca et al., 2012). Such conditions can lead to 'market failures'. The same applies to information asymmetries or cases with powerful monopolists (Akerlof, 1970) or oligopolists. It is therefore understandable that Thomas Hobbes (1991) pointed out that a selfish species would require regulation. The shocks to our economy like bank runs, financial turmoil, public spending crisis, and mass unemployment (particularly youth unemployment) that were previously thought as uncommon and whose cycles were few and far between today seem to have shorten, and they appear to occur more frequently. In response, markets have become more regulated, and societies have become more tense and 'suffocated'.

1.2 OBJECTIVES AND OUTLINE

The failure to understand the causes for the repeated cycles of financial crashes and debt crises continues to haunt the global financial system. Reinhart and Rogoff (2011) contend that the rocky road to defaults (and in most nations, serial defaults) lies in the human nature that makes flawed decisions, putting financial institutions, central banks, and sovereign nations into an economic spiral through overleveraging. They find that across time, place, cultures, institutions, and political systems, financial crises still happen, regardless of the monetary system (viz. gold standard, Bretton Woods, and current floating-rate system). As such, the root cause of these issues seems to be buried deeply in the human psyche and social behaviours. It would be invaluable to know specifics for countries and regions to really understand the mechanics of the processes behind their individual crises. Like Akerlof and Shiller (2010) know that managing these 'animal spirits' requires the steady hand of governance – simply allowing markets to work is not enough. In order to be able to dive into an in-depth analysis of default cycles and financial crises, we realize that classical economic theories and their models may be insufficient to the task. It would require the opening of the proverbial Pandora's box – these animal spirits and psychological fallibilities that are behind the thought processes that drives all decisions – the mysterious internal workings of human cognition and motivation that have been locked up in a 'black box' until recently.

In Chapter 2, we first explore the key economic concepts in classical theory in conjunction with the views from new institutional economics (NIE). The conflict arises between traditional and behavioural economics, where behavioural considerations remain missing from traditional assumptions that people behave rationally and as expected utility maximizers are examined closely. We attempt to systematize the manifold and multifaceted influences on the already complex institutions[1] via an institutional analysis framework developed by Williamson (2000). This is subsequently infused with the general rules of behaviour extracted from the Qur'ān and Sunnah, including the rules for exchange and market behaviour.

The study of behaviours (institutions) is often framed in terms of the structure of incentives. But the human response to the external structure of incentives (payoffs) is itself structured by the learned internal preferences and patterns of cognition. Institutions shape preferences and the external payoffs to different choices. If institutions are both formal rights and informal habits and include things ranging from money, language, contract laws, and constitutional rules, then we need a unit of analysis that can accommodate them all. That concept is the transaction. And game theory is a tool that is able to record transactions as 'observable data' to quantify the performance or outcome of the interaction of players.

The main objectives of the study are as follows:

1. To investigate the level of rule compliance in the members of a society using experimental games, specifically to the institutional rules that can be applied to the society as laid down in the Qur'ān and manifested in the Prophet ﷺ as reported in the Sunnah

[1] Here, institutions are defined as human relationships that structure opportunities via constraints and enablement, where a constraint on one person is opportunity for another (Schmid, 2004). Institutions can be viewed as networks of ordered relationships (connections) amongst people that define their rights, their exposure to the rights of others, their privileges, and their responsibilities. Institutions also enable individuals to do what they cannot do alone. They structure incentives used in calculating individual advantage. They also affect beliefs and preferences and provide cues to uncalculated action whilst providing order and predictability to human interaction.

2. To investigate how Muslims behave in real-life situations measured against what Islam prescribes to them as rules of conduct

The presumption is that since the rules were extracted from the Qur'ān and Sunnah, Muslims would have a higher level of adherence to these rules of behaviour.

Our study also examines the following:

1. To analyse the adherence of the selected rules of behaviours and if Muslims who believe in the Qur'ān and Sunnah would behave differently from non-Muslims.
2. To observe outcomes of transactions in various scenarios. The transaction can be used to conceptualize the formation of habits and ideologies, lawmaking, or setting up rules for governance.
3. To gain insight into changing preferences, rule compliance, and distinction of Islamic versus non-Islamic behaviour. Understanding human behaviours is at the very heart of improving institutional performance in a society.
4. To investigate if there is any co-relation to rule compliance with the background of participants. A full understanding of behaviours must include internalized rules versus external expected rules of behaviours by those of society or enforced by the economic, legal, and political institutions.

In order to operationalize those prescribed behaviours, there has to be a clear understanding of typical human behaviour. Chapter 3 presents a framework for understanding and using recent findings on human decision-making. It develops the four elements of the framework: the individualistic dimension, the social dimension, the mental frame dimension, and the divine dimension.

From a general sense of understanding in decision-making, a deeper understanding of financial decision-making is undertaken. Chapter 4 describes the fundamental heuristics, cognitive errors, and psychological biases that affect financial decisions and begins with the underlying concepts that explain such behaviours. Prospect theory provides better descriptions of choice behaviour than conventional models. This is especially true in a world of uncertainty, which characterizes decision-making in financial markets. Of particular importance is the introduction and development of the concepts of the differential treatment of losses and gains, emotive considerations, loss aversion, and reference points as key decision-making variables.

In Chapter 5, the background on game theory as a tool to analyse real-world behavioural transactions is introduced. We also determine explicitly the documented games that we have selected that are appropriate for testing of the rules we have selected. Also, to statistically control for religious effects, we use a priming instrument used by Shariff and Norenzayan (2007) to segregate the Islamic salient subjects from non-Islamic subjects via sentence-unscrambling task.

The experimental results will be tested for significance, in particular, for the significance of possible differences between Muslim and non-Muslim subjects in Chapter 6. The data will be analysed according to the players' information like age and income group, economic and educational background, and gender. In addition, background information into both countries where the experiments are carried out is also scrutinized; for example, ethnic and religious make-up, population growth, level of income, openness, macroeconomic and financial variables, formal institutional variables, and informal socio-economic variables will be used to act as external control variables. Such information will be useful to check the robustness of the experimental results.

Chapter 7 provides the insights into the influence of behavioural factors that can be mediated by the ability of institutions to contain and reduce aggregate results of human idiosyncrasies. We present broad aspects of policy recommendations that can be considered by any governing institution. The behavioural research in rule compliance explores behavioural approach applications and presents evidence of its use and effectiveness in the areas of fighting corruption and poverty and preserving the environment and depletable natural resources. With respect to financial applications, sections of the chapter dwell on corporate responsibility, financial market regulations, product innovation, and advantages of risk sharing in financial contracts.

Chapter 8 concludes the research by summarizing its findings and contributions. It then discusses the limitations of the study and future directions that can be taken to further such behavioural and experimental research in improving human decision-making behaviour.

CHAPTER 2
Theoretical Frameworks

It is in the admission of ignorance and the admission of uncertainty that there is a hope for the continuous motion of human beings in some direction that doesn't get confined, permanently blocked, as it has so many times before in various periods in the history of man.

Richard P. Feynman (1964)

2.1 NEOCLASSICAL ECONOMICS: CONCEPTS AND LIMITATIONS

In the neoclassical theory, the market is a normal, naturally established order that leads to automatically established economic equilibrium. So, the neoclassicists see the market as the ether in which the given individual preferences and intentions interact and become mutually connected, which results in the exchange of goods and services. At the same time, cooperation takes place without significant costs, that is, it is assumed that the market, as the organizational and coordination mechanism, is free of charge and that transaction costs are equal to zero or negligible. Also, they assert that the market exchange does not operate smoothly, but that the realization of an economic transaction assumes certain costs in connection with negotiating, requires time and resources, and poses a certain degree of risk and difficulties in its execution. The mainstream of neoclassical economics has been successful for a number of reasons. One reason is that it has strenuously pursued a division of labour, assigning itself two courses of action. Firstly, it has projected a pure institutional abstract conceptual model of the economy. Secondly, it has followed a research protocol that seeks unique determinate optimal equilibrium solutions to problems. In pursuit of both, it has assumed one or another version of rational behaviour and of competition. But actual markets are a function of the institutions that form and operate through them; the price mechanism operates only within and through these institutionalized markets. The research protocol seeking unique determinate optimal equilibrium solutions can only be successful by eliminating

Belief and Rule Compliance
https://doi.org/10.1016/B978-0-12-813809-0.00002-3

all variables and considerations that interfere with reaching its goal, variables, and considerations that operate in actual economies. In particular, the common assumptions of rational behaviour and competition tend, in practice, to exclude consideration of factors and forces that not only operate in but also tend to dominate actual economies. The two domains, therefore, that neoclassical economists tend to exclude are institutions and behaviour. Allan Schmid (2004) believes that these two domains are important parts of economics, and institutions and behaviour are both independent and dependent variables – or, as he puts it, from individual experience to institutions and back again. The lubricant that facilitates in both those domains is trust according to Kenneth Arrow (1975). He stresses that virtually, every commercial transaction has within itself an element of trust, certainly any transaction conducted over a period of time. Without trust, cooperation breaks down, investment stops, and markets stop working – for trust is our expectation that another person (or institution) will perform actions that are beneficial (or at least not detrimental) to us, regardless of our capacity to monitor those actions. Bowles and Gintis (2004) note that behaviours based on self-interested exogenous preferences and complete and costless contracting have come under critical scrutiny. First, social norms and psychological dispositions extending beyond the selfish motives of *homo economicus* may have an important bearing on outcomes, even in competitive markets. Second, market outcomes depend on strategic interactions in which power in the political sense is exercised. To them, it follows that economics must become more behavioural and more institutional.

Frydman and Goldberg note that a good forecasting economist not only uses quantitative methods but also studies history and relies on intuition and judgment. Those authors set out an alternative approach to prediction, in which the forecaster recognizes that his model will inevitably be less than perfect (Frydman and Goldberg, 2007) so the pursuit of precision in forecasting is a fallacy. This fact has been lost on some contemporary economists, who continue to pursue the perfect economic forecast despite abundant evidence that it does not, and cannot, exist.[1] They dismiss their repeated failures in much the same way that self-styled socialist planners once insisted that socialism was great but just needed to be carried out better.

[1]Frank Knight of 'Knightian uncertainty' from the 1921 book *Risk, Uncertainty and Profit*, noted that most business decisions involve a step into an unknown that is to some degree unmeasurable. Also, John Maynard Keynes observed that human decisions affecting the future, whether personal, political, or economic, cannot depend on strict mathematical expectation, since the basis for making such calculations does not exist.

In *Debunking Economics*, Steve Keen (2011) similarly argues that the theory of perfect competition is 'mathematically flawed' and that classical economists are using static methods to analyse dynamic problems. The complete failure of neoclassical economics to anticipate financial and credit crises also points to fundamental deficiencies in economic theory and puts neoclassical economists under public criticism and denigration. In rational expectation theory, a range of variables including inflation, interest rates, and growth should have a predictable impact on currency movements, but in practice, this theory has proved less useful for forecasting than tossing a coin. Predictions based on imperfect knowledge (or information) are doomed to have large errors. But when used creatively with experience, intuition, and other qualitative factors when making a decision, these forecasts may provide patterns of behaviour that are observable and somewhat predictable that though not perfect will often give a better clue to the future.

2.1.1 Rational Choice Model & Decision Theory

Rational choice theory starts with the idea that individuals have preferences and choose according to those. Individual decision-making forms the basis for nearly all of microeconomic analysis. In the standard view, rational choice is defined to mean the process of determining what options are available and then choosing the most preferred one according to some predetermined criteria. If policies were to be decided based on attaining the 'greatest good for the greatest number', they would need to find a utility index that could measure how beneficial different policies were to different people. On the other hand, thinkers following Adam Smith were trying to refine his ideas about how an economic system based on individual self-interest would work. Unfortunately, many economists have narrowed Smith as the author of the self-interest motive that is the basis of utility and profit maximization for the individual consumer and producer at any cost to society.[2]

[2]Perhaps the study of *An Inquiry to the Wealth of Nations (1776)* would have been more complete if it had included the study of *The Theory of Moral Sentiments (1759)* as its foundation, the way Smith must have wrote it. The *Theory of Moral Sentiments* explained social cohesion and ethical principles. Smith included the display of self-command as a virtue, which he saw guiding the moral propriety of action in respect of the other virtues and therefore moral autonomy. The four virtues particularly associated with Smith are prudence, justice, beneficence, and self-command. For him, prudence and justice provided the most important link between free markets and virtue. In many respects, the two publications, *The Theory of Moral Sentiments* and *The Wealth of Nations*, can be treated and read as two parts of one work.

Despite the attractions of the rational choice approach, its best-known criticism has been from empirical demonstrations that individuals often violate some of the rationality axioms, even in laboratory demonstrations or thought experiments and even when the subjects are expert decision makers or eminent decision theorists. For example, consider the ultimatum game. In this game, player 1 is given $100 and asked to split it with another anonymous person. Player 1, known as the proposer, offers $X to player 2 and keeps the remainder, $1-X. Player 2 either accepts or rejects the offer; if he rejects, they both get 0, and if he accepts, the proposer keeps $X and the responder $1-X. According to the rationality axioms, a rational responder will accept any offer greater than zero, as he would be economically better off at the margin since he started with nothing. Instead, laboratory experiments indicate that the modal offer is between $40 and $50 (see Camerer, 2003) and that offers below 20% are rare. The fundamental rationality assumption that people are self-seeking and care only about their own payoffs is violated because, in reality, choices are affected by relative payoff as compared with others and of feelings of equity, fairness, honour, justice, etc.

Rational choice theory's empirical failings in economics and psychology experiments have promoted an intense interest in new approaches. A wide range of alternative models have been advocated. Learning models, in which individuals make choices like those that have worked well for them in the past, have attracted particular attention from economic theorists and experimenters (Levin and Milgrom, 2004). Bounded rationality models include decision makers who have adopted rules that evolve slowly. Other models assume that people seek acceptance by imitating their peers, rely on intuition on heuristics, or make choices that are heavily influenced by their current emotional state. Recent research tries to identify the parts of the brain involved in decision-making and model how brain processes affect decisions. Still, others give up on modelling choice mechanisms and simply concentrate on measuring and describing what people choose.

2.1.2 Transaction Costs and Efficiency

Transaction cost economics (TCE) focuses on the organization of transactions that occur whenever a good or service is transferred from a provider to a user across a technologically separable interface. When transactions occur within an organization, the transaction costs can include managing and monitoring personnel and procuring inputs and capital equipment. The transaction costs of buying the same good or service from an external provider can include the costs of source selection, contract management, performance measurement, and dispute resolution. Thus, the organization of transactions, or 'governance structure', affects transaction costs (Williamson, 1989). Simple, short-term contracts involve customization that requires an exchange of information and terms of payment. For more complex customization, longer-term contracts may be required, including adjustment clauses to respond to contingencies over the life of the contract. When the goods or services cannot be well defined in advance, relational contracts may be used. These contracts focus on the terms of the relationship rather than the scope of work, which may be renegotiated as needed.

For many types of transactions, markets are the preferred governance structure because they provide 'high-powered incentives'. That is, the supplier reaps the full benefits or bears the full costs of its own activities and thus has a strong incentive to maximize value net of production costs and to respond quickly to changes in the market prices of inputs or outputs (Eggertsson, 1990). However, transaction cost economics argues that markets have difficulty dealing with some transactions because of asset specificity,[3] bounded rationality,[4] and opportunistic behaviour by the parties to the transaction. Since buyers and sellers can easily walk away from pure, spot-market transactions, they offer no protection against opportunism when transaction-specific assets are involved. Contracts offer some protection for transaction-specific assets by tying the buyer and seller together for a specified period. However, bounded rationality prevents comprehensive *ex ante* contracting that specifies how the parties will behave in all possible circumstances. If contracts are inherently incomplete, parties may perceive potential gains from opportunistic behaviour. As a result, attention must be focused on more complex (or internalized) governance mechanisms to fill gaps in the contract, settle disputes, and adapt to new conditions. Contracting parties may also make *ex ante* efforts to screen counterparties in terms of reliability or reputation (due diligence) and/or design *ex post* safeguards to protect transaction-specific investments.

When asset specificity, bounded rationality, and opportunism make contracting problems severe, vertical integration may be needed to ensure that the value of transaction-specific assets is internalized. It can also allow for flexible redeployment of assets and personnel when the conditions

[3]Asset specificity includes site/location, physical asset, human capital, capacity, and brand capital/reputation.

[4]The rationality of individuals is limited by the information they have, the cognitive limitations of their minds, and the finite time they have to make a decision.

surrounding the transaction change. However, bounded rationality limits the span of effective managerial or governance control. Managers and employees may engage in suboptimizing behaviour, or market players may have insufficient incentives to minimize production costs.

2.1.3 Property Rights and Their Dimensions

Economic, legal, and political institutions – the rules, laws, and customs that guide behaviour – help determine living standards around the world. Using conventional tools of the trade like cross-country regressions, instrumental variables, and more nuanced institutional economics methods, several well-cited studies[5] have asserted the importance of private property for economic growth. Taking this one step further, economist Hernando de Soto put forth the boldest and most articulate version of the property-right claim: "not only are stable, secure and well-defined property rights incidental to growth, but they are necessary for it". Similarly, Acemoglu and Johnson (2005) revealed that amongst these institutions, well-defined and enforced property rights are most important in shaping long-run economic growth and thus prosperity. In any economy, there are two key rules of the game: property-right institutions, which include safeguard against expropriation by the government, and contracting institutions, which assist private contracts between citizens. Acemoglu and Johnson found that, when property-right institutions protect people from expropriation (e.g. via high taxes, price controls, or outright confiscation), individuals can profit from investment in both physical and human capital. This investment produces higher rates of growth, which eventually yield much higher living standards. In contrast, the authors find that contracting institutions (such as those determining how difficult it is to resolve contractual disputes through the legal system) have little effect on measures of long-term prosperity. Instead, when contracting institutions are weak or flawed but property rights are protected, individuals seem to simply alter the terms of their contracts to avoid most of the adverse effects of such flaws. In contrast, the only sure way to avoid predation by the state in the face of weak property rights is to refrain from investing in the first place – which incurs poverty in the long run.

[5]Robert J. Barro, 1996. Determinants of Economic Growth: A Cross-Country Empirical Study. National Bureau of Economic Research, Working Paper No. 5698.See also Daron Acemoglu, Simon Johnson, and James A. Robinson, 2001. The Colonial Origins of Comparative Development. American Economic Review, vol. 91.Oliver C. Williamson, 2000. The new institutional economics: taking stock, looking ahead. Journal of Economic Literature, vol. 38.

2.2 FOUR LEVELS OF INSTITUTIONAL ANALYSIS FRAMEWORK

Before we can operationalize rules of behaviour as prescribed by the Qur'ān and Sunnah, the various influences over economic institutions, such as market behaviour, need to be structured so that an analysis can be carried out. These rules are subjected to influences that are manifold and complex. Fortunately, Williamson (1998 and later 2000) provides such a structure with four levels of institutional analysis to analyse complex institutions. The following includes a brief analysis of Williamson's framework:

Fig. 2.1 depicts the four stages in which an institution functions (according to the NIE framework) and the time it typically takes to change institutions at each stage. The first level is 'embeddedness'. It deals with

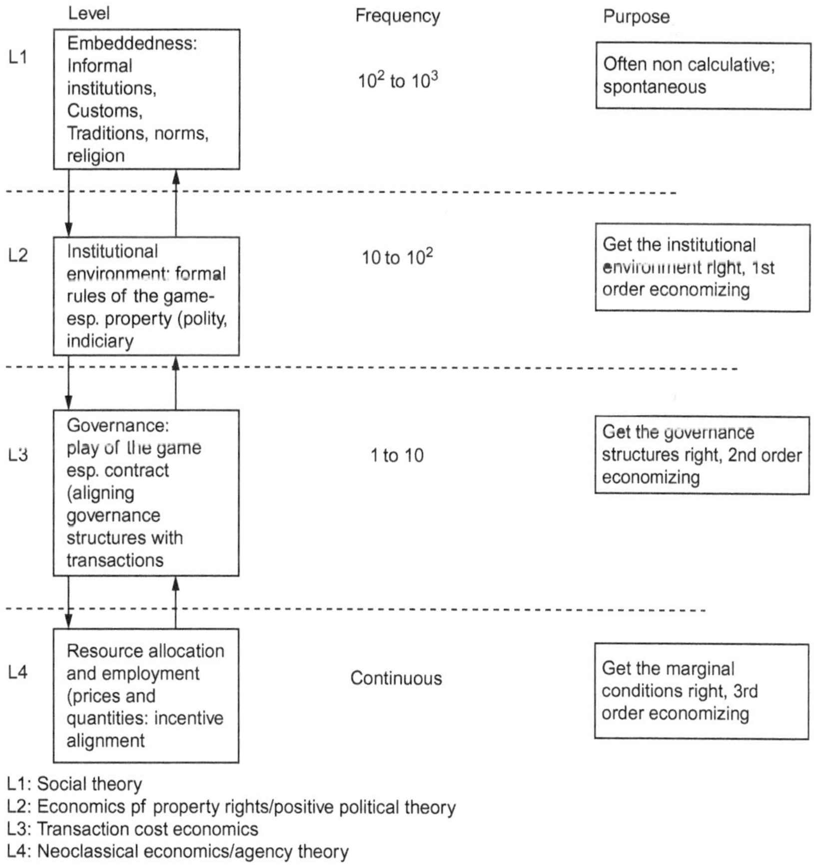

Fig. 2.1 Economics of institutions. *From Williamson, O.E., 2000. The new institutional economics: taking stock, looking ahead, J. Econ. Lit. 38 (3), 595–613.*

the informal constraints such as customs, taboos, and traditional norms that the institution (economic behaviour) is embedded in. Such informal constraints are usually present in a society for a long period, take centuries or millennia to change, and are believed to be spontaneous in origin. The second level refers to the institutional environment that human beings create through formal rules (e.g. constitutions, laws, and property rights). Institutions on this level tend to change faster than at the previous level, with a time frame of decades or centuries. The theoretical framework for this level is given by the economics of property rights, which implicitly assumes costless or easy enforcement of rights. However, this assumption has been disputed and rejected by the advocators of transaction cost economics (Williamson, 1998). As a consequence, level 3 deals with how the game is played or 'the governance of contractual relations'. Here, institutions of governance are discussed, including issues of contract definition and enforcement and conflict resolution mechanisms. The idea is that for each specific transaction, there exists an efficient, that is, transaction-cost-minimizing governance structure. Changes at this level take place within much shorter time than at levels 1 and 2 (1–10 years). The fourth level deals with economic activities and is concerned with getting the marginal conditions right. Neoclassical economics (where continuous adjustment of prices and quantities takes place to optimize marginal conditions) and theories of asymmetric information (including adverse selection and moral hazard problems) are located here. At this level, the incentives are formulated according to the combined effects of the other three levels.

Stages are interconnected with each other in the following manner (see Fig. 2.1). The arrows that connect a higher with a lower level signify that the higher level imposes constraints on the level immediately below. For example, it can be expected that the evidence of centuries-old archetype model management of the economy has a demonstrative role in changing the formal institutional environment (e.g. central banks and finance ministries) and its governance (play of the game) and incentive structures. The reverse arrows that connect lower with higher levels signal their cyclical feedback.

In the subsequent sections, that is, Sections 2.3.1–2.3.4, the four levels of institutional analysis are discussed as they relate to the Islamic economy and its institutions. Section 2.3.1 highlights the role of traditional informal institutions in Islamic economic management and its implications for the outcomes of current Islamic economics (level 1). The formal institutional environment (level 2) is discussed in Section 2.3.2, where detailed analyses of the evolution of property rights in respect to current Islamic economics are presented. Section 2.3.3 analyses the evolution of the current Islamic economic institution from the point of view of transaction costs (level 3). It also discusses more elaborately the issues of rule setting, monitoring, and enforcement within Islamic economic institutions. Section 2.3.4 deals with the fourth level of institutional analysis and focuses mainly on issues related to tenancy, incentive structures, and rule compliance amongst the different stakeholders under Islamic economics.

2.2.1 Social Theory – Embeddedness (Informal Rules of the Game)

Formal institutions are rules devised by human beings, which are socially recognized by everyone and are subject to sanction in case of violation. These rules can be modified or changed easily through legislation whenever there is need for change. Informal institutions are rules, norms, and customs that are typically being practiced for centuries. These rules, norms, and customs take a long time to change and are generally found to have a strong underpinning in the religion, culture, and tradition of a community that is common practice (Berger, 1999). In the case of economics, particularly Islamic economics, it is the historical imprint of the conventional economic system. The tradition of Islamic economics was only revived about 50 years ago, and the 'embeddedness' of the conventional system in Islamic societies today is widespread.

The main conflict that led to the differences between the mainstream economic theories and Islamic economic thought lies beyond *riba* (interest), *maysir* (gambling), and *gharar* (ambiguity). These conflicts are grounded in the very axioms that founded the respective economic theories (Table 2.1) (Mirakhor, 2009).

Table 2.1 Fundamental differences in conventional and Islamic economic axioms[a] (Mirakhor)

Conventional economics axioms	Islamic economics axioms
1. Scarcity	1. *Tauhid* (oneness of God)
2. Rationality	2. *Nubuwwa* (prophethood)
3. Self-interest	3. *Miqat* (accountability)

[a]It should be noted that the table depicts fundamental axiomatic differences between conventional and Islamic economic frameworks. It is not meant to be a line-by-line comparison but rather reassessed comparatively.

Allåh (s.w.t.) has created resources in due amounts that is sufficient to all His creations. The illusion of scarcity is due to several reasons (or transgressions) – unlimited wants, hoarding, poor distribution and coordination, uncooperative and selfish behaviours, etc., all of which is in contradiction to the teachings of Islam and the laws of the Sharī'ah. Instead, Islamic economics should be viewed as the study of sharing of risks and compliance to Islamic rules according to Qur'ān and Sunnah in order to achieve maximum utility on Earth and maximum rewards in the hereafter.

To sum up the discussion, informal constraints such as norms, culture, conventions, and code of ethics evolve over time in a society and are found to be more pervasive than formal rules. These informal institutions do not change immediately in reaction to changes in formal rules. As a result, they play an important role in structuring interactions amongst the users of conventional and Islamic economic systems. However, it can be observed that the resulting tension between changed formal rules and the persisting informal institutions may have implications for the overall socio-economic outcomes.

2.2.2 Institutional Environment (Formal Rules of the Game)

The manner in which people use environmental resources depends on the property rights governing these resources (Tietenberg, 1994). In particular, it has been argued that property rights, whether *de facto* or *de jure*, significantly affect the incentives individuals face, which ultimately determine the final outcome of resource management. It is argued that one of the reasons for the massive degradation of natural resources in developing countries is the lack of well-defined and secure property rights (Panayotou, 1993; Pearce and Warford, 1993). Mirakhor (2009) also presents these arguments as two important issues in market relations: (1) Property rights deter or eliminate the tragedy of the commons and provide incentives to invest; (2) they reduce uncertainty, which also increases incentives to invest in an orderly market. He added that these five pillars – (a) *property rights*, (b) *free flow of information*, (c) *trust*, (d) *contract*, and (e) *the rule of the right not to be harmed by others* – in combination reduce ambiguity and transaction costs and allow cooperation and collective action to proceed unhindered.

2.2.3 Governance of Contractual Relations (Play of the Game)

At this level, the analysis is concerned with the contractual relations (contract laws and enforcement) between the governments, institutions, and people. That is, it deals with how the formal rules are translated or enforced and its implications for different outcomes.

2.2.3.1 Rule Setting

The process of setting rules and regulations for resource use and management is an important issue, and rule setting typically involves complex and complicated procedures as there are layers of hierarchies in bureaucratic and government agencies involved in it. A broad framework is provided by the central government to the local governments under which all the local governments have to bring their own framework of resolution. Within the broad framework of rules and regulations provided by the central government, the local governments have further scope to implement their own resolution of rules and regulations, depending on their prevailing requirements and situations.

On the other hand, Islamic law, in theory, is not created by rulers or legislators but by God; its rules (the *Sharī'ah*) are deduced by legal scholars from the text of the Qur'ān and the words and actions of the Prophet Muhammad ﷺ. The Qur'ān provided broad rules through commandments, clear prohibitions, and declarations. Strictly speaking, what traditional Islamic courts enforced is not pure *Sharī'ah*, which is God's sublime law, but *fiqh*, or jurisprudence, the imperfect human attempt to deduce specificity from religious sources what the law should be at a particular situation or circumstance.

There exist possibilities for the elite groups or interest groups to influence the rule setting. This can also lead to collusion between members of the elite, policymakers, and government officials that could undermine the interests of marginalized sections of the communities. The Qur'ān (3:154) states "...They conceal within themselves what they will not reveal to you... [It was] so that Allâh might test what is in your breasts and purify what is in your hearts". The axiom of accountability warns against such transgressions, the extent of which encompasses our daily lives, not only in government or bureaucracies. Similarly, this concept of responsibility of our actions includes trade and commercial transactions.

Mutual Agreement

In ensuring social justice, a doctrine of options was established in Islamic financial transactions. The idea of optional clauses in a commercial sale was developed from prophetic tradition.[6] There are several main options known

[6]The Prophet ﷺ said, "No deal is settled and finalized unless the buyer and the seller separate, except if the deal is optional (whereby the validity of the bargain depends on the stipulations agreed upon)". Narrated by Ibn Umar, Sahih Bukhari, Volume 3, Book 34, Number 326.

under Islamic contract law that are usually associated with a contract of sale.[7] Options may be classified as 'option by mutual consent' and 'option by law':

(a) Option of acceptance or contract session (*khiyar al-majlis*) occurs during the formation of a contract and allows both parties to either accept or reject an offer. The period of this option lasts until the separation of the contracting parties. It should be noted that the option of acceptance does not apply to unilateral contracts such as endowments or gifts.

(b) Option of condition or stipulation (*khiyar al-shart*) allows both parties to include a condition in the contract that gives them a right to either ratify or cancel the sale. This option cannot be associated with a future event as the latter will encompass uncertainty and thus be voided. It is only a suspended condition for a certain period of time.

(c) Option of designation (*khiyar al-ta'yin*) is in fact similar to the option of condition. The option of designation was developed in the case when the subject matter of the contract was undefined at the point of inception of the contract so as to allow a party to reserve the option to validate the contract. This option was available for a fixed period of time. Thus, the party has an option to either ratify or cancel the contract.

(d) Option of defect (*khiyar al-'ayb*) is a legal right that allows a buyer in a sale to rescind the contract if a defect is to be found after the transfer of property. This also applies to hiring property where the party has to return the subject with no defect to the owner. The importance of this option is that it does not have to be stipulated at the inception of the contract but rather shall be regarded as a condition of termination (of the contract).

(e) Option of inspection (*khiyar al-ru'yah*) is also a legal right that occurs either in the absence of the subject matter of the contract or the physical absence of the contracting parties at the inception of the contract. Thus, a buyer in a contract of sale is given a right to ratify or cancel the contract upon his possession of the property. So upon the delivery of the subject matter, the buyer will have the right to inspect and thus hold or return the property if it does not meet his expectation. The option of inspection is also helpful if there has been a mistake in the contract where the intention of the contracting parties has not been disclosed.

[7]Noel J. Coulson, 1984. Commercial Law in the Gulf States, the Islamic Legal Tradition. Graham and Trotman, London, p. 57.

Ensuring Justice (*Qist*)

Here, *qist* denotes relational justice not general justice (*'adl*). Parties should receive fair share of the benefits derived from the contract entered into.

- Prohibition of Conditions Under Duress

  One of the main conditions for contractual validity in Islamic law (including other laws like the conventional contract law) is that commercial transactions should be concluded at a price that is agreed mutually and not under duress. Clearly, making someone accept contractual conditions under duress goes against the principle of fairness and equality.

- Prohibition of Hoarding of Commodities (*Ihtikar*)

  There is a prohibition that wealth should not be monopolized (including hoarding of commodities) in the hands of a few individuals, since this will create social imbalance. *Sharī'ah* prohibits monopoly and exclusive possession of *al-māl* because monopoly, along with interest, is believed to be the primary vehicles for financial exploitation and wealth concentration. By denouncing monopoly, the *Sharī'ah* mandates that *al-māl* should be distributed in a way that does not confine it to a few wealthy people in society. Therefore, the private owner should adhere to the requirements of the *Sharī'ah* when acquiring, disposing, spending, transferring, or exchanging property.

- Prohibition of Contract with Weak-minded (*Safeeh*)

  Safeeh are people who are incapable of managing their affairs properly, so the *Sharī'ah* invalidates any contract entered with them in order to protect their rights.

- Prohibition of *Gharar/Ghash*

  Following up the notion of protecting the weak against exploitation, the *Sharī'ah* has prohibited any transaction entailing uncertainty, speculation, or asymmetric information (*gharar*). The *Sharī'ah* prohibits any gain that may result from chance or from undetermined causes.

- Prohibition of *Tatfeef*

  The exact meaning of *tatfeef* is to give less in measure or weight to others when they buy, fabric, for example, and to take more when you are the buyer of that fabric. Therefore, *At-Tatfeef* includes weights, measures, lengths, amounts, and numbers in its wide sense, and thus, all kinds of fraudulent activities are considered as acts of *tatfeef*: "And O my people! Give full measure and weight in justice and reduce not the things that are due to the people, and do not commit mischief in the land, causing corruption." (Qur'ān 11:85)

- Prohibition of False Testimony
  Islam guarantees the means that lead to the actualization of justice and its consolidation. One of the means of establishing justice is giving testimony and knowing its importance. Testimony is the criterion with which we distinguish between truth and falsehood and true claims and false ones. Someone said, "Testimony to people's rights is like the soul to the body, for as Allah enlivens bodies with souls, He also enlivens rights with truthful testimony". It is essential in establishing a sound society. Islam forbids concealing the truth by giving false testimony because concealing evidence is something that is disapproved and detested: "... And do not conceal testimony, for whoever conceals it – his heart is indeed sinful..." (Qur'ān 2:283).
- Prohibition of Bribery
  Interest-based transactions, bribery, theft, robbery, breach of trust, and the use of fraudulent weights and measures do not satisfy the definition of *al-māl* and, therefore, are not worthy of ownership. Any contract involving these products is not binding and invalid and, hence, cannot be honoured or enforced.

Distribution and Redistribution

One of the most important economic institutions that operationalizes the objective of achieving social justice is that of the distribution/redistribution rule of the Islamic economic paradigm. The Islamic view holds that it is not possible to have many rich and wealthy people who continue to focus all their efforts on accumulating wealth without simultaneously creating a mass of economically deprived and destitute. The Qur'ān considers the more able as trustee-agents in using these resources on behalf of the less able. In this view, property is not a means of exclusion but inclusion in which the rights of those less able in the income and wealth of the more able are redeemed. The result would be a balanced economy without extremes of wealth and poverty. The operational mechanism for redeeming the right of the less able in the income and wealth of the more able is the network of mandatory and voluntary payments such as *zakat* (2.5% on wealth) and transference of property rights such as *sadaqah* and *infaq*.

The institution of *zakat*, for example, is expected to play an important role in income distribution and resource allocation. First, the *zakat* serves as a safety net designed to provide for the relief of poverty and other forms of social security. Its redistribution effect is expected to increase the aggregate demand in the economy. Second, the *zakat* is expected to have a strong stimulating effect on investment and productivity. By discouraging property owners from holding idle assets, the *zakat* will create incentives for wealth owners to ensure the maximum turnover of their net capital (Gambling and Karim, 1991). Together with the proscription of extravagant spending, the *zakat* is expected to reduce the transaction demand for money. Moreover, the stimulating effect of the *zakat*, together with the ban on interest, is expected to reduce the precautionary demand for money. Furthermore, the redistribution effects of *zakat* are expected to have a positive impact on the level of aggregate savings. Finally, such channels allow for money to flow through the different levels of income in an economic system, and societies that are sharing grow faster than societies that are stratified by large income gaps. Hence, a system like the *zakat* (including *sadaqah* and *infaq*) that channels money back from a section of the society that tends to save to a section of the society that tends to spend actually prospers the nation by increasing its GDP.

2.2.3.2 Enforcement of Rules

The basic purpose of institutions is to structure human behaviour in order to achieve the settled objectives. If the objectives are set and rules are framed to achieve them, an effective mechanism must be implemented to make sure that the rules are enforced and observed. Effective enforcement requires a mechanism to detect the violation and proper sanctions to deter anyone from violating the rules.

In Islamic markets during the Prophet's time, Mirakhor and Askari (2010) reported that "prices were determined by fierce competition amongst suppliers, and every market was supervised by a person called muhtasib, a practice started by the Prophet ﷺ himself. Market supervision was supplemented by the self-regulation by guilds of each profession and trade. Supervision was based on the rule-enforcement mechanism of commanding the good and forbidding the evil in urging with compliance with the rules. These enforcement devices were fortified by the physical architecture of the bazaars, which were constructed such that the grand mosque was located at the centre of the bazaar."[8]

Ibn Khaldun in his *Al-Muqaddimah* noted that "There will also be non-acknowledgement or denial of obligations, which may prove destructive to one's capital unless (the obligation) had been stated in writing

[8]Mirakhor and Askari, 2010. Islam and the Path to Human and Economic Development, pp. 162–163.

and properly witnessed. The judiciary is of little use in this connection, since the law requires clear evidence". Hence, contractual agreements and enforcement mechanisms are the bedrock of efficient institutions. Typically, historians of the economy differentiate between two forms of enforcement. The first is self-enforcement, what Greif (1994) terms 'private-order enforcement mechanism', where the 'credible' threats to reputation and the threat of market exclusion induce contractual compliance. This environment is characterized by 'optimal contracts' that are 'fundamentally self-enforcing', and 'institutions do not matter'. The focus is on the *ex ante* conditions to drafting contracts with watertight clauses that supposedly render them self-enforcing. The second is third-party enforcement, where agreements are drafted between parties in the presence of an independent individual (strongmen, chiefs, or other local authorities) or entity (state or court). Some academic scholars call these 'incomplete contracts' because their enforcement requires public enforcement institutions.

Muslim cases in the trans-Saharan trade community do not fit into either of these distinct scenarios (Lydon, 2008). For them, the act of drafting a contract in a 'session' following formal legal guidelines from the Qur'ān and the Sunnah required third-party enforcement through the use of witnesses. In trade practice, they approached the issue in two ways for enforcing contracts through the mechanism of prevention and the mechanism of remediation:

i. Prevention of contractual failure required literacy skills and legal knowledge (contractual models and principles), resources (writing paper in sufficient quantity for making copies), and connections (witnesses with impeccable reputations and authority (merchants, *muḥtasibs*, and *qāḍis*)).

ii. Remediation took various forms, such as the mediation of third parties (contract witnesses and *qāḍis*), pressuring contracting party directly or via correspondence (threats to tarnishing their reputation, their client base and instilling them with the fear of ex post consequences to future transactions, and pressure on family members), or engaging in costly litigation.[9]

Furthermore, the institution of *al-hisba* is meant to monitor the behaviour of market participants and set the standards for fostering ethical and moral behaviour.

[9]Based on oral historical reports of Tishti, Shinqiti, etc., tribe families by G. Lydon.

2.2.3.3 The Implications of the Rules

Just as there are ideologies and customs that complement formal economic institutions, there are informal rules that complement the formal rules for making rules. Hence, the evolution of institutions is a function of both formal and informal processes. In order to determine which current institutions contribute to optimum or desired performance, policymakers and citizens in their own capacities decide which institutional changes to enact to achieve a particular performance. But the formal constitutional rules for making economic rules are only part of the picture. One purpose of institutional analysis is to inform institutional choice, though all institutions are not the product of explicit choice. People are continuously choosing amongst institutional alternatives at several levels. The first choice is at the constitutional and political level. The second is at the level of everyday working rules of individuals and organizations. The third is within organizations. The actors need information on the consequences (impact) of these alternatives, so they can choose the ones that serve their purposes. The objective of institutional theory is to make these choices less blind.

Often, unclear and overlapping jurisdictions and mandates lead to institutional conflict and struggles for power within a community (Kumar, 2002). In many cases, the influence of government and local elites in the decision-making process is found to be very strong, which may severely dilute community representation. Altering some of the rules and policies to suit one community over another can and will often lead to the collapse of the institution, as history will attest.[10] Fair dispensation of the law and proper observance of the rules will prosper any society, but destruction will follow if they act otherwise:

> *And how many a city did We destroy while it was committing wrong - so it is [now] fallen into ruin - and [how many] an abandoned well and [how many] a lofty palace.*
>
> **(Qur'ān 22:45)**

> *And for how many a city did I prolong enjoyment while it was committing wrong. Then I seized it, and to Me is the [final] destination.*
>
> **(Qur'ān 22:48)**

[10]Most recently, the 2008 global financial crisis. These are examples of injustice and non-compliance of the law. Historical evidences of non-compliance include pre-Islamic and ancient times like the destruction of the tribes of Ad, Noah, Sodom and Gomorrah, Thamud, Al-Rass, etc.

2.2.3.4 The Role of Collective Action

It is hypothesized that in particular situations, individuals sharing a performance preference cannot get what they want acting as isolated individuals at the margin within existing opportunity sets. It is a tragedy when individuals make their most advantageous choice – the tragedy of isolated individualism – without considering the bigger picture or the larger good.

A community's ability for collective action is likely to be an important determinant of its success in organizing community management activities and for monitoring and enforcement of rules. In the case of the trans-Saharan tribes, the representatives of the law, namely, judges often acted as witnesses, scribes, and intermediaries, were found to be contributing to contractual enforcement through information sharing and pressuring services (Lydon, 2008). In other words, not only did private-order and public institutions work in tandem, but also they were frequently indistinguishable. As the letter of the law was developed through collective formative jurisprudence, it was not meant to be politically inspired legislations to benefit a particular entity only. An advantage of religious law is that it is not subjected to the dictates of political power, and this creates a vital distinction between the power of the executive and the rule of law.

2.2.4 Resource Allocation and Employment (Motivation for the Game)

This level consists of the requirements that must be fulfilled to achieve the required level of efficiency. It emphasizes basically the nature of individual stakeholders' incentives to participate in different levels of regulatory (management) decisions and actions and to comply with rules prescribed. Problems occur especially in situations where several stakeholders benefit from rule violations. In such a complex situation, a very strong enforcement of rules is needed, where all the involved agents including governing entities must be accountable for any rule violations.

2.2.4.1 Incentive Systems for All

The principle of accountability mentioned earlier (in Section 2.3.1) keeps alignment to the objectives of the Qur'ānic message and subsequent adherence to rule compliance and serves as an all-encompassing incentive system. Allåh (s.w.t.) has given human beings trusteeship and resources. This means that every single person will be questioned on the Day of Judgment as to how they have behaved in their earthly life, including their economic behaviour. Allåh (s.w.t.) says.

And then on that Day (the Day of Resurrection) you will be called to account for every comfort and delight [we bestowed upon you].

(Qur'ān 102:8)

There is also a verse in the Qur'ān that contains the necessary and sufficient condition for an ideal economy:

If the members of the collectivity were to be rule-compliant (mu'min)1 and ever-conscious (had taqwa) surely We would have opened them blessings from the sky and from the earth. But they rejected (the Divine messages), therefore, we seized them on account of their (non-compliant) deeds.

(Qur'ān 7:96)

The necessary condition is to have *iman* (faith) being rule compliant, and the sufficient condition of *taqwa* requires that there be no lapses in rule compliance.[11]

The incentive system of the Qur'ān spells out that the reward for a just and rule-compliant system is a healthy, just, and prosperous society, as the reward for good is good itself. Although the rules seem to apply to the individual level, the returns are compounded from the individual to the societal level:

That Allah may reward them according to the best of their deeds, and add even more for them out of His Grace: for Allah doth provide for those whom He will, without measure.

(Qur'ān 24:38)

The all-encompassing incentive system continues from this world to the next:

Indeed, those who disbelieve in Our verses - We will drive them into a Fire. Every time their skins are roasted through We will replace them with other skins so they may taste the punishment. Indeed, Allah is ever Exalted in Might and Wise.

But those who believe and do righteous deeds - We will admit them to gardens beneath which rivers flow, wherein they abide forever. For them therein are purified spouses, and We will admit them to deepening shade.

(Qur'ān 4:56–57)

The free flow of information, free entry and exit of markets, according to the rules derived from the Qur'ān, enables a market that is highly competitive. In the long run, it makes it almost impossible for every seller to make

[11]Abbas Mirakhor and Hossein Askari, 2010. Islam and the Path to Human and Economic Development, pp. 95–138.

high profits. From the analysis of early Islamic markets, especially the large competition amongst the participants, a perfectly transparent market makes the long-run profit quite negligible.[12] However, it spurred innovations and new techniques, and in these, any firm could gain considerable profits in the short run. In the free flow of information and depending on the ease of the innovations' utilization, the competing suppliers could quickly adopt it and catch up. This cycle of competitive innovation either increased the quantity (of service or goods) or reduced its related production costs. In the long run, the prices of the goods declined, and new ways or opportunities are needed to be innovated to profit from. This brings on technological advancement and improved human development rapidly and continuously.

2.3 RULES OF BEHAVIOUR ACCORDING TO QUR'ĀN AND SUNNAH

Mirakhor (2009), however, believes that central amongst the rules that constitute the institutional structure of the ideal economy are rules governing property, production, exchange, distribution and redistribution, and market conduct. According to him, from an institutional perspective, "the ideal economy is composed of a collection of institutions – rules of conduct and their enforcement characteristics – designed by the Law Giver, prescribed in the metaframework (specified in the Qur'ān) and operationalized by the archetype model (the way the Messenger understood and implemented the rules) to deal with allocation of resources, production and exchange of goods and services, and distribution-redistribution of resulting income and wealth". Mirakhor and Askari (2010) noted that Adam Smith (in *The Theory of Moral Sentiments*) concisely and clearly shares some of the foundational scaffolding of Islam: belief in the One and Only Creator, belief in the accountability of the Day of Judgment, belief in the necessity of compliance with the rules prescribed by the Creator, and belief that justice is achieved with full compliance with rules. This underlines the productive role that religion can play in markets, and the Islamic market principles deriving from the Qur'ān and the teachings are a perfect example. To them, it is clear that Smith considers the internalization of the rules, being consciously aware of the ever presence of the Creator and acting accordingly, as crucial to all productive human conduct, including economic transactions. They stressed that these rules reduce uncertainty and transaction costs and that

[12]Seyed Kazem Sadr, 2016. The Economic System of the Early Islamic Period: Institutions and Policies. Palgrave Macmillan.

they promote coordination and make collective action possible. In addition, they believe that rule compliance promotes social solidarity. Social cohesion can enhance growth via reducing transaction costs, that is, the costs incurred in making economic exchanges, such as information gathering, communications, and contract enforcement (Coase 1960). The concept of transaction cost has also been applied to the effects of informal institutions, including trust and non-discrimination. In societies where norms of trust or cooperation between differing ethnic, sectarian, or other identity groups are low, the costs of economic cooperation will be higher, thereby inhibiting economic activity. Empirical studies have also shown generalized social trust to be a predictor of future rates of economic growth (Knack and Keefer, 1997).

Since behaviours prescribed according to Islamic tenets can strengthen the case for guidance in addressing market failures like negative externalities from narrow decision-making and their eradication through ethical, social, and legal means, in this thesis, we draw upon those rules of behaviour from the Qur'ān and Sunnah and then use those rules towards testing the level of adherence of those rules via experimental games on a sample of society grouped into Muslims and non-Muslims. Specifically, in Sections 2.3.1–2.3.9, we select and discuss those rules in more detail.

2.3.1 Rule-Compliance and Discouraging Noncompliance (Capstone Rule)

The duty of commanding the good and forbidding evil, incumbent on individuals and the whole community, is the most important means of enforcement of prescribed rules of the metaframework and the archetype model by Mirakhor (2009). It is also an effective promoter of social solidarity and preserver of social order. Existence of oppression, corruption, massive inequality, and poverty in a society is *prima facie* evidence of non-compliance with or outright shirking of this duty. No one is absolved from the necessity of performance of the duty of commanding rule compliance and forbidding rule violation. This is particularly binding vis-à-vis the rulers. Even though there is particular emphasis both in the Qur'ān and in the *Sunnah* of the Messenger on just political authority, the individual members of the society are not absolved from the duty of commanding the authorities, at all levels, to righteous conduct and forbidding them from rule violations whenever the individuals recognize the necessity of doing so.

Rules governing the market relate to appropriate behaviour of all participants in the market. The Qur'ān acknowledges the need for markets and affirms their existence, placing emphasis on contracts of exchange (*bay'*) and trade (*tijarah*). As a rule, the Qur'ān places emphasis on market transactions based on mutual consent, therefore, based on freedom of choice and freedom of contract that, in turn, requires acknowledgement and affirmation of private property rights. Also, the proper structure of institutions and adherence to rule compliance are crucial in achieving the objectives of institutions: "The Messenger ﷺ specified operational rules of conduct in the market place, appointed a market supervisor to ensure rule compliance, and encouraged internalization of these rules by participants before their entrance into the market. Compliance with the rules of market behaviour ensures the emergence of prices that are fair and just. So long as market participants are rule compliant, no direct interference with the price mechanism is permitted, even though the legitimate authority has the power and the responsibility of supervision of market operations" (Mirakhor, 2009).

2.3.2 Cooperation

The rule of consultation subsequently involves the rules of cooperation; for to enact regulations and secure compliance and accountability, there has to be cooperation amongst the institutions involving the regulators, agents, and market players. The Qur'ānic verse that underlines this behaviour rule is "...Help (cooperate) one another in Al-Birr and At-Taqwa (virtue, righteousness and piety); but do not help (cooperate) one another in sin and transgression..." (Qur'ān 5:2). The fulfilment of God's trust or (see Section 2.3.9) is a prerogative and responsibility of the human community; the individual is just an active partner in the process. Since no individual can survive alone, the personal needs of an individual necessitate human cooperation in society. The community as a whole becomes responsible for the accomplishment of the trust. However, no meaningful, extensive, and long-lasting cooperation is possible without its effective understanding of goals and proper governance. The more people there are who participate in the process of cooperation, the more effective the outcome becomes.

2.3.3 Consultation

The Qur'ān (42:38) states that "...whose affair is [determined by] consultation among themselves..." and (3:159) that "...and consult them in the matter. And when you have decided, then rely upon Allah...". Clearly, in Islam, coming to consensus (and subsequent cooperation) through a *shura* or consultation collectively is encouraged and brings benefit to both parties. Consulting parties involved in the decision-making ensures motivation to comply with the final decision as it had been a mutual consensus.

It brings people together, enjoins cooperation, instills amity, and promotes understanding. The independence of the *fiqh* institutions was the catalyst in allowing the Islamic jurists to freely interpret relevant and applicable *Sharī'ah* rules and perform *ijtihad*. The *shura* institutions (e.g. consultative committees), on the other hand, are needed to enact regulations and secure compliance and accountability.

2.3.4 Contract

In general, Islam secures all worldly activities, including economic transactions, on contracts. The primordial covenant[13] between the Creator and humans – the *Mithaq* – is basically a contractual agreement between creation and the Creator, which imposes the obligation on humans to recognize the Creator as their provider and sustainer (*Rabb*). From an operational standpoint, that cognizance is an affirmation that in their conduct on the earth, they will comply with the rules prescribed by their Cherisher Lord. Faithfulness to the terms of all contracts entered into, establishing justice; reward for rule compliance; and punishment for rule violation on the day of accountability are linked to the fulfilment of obligations incurred under the stipulation of terms and conditions of the primordial covenant. This proposition links humans directly to their Creator and to one another.

In a direct, clear, and unambiguous verse, the Qur'ān commands "... fulfill the Covenant of Allåh" (Qur'ān 6:152). In an equally clear verse, it generalizes this imperative to all contracts: "...fulfill all contracts" (Qur'ān 5:1). Thus, faithfulness to the terms of every covenant, contract, or oath to carry out obligations one has committed to becomes a reflection of the primordial covenant.

2.3.5 Free-Flow of Information

In its practice, Islamic markets during the Prophet's time in Madinah demonstrated a network of microlevel rules that ensure transparency and unhindered flow of information. In endorsing economic freedom and allowing maximum scope to market forces, the *Sharī'ah* acknowledges the market mechanism as a vehicle for the determination of commodity prices. Full and unlimited access to the market, by all buyers and sellers,

[13]"And (remember) when your Lord brought forth from the Children of Adam, from their loins, their seed (or from Adam's loin his offspring) and made them testify as to themselves (saying): 'Am I not your Lord?' They said: 'Yes! We testify', lest you should say on the Day of Resurrection: 'Verily, we have been unaware of this'." (Qur'an 7:172).

is advocated as a prerequisite for the free working of a just economy. Moreover, full disclosure of the quality of goods being offered for sale and non-interference with suppliers before entrance into the market is required. Above all, specific norms of behaviour have to be observed by all market participants if the interests of all parties are to be safeguarded (Ahmad, 1981). For example, the parties entering any sale-purchase transaction have free consent (*khiyar*) in reaching an agreement. However, once the transaction is completed, fulfilment of all terms of the contract is required. In addition, the *Sharī'ah* prescribes certain norms to enhance the market behaviour. Adulteration, hoarding, and cornering of stocks with a view to creating artificial scarcity and profiteering; collusion amongst buyers or sellers to hurt the interest of one party; and bidding up prices without the intention to purchase are all severely condemned (Ahmad, 1981). Strict adherence to correct weights and measures is also emphasized.

Historically, market supervisors, appointed by the Prophet ﷺ, ensured there was no fraud, cheating, withholding of information, or other practices that could lead to the malfunctioning of the price mechanism. Subsequently, independent regulatory agencies were established to monitor trading practices and other fraudulent market behaviours. These medieval Islamic institutions included *al-hisba*, *diwan al-azimmah*,[14] and real estate registry. Currently, *Sharī'ah* committees affiliated with Islamic banks are established for the same purpose. Meanwhile, the state is enjoined to institute whatever procedures are needed to regulate the market. Certainly, this can be interpreted as part of its duty of propagating good and suppressing evil (*amr bil ma'ruf wa nahi 'anil munkar*). The Qur'ān (22:41) states "(They are) those who, if we establish them in the land, establish regular prayer and give regular charity, enjoin the right and forbid wrong...". Islamic 'preferred market behaviour' provides the moral scaffolding for market institutions that cannot be perfect (importantly, contracts). In the purview of institutional economics, these are the foundations of a market system that provides guarantees (protection of property and covenants) and incentives to invest and work.

[14] A supreme audit office established by Abbasids (AD 750–945) to control and check the accounts of other *diwans* (registries where records of all decisions were stored).

2.3.6 Property Rights

In Islam, God's ultimate ownership of property supersedes that of the individual. The Qur'ān and the Sunnah (records of the Prophet's ﷺ actions and speech) clearly and explicitly state that God is the sole owner[15] of wealth and that people, as vicegerents of God, are merely trustees or custodians.

In practice, the individual claims to *al-māl* (which denotes all the resources made subservient to man) are recognized and safeguarded by law.[16] The sanctity of private property rights has been affirmed by Prophet Muhammad ﷺ when he delivered his last sermon (known as *Khutba-e-hajjatul Wida*): "O people! Verily your blood, your property and your honour are sacred and inviolable as the sacred inviolability of this day of yours, this month of yours and this very town (of yours)".

The use of property owned is restricted, however, by the prohibition of *ribā* (usury) and the legal obligation to give *zakat* (alms). The Qur'ān (57:7) explicitly states "Believe in Allah and His Messenger, and spend of that whereof He hath made you trustees...". By implication, the ownership of *al-māl* is understood to be a trust, and its disposal is considered to be a test of faith since the owner has to use it in accordance with God's revealed wisdom. The Qur'ān (6:165) states "It is He who hath made you (His) vicegerents (or stewards), successors of the earth. He hath raised some of you above others in degrees [of rank] that He may try you through what He has given you...". Hence, a person entrusted with wealth can achieve the highest degree of virtue (*falāh*) by spending out of his wealth within the boundaries prescribed by the *Sharī'ah*.[17]

Interestingly, economists have recognized that market transactions are exceptionally productive in reconciling private desires with public purposes. One central component of the legal foundation of the market relates to property rights over objects and circumstances. As previously underlined, effective and properly defined property rights are deemed essential in providing the preconditions for economic growth. In so doing, the *Sharī'ah* explicitly specifies a set of rules and principles that regulate

[15]See Qur'ān (20:6): "To Him belongs what is in the heavens and what is on the earth and what is between them and what is under the soil".

[16]The concept of *al-māl* in Islam denotes all the resources that God made subservient to man on land, in the sea, and beneath the surface of the earth. *Al-māl* is also defined as anything (property) that can be owned and has value, including the rights and benefits of ownership.

[17]See Qur'ān (2:261): "The example of those who spend their wealth in the way of Allâh is like a seed [of grain] which grows seven spikes; in each spike is a hundred grains. And Allâh multiplies [His reward] for whom He wills. And Allâh is all-Encompassing and Knowing".

the legitimate sources of acquiring *al-māl* (property), its growth, and its disposal. These moral limits, which will be discussed in detail below, are meant to achieve two vital objectives: restoring *al-adl* (socio-economic justice) and promoting *al-ihsān* (mutual benevolence) (Qur'ān 16:90). *Al-adl* and *al-ihsān* are meant to articulate the notion that people should have equal opportunities, not necessarily equal riches.

More specifically, by emphasizing *al-adl*, the *Sharī'ah* intends to eliminate all forms of economic inequality, injustice, exploitation, oppression, and wrongdoing, whereby a person either deprives others of their rights or does not fulfil his obligations towards them. The concept of *al-adl* forbids gross inequalities in the distribution of goods and indicates that the ownership of wealth has social and economic dimensions.

Al-ihsān, on the other hand, is a reassurance that *al-māl* (property) is to be used to protect the welfare of the community (*ummah*). Restoring both *al-adl* and *al-ihsān* is necessary and sufficient condition for equitable distribution of income. Other precepts specified by the *Sharī'ah*, to restore *al-adl* and *al-ihsān*, include the prohibition of both avarice and wasteful spending (Qur'ān 17:27). Overspending (*israf*), waste (*itlaf*), and ostentatious and opulent spending (*itraf*) are prohibited because they entail consumption beyond the average standard for society and, therefore, violate the principle of responsibility. Hence, people are encouraged to be modest and utilize the available resources to attain both the mundane and the spiritual objectives of the *Sharī'ah*. Another important injunction required for the restoration of *al-adl* and *al-ihsān* is the proscription of hoarding (e.g. commodities and *kanz*). Hoarding is prohibited due to its negative externality on wealth and income distribution. In today's economic thinking, hoarding can be harmful because it limits the productive capacity of resources and leads to the concentration of wealth in the hands of few. Chapra (1985) writes, "Islam provides an economic system that makes it absolutely imperative to use God-given resources for fulfilling the essential needs of all human beings and providing them with decent living conditions".

In addition, ibn Abbas reported that the Messenger of Allåh ﷺ said "The people (i.e. humanity) are partners in three things – in water, herbage and fire". Water, trees, pastures, and fire, being things of natural resource and common use, are considered public property in Islamic thought. This does not mean, however, that humans are given free rein to use (and abuse) the resources God has provided us however we choose – even collectively. Humankind is urged to harness the various resources (public property) that God has made available to them on this earth responsibly. Humans are encouraged to enjoy of the good things that God has created, but they are to do so within the boundaries that He has given. Doing so is not regarded as sinful as long as it follows His path and does not transgress His limits. Allåh (s.w.t.) says "It is He Who produces gardens, with trellises and without, and dates, and tilth with produce of all kinds, and olives and pomegranates, similar (in kind) and different (in variety): eat of their fruit in their season, but render the dues that are proper on the day that the harvest is gathered. But waste not by excess: for Allåh (s.w.t.) loves not those who waste" (Qur'ān 6:141).

In line with our arguments earlier in this section, the fundamentals of Islamic law lay the legal foundation for internalization. Private property must be used and disposed of in favour of public good and should not cause public harm. Here, the Islamic principles exhort justice and benevolence in the name of the Creator, the ultimate owner of all property *in perpetuum*. Thus, an ethical and legal basis is provided to overcome the barriers of transaction costs for a fair and ethical solution to internalizing externalities that may arise as a result of property rights.

2.3.7 Reciprocity

The concept of reciprocity revolves around in-kind responses for the actions of others, which are in relation to justice, and related ideas such as gratitude, mutuality, and the Golden Rule. This concept describes a 'reciprocal', or 'two-way', relationship between one's self and others that involves both sides equally and in a mutual fashion.[18] The Messenger of Allåh ﷺ advises Muslims that whoever passes his night satiated and restful in his home with his family whilst he has poor neighbours who pass their night hungry has no true belief.

From the macro view of the market, the rule of reciprocity can be similarly applied to other facets of the economy like trade concessions, for instance, whereby governments make those concessions through multilateral bargaining that are mutually beneficial. When one country agrees to reduce tariffs on imports from a second country, it has the right to expect the other country to make tariff concessions of equal value in return. The principle of reciprocity, therefore, attempts to ensure that the concessions that each country makes in the multilateral trade negotiations are equalled by the concessions it gains from its trading partners. The rule of reciprocity may be able to address market failures (related to mistrust, asymmetric information, etc.) in persuading their interlocutors to act cooperatively and maintain their bargain, even without explicit incentives and assurances, and keep markets efficient.

[18]Marcus George Singer, 1955. Generalization in Ethics, Mind LXIV, p. 119.

2.3.8 Right Not to Be Harmed, and the Obligation Not to Harm (Golden Rule)

This rule is essentially known as the Golden Rule. It is a maxim,[19] ethical code, or a universal morality[20] that fundamentally states either of the following:

One should treat others as one would like others to treat oneself.

(Positive form)

One should not treat others in ways that one would not like to be treated.

(Negative form, also known as the Silver Rule)

Simon Blackburn also states that the Golden Rule can be 'found in some form in almost every ethical tradition[21]'. Not surprisingly, this rule of not to harm is also a generally accepted rule that can be found in the first rule of patents,[22] Three Laws of Robotics,[23] and under the UNWC convention.[24] All belief systems, including Islam, attach great importance to protecting people from harm. The Qur'ān states.

...and you should forgive and overlook: Do you not like God to forgive you? And Allåh is The Merciful Forgiving.

(Qur'ān 24:22)

[19]Antony Flew (Ed.), 1979. 'Golden Rule'. A Dictionary of Philosophy. Pan Books in association with The MacMillan Press, London, p. 134. ISBN 0-330-48730-2. This dictionary of philosophy contains the following exact quote under the entry for 'Golden Rule': "The maxim 'Treat others how you wish to be treated'. Various expressions of this fundamental moral rule are to be found in tenets of most religions and creeds through the ages, testifying to its universal applicability".

[20]Walter Terence Stace argued that the Golden Rule was much more than simply an ethical code. Instead, he posits, it 'express[es] the essence of a universal morality'. The rationale for this crucial distinction occupies much of his book *The Concept of Morals* (1937): Stace, Walter T. (1937, reprinted 1975 by permission of MacMillan Publishing Co. Inc., also reprinted January 1990 by Peter Smith Publisher Inc). The Concept of Morals. The MacMillan Company and also reprinted by Peter Smith Publisher Inc., New York, January 1990, p. 136. ISBN 0-8446-2990-1 (above quote found p. 136, Chapter 6).

[21]Simon, Blackburn, 2001. Ethics: A Very Short Introduction. Oxford University Press, Oxford, p. 101.

[22]http://online.wsj.com/news/articles/patent_reform

[23]Isaac Asimov, 1942. Runaround. Street and Smith, New York.

[24]Article 7 of the UN Watercourses Convention codifies and clarifies the scope of the duty *not to cause significant harm*. This obligation, otherwise known as the 'no significant harm' rule, requires that 'in utilizing an international watercourse in their territories, take all appropriate measures to prevent the causing of significant harm to other watercourse States'.

and the Prophet ﷺ is reported to have said.

to cause harm to others is not allowed in Islam.

Anas related that Prophet Muhammad ﷺ said 'None of you is truly a Muslim until he loves for his brother what he loves for himself'.

(reported in Sahih Muslim and Sahih Bukhari)

Whoever wishes to be delivered from the fire and to enter paradise should treat other people as they wish to be treated themselves.

(reported by Sahih Muslim)

Do unto all men as you would wish to have done unto you; and reject for others what you would reject for yourself.

(reported by Abu Dawud)

It may appear that the world may be a better place if we treated each other as the Golden Rule suggests. The Golden Rule simply states that all of us are to treat other people as we would wish other people to treat us in return. Almost all organized religions, philosophical systems, and secular systems of morality include such an ethic. It is normally intended to apply to the entire human race. To apply the Golden Rule adequately, we need to have great empathy for others – we need to be able to imagine ourselves, vividly and accurately, in the other person's position and circumstance. We also need to know what effect our actions have on the lives of others. And for many centuries, the idea has been influential amongst people of very diverse cultures that suggest that the Golden Rule has an important moral value. In addition, it is arguably the most essential basis for the modern concept of human rights, in which each individual has a right to just treatment and a reciprocal responsibility to ensure justice for others. There has been research published arguing that some 'sense' of fair play and the Golden Rule may be stated and rooted in terms of neuroscientific and neuroethical principles.[25] Also, markets thrive where there is justice, equality, and fairness.

In other scriptures, the Golden Rule is similarly emphasized:

All things whatsoever ye would that men should do to you, do ye so to them; for this is the law and the prophets.

(Christianity: Matthew 7:1)

[25]Pfaff, Donald W., 2007. The Neuroscience of Fair Play: Why We (Usually) Follow the Golden Rule. Dana Press, The Dana Foundation, New York, 2007.

Do not do to others what you would not like yourself. Then there will be no resentment against you, either in the family or in the state.

(Confucianism: Analects 12:2)

Hurt not others in ways that you yourself would find hurtful.

(Buddhism: Udana-Varga 5,1)

This is the sum of duty; do naught onto others what you would not have them do unto you.

(Hinduism: Mahabharata 5,1517)

What is hateful to you, do not do to your fellowman. This is the entire Law; all the rest is commentary.

(Judaism: Talmud, Shabbat 3id)

Regard your neighbor's gain as your gain, and your neighbor's loss as your own loss.

(Taoism: Tai Shang Kan Yin P'ien)

That nature alone is good which refrains from doing another whatsoever is not good for itself.

(Zoroastrianism: Dadistan-I Dinik, 94,5)

In 1993, the second Parliament of the World's Religions met in Chicago. The 8000 attendees represented many faiths and many branches of faiths like Buddhism, Christianity, Hinduism, Islam, and Judaism. The parliament tried to reach an agreement on a global ethics document that supported common values. Most agreed on the need for this document and the central place of the Golden Rule. The Golden Rule is arguably the most essential basis for the modern concept of human rights, in which each individual has a right to just treatment and a reciprocal responsibility to ensure justice for others.

Imam ʿAlī (about AD 600–660), a cousin and son-in-law of the Prophet ﷺ and later became the fourth rightly guided caliph, gave a longer statement of the Golden Rule in a documented text to his son Hasan ibn ʿAlī:

O my son, regard yourself as a scale [against which you measure your behavior] with others. Hence, what you prefer for yourself, prefer for others; what you find objectionable for yourself, treat as such for others. Do not wrong anyone, just as you would not like to be wronged; do good to others just as you would like others to do good to you; that which you consider immoral for others, consider immoral for yourself.

This deals with both desires and actions ('prefer' and 'do not wrong') and with both doing good and refraining from harming ('do good' and 'do not wrong'). And there is no suggestion that these 'others' are limited to fellow Muslims.

The renowned scholar and eminent thinker Abu Hāmid al-Ghazāli (AD 1058–1111) in his *Disciplining the Soul* gave this statement of the Golden Rule: 'Were all people only to renounce the things they dislike in others, they would not need anyone to discipline them'. Thus, the Golden Rule is an important help for disciplining ourselves towards greater perfection.

The Grand Sufi mystic saint and philosopher Ibn ʿArabī (AD 1165–1240) stated the Golden Rule this way: "All the commandments are summed up in this, that whatever you would like the True One to do to you, that do to His creatures". Here, the Golden Rule applies to how we are to treat all creatures that would include not only all humans but also all animals. And the Golden Rule, formulated in terms of how we want God to treat us, is given as the summary of how we are to live.

The enigmatic Persian poet Saʿdī (about AD 1213–92) in his *Gulistan* (Chapter 1, Story 10) had these verses, which accord with the spirit of the Golden Rule and are now displayed at the entrance of the United Nations Hall of Nations:

Human beings are members of a whole, In creation of one essence and soul.

If one member is afflicted with pain, Other members uneasy will remain.

If you have no sympathy for human pain, The name of human you cannot retain.

The context here is a story about an evil king who thinks nothing of breaking the fingers of a poor man. Many of Saʿdī's stories involve the idea that the good or evil that we do to others will somehow come back to us (sometimes through divine action). So, the good or evil that we do to another, we really are doing to ourselves.

Gensler (2013) notes that Islamic golden-rule formulas deal with our desires towards others (what we wish, love, or prefer) instead of just actions (what we do), as in the examples given earlier from the Qur'ān and Sunnah, Imam ʿAlī, and Ibn ʿArabī. So, this tradition has both golden-rule forms: about desires and about actions. Gensler observes that the forms about desires are more distinctive and that very few other traditions have golden-rule forms about desires.

2.3.9 Trust

Economies and societies with lower levels of trust tend to be less productive and have more stifling levels of regulation – higher barriers to entry, lower freedoms in price setting, more formalistic legal systems, reduced product, and labour market flexibility – to try and compensate (Aghion et al., 2010) for that lack.

God expressed His will to the angels about creating on earth a new being who would be the best of all His creations and would be assigned the status of His vicegerent (*khalīfah*). The angels expressed their reservations, fearing that the new being would create chaos and disorder in society and shed blood and would bring suffering to his own species. In response, God only said to the angels that they did not know what He knew. God then breathed into Adam (a.s.) His Own Spirit (Qur'ān 15:29; 32:9; 38:72). Thus, not only Adam was created with such faculties of hearing, seeing, and understanding, but also he received the potential to develop advanced qualities such as being caring, responsible, kind, just, wise, and forgiving. Human beings, therefore, are unique and privileged as compared with other creation. The Qur'ān also speaks of a covenant between man and God (Qur'ān 7:172) in which man recognized God's position as his Creator. In other words, the ability to perceive the existence of the Supreme Being is inborn in human nature.

The role of *khalifah* (God's vicegerent) is essentially a trust (*amanah*). God has invested man His trust – a trust that the heavens, the earth, and the mountains refused to accept because they were afraid of its heavy burden (*Surah al-Aĺzab*, Qur'ān 33:72) – a trust that defines the rights and responsibilities in relation to humans, the environment, and the rest of God's creation. As a *khalifah*, man is entrusted with an *amanah* to establish responsibility on earth by means of virtues and bounties endowed to him by God, his initiative, creativity, and labour (*isti'mar*). "He brought you forth from the earth and settled you therein" (Surah Hud, Qur'ān 11:61) to fulfil God's creative work in the universe. Nature has been created for human beings, but man is also required to establish a moral social order on earth. The concept of *amanah* determines the individual's relationship with the society, state, government, and humanity at large. Man is attached to these institutions both procedurally and spiritually. The individual has a weighty contract with his society, with the animal world, with the plant and mineral worlds, and with the universe. The concept of *amanah* implies that in all his actions, man should choose to prosper the earth (*islah*) by making the best use of resources and to fully utilize the virtues inherent in him to *isti'mar* the earth. *Ifsad* (*fasad*) or adversity or corruption is to be avoided in managing one's role as a *khalifah*. Being a *khalifah*, man has also been granted authority to freely manage nature/universe and to cooperate with his fellow beings to complete the task of *khalifah*. This part, Izutsu[26] says, is in the realm of 'human ethics' that should be guided by those 'divine ethics'. *Amanah* makes human life meaningful because it makes him squarely responsible for creating a moral social order. It provides him with the opportunity to demonstrate his ability to be God's vicegerent on earth. In other words, the Qur'ān, like the Old Testament, gives the human being dignity; it presents unity and nobility of purpose.

Similarly, the Holy Prophet ﷺ said "One who is dishonest in this world and does not return the trust to its owner and dies in this state has left the world being out of my ummah nation and is not considered as my follower and he will meet Allah making Him angry and furious, that is, he will meet with Divine chastisement".

These selected set of nine rules (capstone rule, cooperation, consultation, contract, free flow of information, property rights, reciprocity, Golden Rule, and trust), which we extract from the Qur'ān and Sunnah, underpin the very behaviours prescribed according to Islamic tenets, and they strengthen the case for the guidance that the Islamic principles provide in addressing market failures such as those concerning negative externalities from narrow decision-making and their eradication through ethical, social, and legal means. Faith-based rules may also reduce economic uncertainty by establishing behavioural compliance and by promoting social trust, cooperation, and solidarity, thus generating positive externalities (Erbaş and Mirakhor, 2013).

2.4 POSITIVISM VERSUS ETHICISM

Positivism, in the conventional economics sense, is being 'entirely neutral between ends' (Robbins, 1935) or 'independent of any particular ethical position or normative judgment' (Friedman, 1970). The nature of human being in this regard is defined as an autonomous individual in all his activities where he measures value at the level of personal impulses, desires, and preferences.[27] He is independent of any external elements of society, environment, and even God.

[26]Toshihiko Izutsu, 2004. Ethico-Religious Concepts in the Qur'ān. Islamic Book Trust, Kuala Lumpur.

[27]Frank Ryan, 2003.Values as consequences of transaction: commentary on reconciling homo economicus and John Dewey's ethics, Journal of Economic Methodology, 10 (2), 249.

In direct contrast, all major religions present an opposite view – even Asimov's 'Three Laws of Robotics[28]' requires basic ethical principles ('do no harm to human beings') for these somewhat autonomous beings to regulate their behaviours. Islam (and the other major religions) acknowledges the freedom of choice and free will, but does not see humanity as being independent of God, society, and environment. Since all resources at the disposal of human beings are a trust from God and human beings are accountable before Him, there is no other option but to use them in keeping with the terms of trust. These terms are defined by beliefs and moral values. Humanity as a brotherhood, one of the central concepts of Islam in the Qur'ān, would be meaningless if it is not reinforced by justice in the allocation and distribution of resources. Whilst conventional economics separate characteristics such as benevolence and equality in just distribution of economic resources and products, these ideals are greatly encouraged in the practice of Islamic economics. The presence of *al-jannah* (Heaven) and *al-jahannam* (Hell) provides 'the form of the moral conscience' whenever a man chooses to do anything in this world. It is the very source of moral values – through accountability. Man, as long as he lives as a member of the Muslim community, is morally required to always choose certain ways of acting that are connected with *jannah* and to avoid those that are connected with *jahannam*. By this, definitely, the choices of the *Islamic economic man*[29] will be different from his conventional *economic man*[30] counterpart in market behaviour and decisions in the economic development. Similarly, in terms of social connectedness and its influence on individual decisions, several notable literatures (e.g. Christakis and Fowler, 2010; Nowak, 2011) have pointed to our social aspect of human nature, to need people in order to

[28] A robot may not injure a human being or, through inaction, allow a human being to come to harm. A robot must obey orders given it by humans except where such orders would conflict with the first law. A robot must protect its own existence as long as such protection does not conflict with the first or second law.

[29] The *Islamic economic man* as the economic agent sees economics and other 'worldly' activities as being supportive in the worship of God. In Islamic economics, the fundamental 'vertical' relation between God (the Creator) and man (the created), Allåh and *insan* and the 'horizontal' man-man relationship define and guide human behaviour that will be applied in various economic-related concepts.

[30] Mainstream economics has established the *economic man* as the ideal type of economic agent who acts rationally by pursuing his own self-interest and maximizing his own utility. A person is seen as maximizing his utility function, which depends only on his own consumption and which determines all his choices. He is characterized by an individualistic self-interested, utility-maximizing, 'rational' characterization, whilst any ethical consideration is an exogenous variable in his preference.

succeed and how our own lives are shaped by others. They reveal intriguing and (to the purely *economic man*) startling implications of social networks on our personal decisions and the connectedness of communities and ultimately as society as a whole.

Erbaş and Mirakhor (2013) provide some understanding on the symbiotic relationship between *homo economicus* and *homo ethicus*. They argue that compromising moral and rational rules of behaviour is an inevitable consequence of limited human cognitive abilities, limited information, and substantive uncertainty. Given human frailties and inclination towards temptations like greed, faith-based rules, with their age-old traditions and embeddedness in the human mind, urge decision makers to pursue moral market behaviour in the face of uncertainty. 'Nudges[31]' appear to reduce decision uncertainty by appropriately framing choice alternatives and steering decision makers away from errors in decision-making when choices must be made with limited information and often in ignorance. Faith-based rules can be interpreted similarly, even though they often *urge* rather than *nudge*, and sometimes narrow down decisions to a single alternative. This is far from the libertarian spirit but should instead be viewed as a complete trust in the wisdom of guidance from the all-knowing God in the face of uncertainty.

John Haidt's book, *The Righteous Mind* (2012), takes on scientific, evolutionary, and rational perspective to understand humanity. From a scientific standpoint, the passive and empirical view of human nature is that man is irrational, impulsive, and self-interested. From an evolutionary perspective, although universal cooperation is implausible, parochial cooperation can be amplified by similarity and a sense of shared purpose. From a rational standpoint, Haidt calls on the capacity for reason and a sense of common humanity as though we are capable of something greater. This opens a Pandora's box of questions like if intuitions are unreflective and if reason is self-serving, then what part of us can we expect to regulate and coordinate these faculties? How can we attempt to integrate a better understanding of human nature – our sentiments, sociality, and morality – into the ways we act, make decisions, and govern ourselves?

[31]Thaler and Sunstein (2008) illustrated paternalistic 'nudges' that helped in inducing better preferences with long-term consequences (such as a nudge to choose a higher savings plan for retirement and higher health insurance coverage for old age).

CHAPTER 3

Game Theory and Human Behaviour

> *The chess-board is the world; the pieces are the phenomena of the universe; the rules of the game are what we call the laws of Nature. The player on the other side is hidden from us. We know that his play is always fair, and patient. But also we know, to our cost, that he never overlooks a mistake, or makes the smallest allowance for ignorance.*
>
> ***Thomas Henry Huxley (1868)***

Helbling (2013) believed that there are in reality two types of man, the *economic man* and the *social man*, whom he calls *homo economicus* and the *homo socialis*, respectively. According to him, the difference between the *economic man* and the *social man* is that the latter takes into account the interests of others when making decisions, which implies interdependent decisions or 'networked minds'. The different nature of the *social man* reflects a different side of the human being whose dynamics seem more complex than the rational *economic man* and one that seems to be interconnected and influenced to his social relationships. In the case of public goods problems, for example, interactions of agents with strictly self-regarding preferences will lead to 'tragedies of the commons', whilst the self-regulation of the *social man* can overcome this undesirable state and foster cooperation, leading to higher individual and social benefits. Due to the different system dynamics and different systemic outcomes, both types of agents cannot be described by the same body of theory. Helbling suggests that they require separate sets of literature and different institutions. Further to his observations, we postulate that to complete the facets of man, a three-dimensional view is required, and the third dimension may be referred to as the *intuitive man*. This dimension of the human being covers the instinctive ability of man to make decisions automatically. Unlike the presumptions of the previous facets, this model does not need to ruminate over information, take time to assess the situation, nor consider repercussions of decisions made. It is the perceptive knowingness that is an essential aspect of the overall intelligence.

Belief and Rule Compliance
https://doi.org/10.1016/B978-0-12-813809-0.00003-5

When intuition is engaged, our awareness is expanded beyond linear logical thinking. The rationalizing and reasoning come later, *after* the decisions have been made, which, in the end, only tries to justify the actions (Haidt, 2012).

Consequently, if we modify Haidt's concepts to reflect Islamic precepts, we can visualize how the primordial instincts (*fitrah*) natural to man contribute to making moral judgments, and the more iterative role is administered over by the deliberate reflective faculty of reason (*'aql*) known as the intellect. Ibn Arabi saw the intellect as the prime minister of the human kingdom (self) created to oversee the City of Man, from high above in the lofty towers built with refined materials called the mind (Bayrak, 1997). Ibn Arabi noted that although God made the human being the vicegerent (*khalifah*) of the Earth, He made the soul His deputy and gave it divine secrets that man is unaware of. God assigned the soul a special place at the centre of the City of Man – the place called the heart. If God's deputy, whom He sent to govern, is immoral and corrupt and betrays His trust, his people will be corrupt and immoral as well. If he fears and respects the One who entrusted him with knowledge and power, the inhabitants of the city will also be heedful and morally upright.

> *Allâh (s.w.t.) says, 'It is not their eyes that are blind, but their hearts that are in their breasts.'*
>
> ***(Qur'ān 22:72)***

> *The Holy Prophet ﷺ said, 'There is a small piece of meat in the body of man: If it is clean and righteous, the whole being is clean. If that piece of meat is rotten, the whole being is rotten. That piece of meat is the heart.'*

The source of reason has been replaced with the *'aql* or intellect because this deliberate thought process involves an active reflection process for arriving at a decision or a desired result by repeating (iterative) rounds of analysis. This often requires cognition from *both* the intellect of the mind and intelligence of the heart. When reason is overcome by passions (*hawa*) or desires (*nafs*), one will frequently find a person making constant excuses for his/her behaviour, in effect putting one's powers of reasoning in the service of one's desires.[1] In the 32nd book of the Revival, the Book of Patience and Thankfulness (*Kitāb al-Ṣabr wa-l-shukr*), al-Ghazāli further expands on the notion that in a disordered soul, reason is made into a slave of the passions where instead reason should rule over the passions. However, where the desires suppress the religious impulse (*bāʿith al-dīn*), "the intellect

[1]al-Ghazāli, Iḥyā', 9:1527.5–11 (XXIII,qawl fī shahwat al-faraj); cf. *idem, al-Maqṣad*, 74.

of such a person has become a slave to his appetite, so that he does not use his intellect for anything except for crafting subtle plans as the means to satisfy his appetites". Enslavement to the passions leads to error, which in turn will lead only to worse laxity in religious observance and the consequent further erosion of one's moral fibre.

3.1 UNCERTAINTY AND DECISION-MAKING IN UNCERTAINTY

Mainstream economics and finance is dominated by models of decision-making under risk under the rationality axioms, where modern macroeconomics has its analytical roots in the general equilibrium framework of Kenneth Arrow and Gerard Debreu (Arrow and Debreu, 1954). In the Arrow-Debreu framework, the probability distribution of future states of the world is known by agents. Risk can be securitized and thereby priced and hedged. As for modern finance, its origins begin in the portfolio allocation framework of Harry Markowitz and Robert Merton (Markowitz, 1952; Merton, 1969). This Merton-Markowitz framework assumes a known probability distribution for future market risk. This enables portfolio risk to be calculated and thereby priced and hedged. Together, the Arrow-Debreu and Merton-Markowitz frameworks form the bedrock of modern macroeconomics and finance. They help explain patterns of behaviour from consumption and investment to asset pricing and portfolio allocation. This has been a well-trodden path for the past 50 years.

However, economic actors do not necessarily abide by the neoclassical rationality axioms and information available to them is incomplete. The recognition of the limitations of rationality and general equilibrium models in capturing key contributors to financial crises began to attract interest in decision-making under uncertainty. The study of optimal choice under uncertainty first requires the distinction between measurable risk and unknown risk factors that may affect outcomes. In other words, it is a study into the inability to form priors on the distribution of future outcomes rather than risk (Knight, 1921). Neither the Arrow-Debreu nor Merton-Markowitz frameworks reflect such uncertainty. Instead, economic and financial models have been built on often unrealistic assumptions about humans' state of knowledge and cognitive capacity.

Only recently have those strong assumptions about states of knowledge and cognition been questioned and investigated. Many of the dominant figures in twentieth-century economics – from Keynes to Hayek and from

Simon to Friedman – placed imperfections in information and knowledge centre stage. Uncertainty was for them the new 'normal' in decision-making affairs. In complex environments, Simon (1955) believed human behaviour followed simple procedural rules. Simon thus underlined 'procedural rationality' or decision-making using heuristics or procedural rules. These heuristics were evolutionary responses, honed in the light of experience passed down generationally from the past (nature) or accumulated locally in the present (nurture). Neurological and experimental research has since lent support to Simon's thinking (e.g. Selten, 2001). As the individual develops these 'mental shortcuts' in making decisions in such an environment of uncertainty, the importance of ethical rules in that environment is also just as necessary in order to prevent unwanted outcomes or negative externalities that may have wider consequences socially and now internationally.

3.2 PRINCIPLES OF HUMAN DECISION MAKING

A very recent world development report by the World Bank Group entitled *Mind, Society, and Behaviour* (2015) captures the idea that paying attention to how humans think (the processes of the mind in decision-making) and how social networks, history, and context shape thinking (the influence of society) can improve the design and implementation of any institutional policies and interventions that target human choice and action (behaviour). That is to say, institutional policies can be redesigned and fine-tuned based on careful consideration of human factors. In the business world, when failure affects the profit-making bottom line, product designers begin to pay close attention to how humans actually think and decide. Product developers, engineers, private firms, and marketers of all major producing industries have long paid attention to the inherent limits of human cognitive capacity, the role that social preferences and the context play in our decision-making, and the use of mental shortcuts and mental processes for filtering and interpreting information. This often involves many diverse disciplines, including neuroscience, cognitive science, psychology, behavioural economics, sociology, political science, and anthropology.

The oversight of standard economic theory is that it places human cognition and motivation in a 'black box', intentionally simplifying the 'messy and mysterious internal workings of actors' (Freese, 2009) by using models that often assume that people consider all possible costs and benefits from a self-interested perspective and then make a contemplative and rational decision. This approach can be useful to utilize models to explain economic behaviour but in many ways is deficient in capturing other impacting factors and conditions; it ignores the psychological and social influences on behaviour. It is imprudent to treat individuals as deliberate and calculating machines only. Rather, people are highly emotional actors whose decision-making is influenced by contextual cues, local social networks, contemporary norms, culture, and shared mental models. This new view based on the full consideration of human factors does not displace existing policy approaches based on affecting self-interested personal incentives; it works with man's natural instincts instead of unlearning it. Rather, they complement them and enhance existing policy mechanisms.

From the hundreds of empirical papers on human decision-making that form the basis of this thesis, three principles stood out as providing the direction for new approaches to understanding behaviour and implementing adjustments to policies. First, people make most judgments and most choices automatically, not deliberately, which we call as the 'individualistic dimension'. Second, how people act and think often depends on what others around them do and think: we term as the 'social dimension'. Third, individuals in a given society share a common perspective on making sense of the world around them and understanding themselves, which we call the 'mental frame dimension'. We add a fourth dimension to the empirical findings of those three principles, and we call it the 'divine dimension' to encapsulate all avenues that can influence decision-making. Although the first three principles are based on recent groundbreaking research from across the social sciences, it is worth emphasizing that the new research, in some ways, brings the discipline of economics full circle to where it began; with the father of modern economics, Adam Smith (largely grounded in *The Theory of Moral Sentiments*) – a revivication of the fundamental economic – thought that began in the second half of the eighteenth century. A vindication for a grand holistic multi-faceted idea of the economy had been reduced by classical economists to the rational *economic man*, the 'invisible hand', and the oversimplifying assumptions of ceteris paribus.

3.2.1 Individualistic Dimension

In routine situations, people use two systems of thinking. The two systems are also called system 1 (automatic system) and system 2 (deliberative system) (Stanovich and West 2000; Kahneman, 2003). Thinking in system 2 is deliberative, reflective, and intensive – as when solving a difficult logic-based puzzle or understanding a perplexing mystery or in trying to overcome moral dilemmas. This type of thinking is hard and time-consuming.

It is cognitively taxing and can be exhausting. Our capacity to engage in it is limited. Sometimes, it may be difficult to spend even a few minutes focusing attention in a concentrated manner. So, in order to make multiple quick judgments or decisions, individuals simplify the problem. They construct a representation in their heads and then reach a judgment or decision based on that simplification. This type of thinking is effortless, fast, and dominantly outside voluntary control. The mental reserves for this kind of cognitive activity are vast – this is where our minds are operating in automatic mode. It allows us to make sense of a situation in a fraction of a second or detect danger and threat.

The psychologists Daniel Kahneman and Amos Tversky established that people tend to rely on the automatic system to make decisions. People evaluate alternatives quickly, based on what automatically comes to mind. People rarely, if ever, consider all alternatives. Although human beings are often perfectly capable of more careful analysis, people are hard-wired to use just a small part of the relevant information to reach conclusions (Kahneman and Tversky, 2000; Kahneman, 2011). By observing mental processes under controlled experimental conditions, they developed a new understanding of human action that helped lay the foundation for the field of behavioural economics that draws on the psychological, social, and cultural foundations of human decision-making. The automatic system effortlessly generates impressions and feelings that are the main sources of the explicit beliefs and reflective choices of the deliberative system. In everyday life, we use the automatic system without much oversight from the deliberative system, unless the deliberative system is provoked to check it (Table 3.1).

Table 3.1 Automatic versus deliberate thinking

Individualistic dimension	Automatic	Deliberate (reflective)
Characteristics	Instinctive (uncontrolled)	Controlled
	Emotional (irrational)	Deductive (rational)
	Unconscious	Self-aware
	Fast	Slow
	Effortless	Tedious
Specificity	Appetite for food	Fasting/weight-watching
	Speaking the mother tongue	Learning a foreign language
	Taking familiar daily routes	Traversing unfamiliar travel routes

The analytical foundations of public policy have traditionally come from standard economic theory. In standard economic theory, an important behavioural assumption is that people use information in an unbiased way and perform careful calculations. The calculations allow them to make choices based on an unbiased consideration of all possible outcomes of alternative choices that might be made. After people make a choice and observe the outcome, they use the information in an unbiased way to make the next decision and so on. But confronted with the mounting empirical evidence on large and costly errors that people often make in critical choices – such as poor financial decisions and the failure to adhere to health regimens, take health precautions, and adopt income-increasing techniques after receiving new information – economists have come to recognize the importance of considering the possible impacts on behaviour of our dual system of thinking, automatic and deliberative, in the design and testing of policy (World Bank, 2015). A more behavioural model of decision-making entails two key concepts that are most relevant for policy-making:

- People may process only the information that is most salient to them, which may lead them to miss key information and overlook critical consequences.
- There may be a mismatch between intentions and actions (the intention-action divide). Even if people understand the full consequences of their actions, they may make decisions that favour the present at the expense of the future, so that they consistently fail to carry out plans that match their goals and fulfil their interests.

3.2.1.1 Biases in Assessments of Information

Automatic thinking is shaped by the accessibility of different features of a particular situation. When trying to make a decision, the automatic thought process is relying on a structure of understanding to organize information and distinguish between the things one needs to consider and the things one can ignore. What we think as unimportant features of the context of decision-making can all affect accessibility and therefore judgment (and behaviour). These include how many choices one must make sense of, whether it resonates with us emotionally, and whether it activates events in recent memory that are deemed relevant to the decision. Affective (or emotional) states, including depression, can strongly affect cognitive processes in attention, memory, and appraisal, which are crucial to effective decision-making (Beck, 2008; Disner et al., 2011).

3.2.1.2 Subjective Assessments of Value

Plato pointed out, "Human behaviour flows from three main sources: desire, emotion, and knowledge'. Our assessments of value are subjected to our emotions and desire for the object or outcome without complete knowledge. Bernoulli's (1738) analysis of the dynamics of the St. Petersburg paradox[2] led him to be aware that the subjective value, or utility, that a payoff has for an individual is not always directly related to the absolute amount of that payoff or expected value. Rather, the value a person attaches to an outcome can be influenced by such factors as the likelihood of winning, or probability, amongst other things. In this way, Bernoulli showed that people would not always bet solely on the basis of the expected value of a game.

Today, our own experience and observations like those in Daniel Kahneman's *Thinking, Fast and Slow* (2011) have confirmed an even broader range of behavioural vulnerabilities and vagaries in our abilities to make decisions as human beings (see Table 3.2). The heuristics may have served us well as human beings when we were employed in physical work such as cultivating the land in a largely industrial economy. They do, however, open us up for biased (risk versus reward) decision-making when applied to today's knowledge-based work.

When people think automatically, the way in which their choices are presented and the context in which they make decisions may systematically influence their preferences. Factors that would be unimportant under the standard assumption that people have unlimited capacities to process information but that in fact can be quite important include the following:

- The default option, to which decisions would revert if no other decision was made or no other action taken
- The number of options
- The sequence in which the options are presented
- The connections, if any, that are drawn between the current decision problem and decisions that the individual made earlier
- The gap between the period when a decision maker forms an intention and the period when he has funds available to pay for it
- The salience of a social identity and relevant norms

[2]The Saint Petersburg paradox is a theoretical game used in economics, to represent a classical example whereby if only the expected value is taken into account as the only decision criterion, the decision maker will be misguided into an irrational decision. This paradox was presented and solved in Daniel Bernoulli's 'Commentarii Academiae Scientiarum Imperialis Petropolitanae' (translated as 'Exposition of a New Theory on the Measurement of Risk'). The game was first proposed by Bernoulli, where a player bets on how many tosses of a coin will be needed before it first turns up heads.

Table 3.2 Selected decision bias concepts

Decision bias	Cognitive distortion
Anchoring	An anchor is an aspect of the environment that has no direct relevance to a decision but that nonetheless affects judgments. For example, our questions prime our attention for certain information, ignoring contradictory data
Availability heuristic	Recent events are weighted disproportionately higher than past events Vivid and unique events are highly weighted too
Confirmation bias	Evidences that confirm our earlier decisions are sought, ignoring new information against them. Judgments of what is fair or right are biased towards own self-interests
Framing	Decisions are made based on how it is framed. In financial situations, our pain of losing is stronger than our pleasure of winning; as such, we are risk averse to gains and risk-seeking to avoid further losses
Hindsight bias	The tendency to view the past as having been more predictable than it actually was. Hence, the challenge to our ability to learn from past errors/events.
Salience	The tendency to overestimate the causal role (salience) of information we have available to us

Well-thought-out policy can improve development outcomes by changing the context of decision-making. And all of this can be viewed as taking place under the overall cloak of uncertainty (see also the processes described in Fig. 3.1A and B and in Fig. 3.2). The fact that the universe is too complex for the human mind points at the need for decision heuristics with guidance from experience, tradition, and last but not least divine revelation.

3.2.1.3 Choice Construction

A lot of consequences on constructing a choice fall on context, options, and simplicity. Choice construction influences decision-making by simplifying the presentation of options, by automatically evoking particular associations, or by making one option more salient or easier to choose than the alternatives (Thaler and Sunstein, 2008). Thaler coined the term *libertarian paternalism*. The *libertarian* part of the idea is that individual choice should be free and not interfered with by others, especially the government. Yet, there is a need for interference in most cases for better social outcomes, that is, a need for a measure of *paternalism*. How does one reconcile the two seemingly contradictory ideas in line with the neoclassical choice models

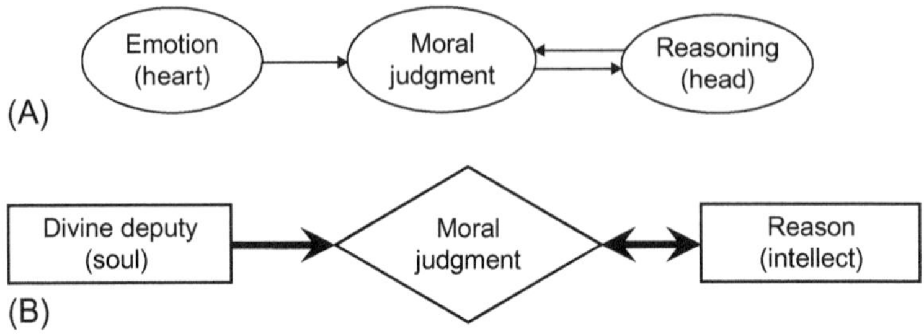

Fig. 3.1 (A) Thought processes to moral judgment according to Haidt (2012). (B) The deputy of God and prime minister of the City of Man decide moral judgment according to ibn Arabi (Bayrak, 1997).

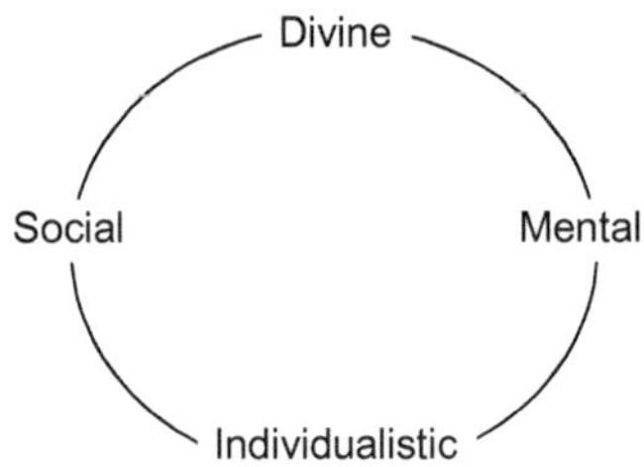

Fig. 3.2 The four dimensions in principles of human decision-making.

and their foundational axioms and philosophical tenets? You nudge the decision maker and frame the better choice as default but give alternatives at the same time. For example, in retirement plans, one could offer a preferred high savings plan and also offer a few low savings plans but frame the offers in such a way that the higher savings plan is salient and, hence, the *paternalistic* but seemingly *libertarian* 'nudge'. A component of choice architecture is simplicity. Too many options or too much complexity may lead individuals to avoid thinking through a decision, to postpone indefinitely making an active decision, or to make mistakes. It is unreasonable to expect individuals to make choices in scenarios for which they have limited experience and have little education or no training to prepare them. Hence, it is worth noting that in 'choices' inspired by divine revelation, often, there are no alternatives or seemingly so because of its saliency, and so, the 'choice' becomes singular, and the nudge is deemed 'ordained'.

3.2.1.4 *Willpower, Procrastination and Temptation*

Human beings experience self-control problems when their preferences are not consistent across time. One form of self-control problem concerns persistent bad habits or addictions, such as cigarette smoking, overeating, or just plain laziness (Burger et al., 2008). People know that they will later regret a current choice of self-indulgence but nevertheless still choose to engage in such activity or the lack of it. In another scenario, an individual is faced with a productive activity that will lead to future benefits but is unappealing at the moment because it requires work and sacrifice to forego some immediate gratification (Burger et al., 2011). This often leads to procrastination (an intention-action divide), common in everyday life. Our inability to fulfil good intentions – to diet, exercise, or save for retirement – can be explained with a mathematical theory termed as *present bias* (Phelps and Pollak, 1968; Akerlof, 1991; Laibson, 1997; O'Donoghue and Rabin, 1999). Present bias gives full weight to the rewards and costs that happen right now and gives half weight to rewards and costs that happen in the future, which leads to a cycle of procrastination. In his 2011 TED Talk[3] on the failure of self-control, Laibson explored why we are tempted to put hard work off for our future selves – "we all have this robust gap between what we intend to do and what we actually do". He believes that gap comes from an inherent focus on the present and a desire to delay the weight of our responsibilities. Psychologically, pushing unpleasant tasks into the future is like getting a 50% discount on them. In other words, delaying unpleasant chores only feel half as bad when we imagine doing them tomorrow. It is the foundation of failures of self control and why good intentions are so often incongruent with good behaviour.

As such when automatically enrolling people into opt-in retirement savings plans (i.e. making 'opt-in' as the default option), 'procrastination is working in your favour', Laibson and his colleagues observed, and participation rates rise from 40% to 90% (Beshears et al., 2008). Laibson showed that the higher the penalties imposed on savers for early withdrawal of funds, the more money they deposited – from 35% of funds at a 10% penalty to 56% of funds when the account was completely inaccessible (Laibson, 1997). Commitment devices, like the 'tying of hands' example above, are an additional promising area of intervention to address present bias. They combine an awareness of the intention-action divide with an understanding of loss aversion.

In Islam, procrastination is closely related to laziness, which is classified as a disease that the Prophet ﷺ sought Allåh's (s.w.t.) protection and refuge against. The Prophet ﷺ was reported to have said, "O Allåh, I seek refuge in You from helplessness, laziness…". To fight it, Muslims are recommended to first make a sincere intention to overcome it and then

[3]Professor David Laibson of the Harvard Business School (2011) at the TED@AllianzGI conference at the Time Warner Center, New York.

strive with consistent action; "And those who shall strive for Our Sake, We shall surely guide them unto Our ways". (Qur'ān 29:69). It is the fact that we persist in it is because we find some comfort and pleasure in it, and in time, it forms into a habit. So, we cannot be expected to get rid of it entirely unless we also learn to link this habit with pain and suffering. One example is www.StickK.com founded by Yale University economics Prof. Dean Karlan and two colleagues to help people fulfil their goals by allowing them to risk their own money. They set up monetary contracts against themselves to fight procrastination and lose the money if they do not complete their self-described objectives. The Prophet ﷺ also said, "The most beloved of deeds to Allåh (s.w.t.) are those that are most consistent, even if it is small" (Sahih al-Bukhari 6464 Book 81, Hadith 53), which also underlines the importance of good habit forming to counter laziness that leads to procrastination.

Although self-control theories model willpower as a depletable (although renewable) resource (Baumeister and Vohs, 2003; Ozdenoren et al., 2012), we do not *realize* that willpower and motivation get progressively depleted throughout the day. When your willpower is exhausted, you are even more likely to make decisions based on the environment around you. This is where choice architecture and self-control (or rather the lack of) come together. Since every choice set is presented in one way or another, making the vital aspects of the choice prominent and making it cognitively less burdensome to arrive at the right decision (such as choosing future benefits over present bias) can help people make better decisions. Prayers are also a way to instill intent and to develop willpower by constant affirmation to regain self-control. Constant striving against the 'comfort' of laziness and inaction will strengthen the muscle of productivity, and sufficient rest through prayer and contemplation will renew depleted willpower (Fig. 3.3).

Verily, the prayer keeps one from the great sins and evil deeds.

(Qur'ān 29:45)

Verily, man was created impatient, irritable when evil touches him and niggardly when good touches him. Except for those devoted to prayer those who remain constant in their prayers...

(Qur'ān 70:19–23)

3.2.2 Social Dimension

The social dimension of humanity is the tendency amongst humans to associate and behave as members of groups. Our beliefs, desires, and behaviours are affected by social preferences, our interconnectedness and the social contexts

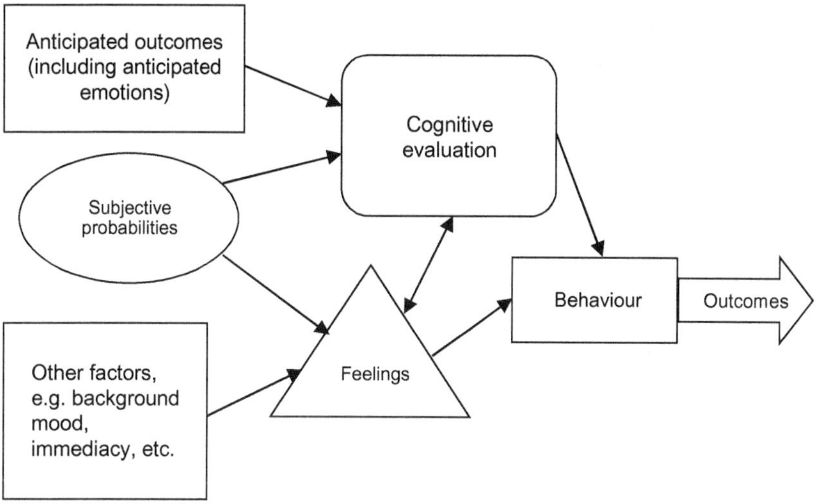

Fig. 3.3 The individualistic dimension of decision-making.

in which we live and make decisions. We are 'group-minded individuals' who see the world from a social and an individual perspective; we understand what is in the minds of others and often act as if our brains are networked with the brains of other people (Christakis and Fowler, 2010; Tomasello, 2014). Our social tendencies mean that we are not purely selfish and wealth-maximizing actors, as many economic models and policies assume; rather, we value reciprocity and fairness, we are willing to cooperate in the attainment of shared goals (World Bank, 2015). We have a tendency to develop and adhere to common understandings and rules of behaviour, whether or not they benefit us individually and collectively. We are subtly (and often unconsciously) influenced by people around us (and our friends' friends' friends) – the power of influence extends out by three degrees – and whilst the impact weakens, the geometric number of influence points grows (Christakis and Fowler, 2010). These shape many parts of our life (including our beliefs, our careers, our health, and how we feel) – some for better and some for worse.

According to Christakis and Fowler in their book, *Connected*, the four key rules to networks and being interconnected socially are as follows:

i. We affect our networks, and our network influences us. We turn out to be like the people we spend time with. *Transitivity* (i.e. the amount of connections we have) affects the quality of our lives (it influences our expectations, our chosen life partners, where we live, the type of jobs we get, our emotions, and our well-being).

ii. Our friends affect us and we often mimic our friends. Friends give us confidence (and indicate safety) to do things. If a friend has done something/bought something/been somewhere, then we are much more likely to also do it/buy it/go there.

iii. Our friends' friends' friends affect us, as we are influenced not only by what our friends do but also by our friends' friends and surprisingly by their friends. Likewise, what we do echoes out through three levels of friends before it loses its energy and impact.

iv. Networks have a life of their own, and no one controls or owns the network much like a river. It is complex, dynamic, and constantly flowing. A flock of geese has no leader but it self-organizes. It has no central control point but rather a 'directed intelligence'.

Some people are on the edge of networks, others at the very heart of them. Some people have lots of connections with others and thus their networks, whilst others are not. For networks to be effective, they also need ties into other networks; for example, those people who have different circles of friends/acquaintances are the critical connectors that allow information to flow between networks. Furthermore, social networks that are more insular are less equipped to solve novel problems than those networks with lots of interconnections with other networks.

The circles we live and work in are fundamental to the opportunities and quality of lives we get to lead (so, it is less about absolute ability as it is about the connections one has around you as they create the initial opportunities and levels of expectations). As such, the old adage 'it's not what you know, it's who you know' is still true. Human sociality can be a lever for new types of behavioural interventions that harness the tendencies of individuals to seek social status, to build and maintain social identities, and to cooperate with others under specific conditions.

3.2.2.1 Social Preferences

Social rewards, such as status and recognition, can motivate people to exert effort and can even substitute for monetary rewards in some situations. Behavioural interventions can harness this human desire for status and recognition.

Firms use employee-of-the-month clubs alongside traditional salaries to recognize and incentivize contributions to organizational goals that are advantageous and exemplary but often difficult to quantify. In fact, humans may have an innate, unconscious tendency to reward strong contributors to group goals with esteem, which helps groups overcome barriers to collective action (Willer, 2009).

Prestige can incentivize people, groups, and even countries. When nations' different values and norms inhibit cooperation, status awards in the form of participation in international summits and strategic partnerships may be more effective than conventional strategies of containment and integration for achieving cooperation on global governance initiatives (Larson and Shevchenko, 2010).

Ranking schemes, which bestow status on exemplary states and shame underperforming ones, may be a cost-effective means of shifting state actions. Numerical indicators, such as the World Bank's Governance rankings and the Islamicity Index,[4] do not only provide performance information but also serve as 'rules of thumb' that simplify and frame information according to an ideology of what a rule-compliant society looks like. Indicators enable comparisons that motivate a variety of economic actors, including bureaucrats, citizens, elites, and governments (Davis et al., 2012).

3.2.2.2 The Influence of Social Networks

We are heavily influenced by the norms of our social networks. We unconsciously mimic others to be part of that group. The more we relate to a group or want to be a part of it, the more influential their norms will be upon us. We are more influenced by people of the same sex and socially, people at the centre of a network have more influence than those on the periphery. Not only networks provide scope for individuals to reinforce existing behaviours amongst one another, but also they can transmit novel information and normative pressures, sometimes sparking social change. The ability of social networks to both stabilize and shift patterns of behaviour means that they may be able to play an important role in social settings where formal institutions are lacking.

Groups such as weight watchers and other interest groups form powerful social networks of influence where it is the people and not the techniques that drive success. An individual's success story at 'The Biggest Loser'[5] resonates throughout the network. This provides a positive reference experience of success, so building their own belief that success is also possible for them.

Sometimes, interventions can initiate broad changes in the social fabric that are difficult to foresee. For example, offering insurance to only those farmers who possess an insurable asset (common in developing countries) may actually increase the wage risk for assetless labourers in Indian villages

[4]A study conducted by Prof. Hossein Askari and Dr. Scheherazade S Rehman that examined 208 countries and determined the greatest economic and social success by the criteria spelt out in the Qur'ān.

[5]A TV show where participants compete to lose the most weight over a set period of time and tasks.

by increasing labour demand volatility (Mobarak and Rosenzweig, 2013). This is an example of *adverse selection* of insurance coverage affecting the labour market. In light of these studies, when policies that target social networks are being considered, it is imperative to pay close attention to how interventions affect social relationships in the population.

3.2.2.3 The Role of Social Norms

Social norms are the 'glue' of society and serve as informal governance mechanisms that exert a powerful influence on individual decision-making and behaviour. Humans are hard-wired to develop and adhere to norms – young children quickly learn the 'social rules of the game' – following norms and punishing norm violators. Imitating behaviours is one of the key ways humans learn strategies for interacting in the world.

The strength of social compliance is often underrated. Muhammad Yunus of the Grameen Bank saw that people would never lend to poor Bangladeshis, as they had no collateral to hold against the loan. By lending to small communities, he harnessed the power of peer group pressure that ensured that the loans were repaid. Another example is Wikipedia, which is an open system that anyone can edit. It is not centralized and like many self-organizing teams with no formal authority, manages to resist abuse by applying self-policing, peer group pressure.

However, inefficient social norms may be sustained because of the coordinating role they play in a society or being heavily entrenched in the social psyche. Norms can evoke strong emotions in people, and they often possess an expressive value in the communities in which they operate. In these ways, social norms can have large effects on both collective welfare and individual agency (Boudet et al., 2013), for instance, social and legal norms around gender and the prejudice of the fairer sex. Altering social norms that contribute to undesirable social outcomes is an obvious policy goal. However, predicting how norms may interact with policy is difficult. In a recent field experiment, a civic education course in Mali actually widened the gender gap in civic participation by increasing the salience of civic activity, which increased the social costs for females who participated in civic life (Gottlieb, 2014). The intervention reduced knowledge gaps, but it exacerbated gender inequality.

3.2.3 Mental Frames Dimension

Mental frames help people make sense of the world – to interpret their environment and understand themselves. Al-Ghazāli suggests that our very perceptions and experiences serve to frame our understanding of the world, so that most of us end up viewing it in more and more mundane terms. This is because the sensory world and our personal experience of it are for most of us all that we have time for and all that we have to go by; an easy familiarity with our daily surroundings leads to jurists dreaming only of jurisprudence and traders only of trade and in general for each of us to perceive in the world only that to which their attention is customarily drawn.[6] This mental framing of an individual perspective includes categories, concepts, identities, prototypes, stereotypes, causal narratives, and worldviews. Although mental frames are often shared and arise from human sociality and social norms, they differ in that they do not need to be enforced by direct social pressure, often capture broad ideas about how the world operates and how they fit in it. In contrast, social norms tend to focus on particular behaviours and to be socially reaffirmed and consequently enforced. Without mental concepts and frames, it would be impossible for people to make most decisions in daily life. And without shared mental models, it would be impossible in many cases for people to develop institutions, solve collective action problems, feel a sense of belonging and solidarity, or even understand one another.

There is immense variation in mental frames across societies, including different perceptions of the way the world functions. Individuals can adapt their mental models, updating them when they learn that outcomes are inconsistent with expectations. However, individuals may hold on to mental models that have destructive consequences for their lives and may continue to use them to validate their interpretations, even when those concepts and interpretations are evidently false. Some mental concepts can have huge consequences, even leading to an entrenched understanding of nature (or way of life) that causes intergenerational transmission of corruption, crime, and poverty. Individuals can also hold onto multiple and sometimes even contradictory mental frames – drawing on one or another mental frame depending on the context triggered by looking at different situations.

Understanding the role that mental concepts and frames play in individual decision-making opens up the possibility of new levers for policy enhancement whilst at the same time highlighting potential problems in design and implementation. Behavioural interventions can be ineffective when policy designers have a faulty mental frame of how a population will react to a program or a policy tweak.

[6]Al-Ghazāli, *Iḥyā'*, 13:2377.15–17 (XXXIII, shaṭ 2,bayān 7).

For example, Tversky and Kahneman (1981) explored how different framing (positive framing, i.e. how many people would live, or negative framing, i.e. how many people would die.) affected participants' responses to a choice in a hypothetical life and death situation:

> Imagine that the United States is preparing for the outbreak of an unusual Asian disease, which is expected to kill 600 people. One possible program to combat the disease has been proposed. Assume that the exact scientific estimate of the consequences of this program is as follows:

Framing	Treatment A	Treatment B
Positive	'Saves 200 lives'	'A 33% chance of saving all 600 people, 66% possibility of saving no one'.
Negative	'400 people will die'	'A 33% chance that no people will die, 66% probability that all 600 will die'.

Treatment A was chosen by 72% of participants when it was presented with positive framing ('saves 200 lives') dropping to only 22% when the same choice was presented with negative framing ('400 people will die'). Here, we can clearly see decision reversals when choices are framed differently.

3.2.3.1 The Impact on Thoughts and Actions

In the standard economic model, if beliefs are inconsistent with outcomes, then the decision maker would revise his beliefs as he observes new information. In contrast, what an individual displaying psychological, social, and cultural influences sees and infers in his mind are affected by his mental frames. The consequence is that we create a world that Hoff and Stiglitz (2010) describe as an *equilibrium fiction.* A conviction in a race-based or gender-based hierarchy can affect self-confidence in ways that create productivity differences that sustain the beliefs, although no underlying differences exist.[7] The skewed features of reality appear when we differentiate between our personal conceptualization of 'a truth' and a universal ideal of 'the truth'. We argue that the basic associations and mental concepts that we hold in our minds are unique to us and this therefore gives us an opportunity to craft our unique experiences.

[7]This is akin to the *Pygmalion effect* (or Rosenthal effect) whereby the greater the expectation placed upon people, the better they perform. It is a type of self-fulfilling prophecy where if you think something will happen, you may unconsciously make it happen through your actions or inaction.

3.2.3.2 The Effects of Identity Saliency

In *Identity Economics*, Akerlof and Kranton (2000) observed that identity in economics showed that social context matters in the following way: since 'people have a notion of who they are', that is, a self-image or what their identities are, social group norms influence their 'beliefs about how they and others are supposed to behave' and that identity (as defined by culture, religion, environment, so on) can influence economic performance.

The identity-salience principle asserts that increases in the salience of an identity within a person's self-concept increase the likelihood of subsequent identity-driven attitudes and behaviour. One way to test the influence of mental models on behaviour is to experimentally manipulate the salience of a mental model. A research on a maximum security prison in Zurich, Switzerland, established that increasing the salience of an individual's criminal identity increased his dishonesty (Cohn et al., 2013).

Reed et al. (2012) propose five basic principles that can help researchers model the process of identity formation and expression:

- **i.** *Identity salience*: identity processing increases when the identity is an active component of the self
- **ii.** *Identity association*: the nonconscious association of stimuli with a positive and salient identity improves response to the stimuli
- **iii.** *Identity relevance*: the deliberative evaluation of identity-linked stimuli depends on how diagnostic the identity is in the relevant domain
- **iv.** *Identity verification*: individuals monitor their own behaviours to manage and reinforce their identities
- **v.** *Identity conflict*: identity-linked behaviours help people manage the relative prominence of multiple identities

Research on performance and identity shows that context also influences the ability and motivation to learn and to expend effort, with potentially large effects on human capital formation. Context seems to trigger beliefs about what one is capable of and what one should achieve. An experiment on caste in India finds that context can have an important impact on performance. The experiment assessed the effect of manipulating the salience of caste on children's intellectual performance in classrooms (Hoff and Pandey, 2006). The control condition, in which caste identity was not revealed, demonstrated that low-caste boys solve mazes just as well as high-caste boys. However, publicly revealing caste in mixed-caste groups reduced the performance of the low-caste boys, which (controlling for individual characteristics) created a 23% caste gap in total mazes solved in favour of the high castes.

3.2.3.3 Shaping Beliefs, Ideologies and Biases

Beliefs can lead people to ignore, suppress, or forget observations that would tend to undermine their beliefs. Confirmation bias, discussed in Section 3.2.1, is the tendency to search for and use information that supports one's beliefs. If the bias is sufficiently strong, it is possible that the false hypothesis will never be discarded, no matter how much evidence exists that favours the alternative hypothesis (Rabin and Schrag, 1999).

Magzan (2012) believes that since our social conditioning provides us with a stable environment, mental frames function as 'filters' in our brain that allow only certain limited portion of the external stimuli to actually enter our consciousness. This is useful in terms of filtering information for our sanity and risk reasons or for quick decision-making, but the problem is that humans generally have a tendency to reject data that do not support an already existing assumption. In other words, the trouble begins when we begin to comprehend everything through categories that worked for us in the past. For this reason, not only mental models are often the greatest barriers to implementing new ideas in organizations, but also they are the area of organizational learning where organizations can make the most significant impact.

Economic and political forces influence mental models, but mental models can have an independent influence on development by shaping attention, perception, interpretation, and the associations that automatically come to mind. Behavioural policy interventions may be able to expose people to alternative experiences, ways of thinking, and role models that expand mental concepts and frames, thereby overcoming stereotypes, improve trust, encourage collective action and increase risk-sharing transactions.

Most economists view human behaviour as intentional or reason-based. That is, an individual acts because it is seen as being in the individual's interest; actions are judged by their expected ends, and the belief that the act will generate a positive result motivates it. This suggests two main avenues of extension to conventional economic analysis: first, the nature of desires, and second, cognitive limitations. From a cognitive view, beliefs about the world and about what one values, as well as learning that modifies such beliefs, are key to understanding decisions. These principles of human decision-making, their complex, and at times perplexing processes create mental patterns that defy conventional wisdom and classical economic models that supposes purely rational calculations lie behind economic decisions. Behavioural economics and behavioural finance (as we will describe more in detail in the next chapter) are raising awareness of a more value-based, emotionally literate approach to the art of choosing. This not only opens up new avenues for productive research but also provides new understanding for why policies based on standard economic assumptions have failed. At the same time, it provides limitless opportunities to develop new tools for promoting mindset shift for development and modifying current approaches to maximize their intended effect.

3.2.4 Divine Dimension

On a different scale of existence, spirituality and divine inspiration cannot be ignored when human behaviours and decision-making are being investigated. It is a significant aspect of gaining knowledge and information for moral and beneficial decision-making. However, it may often be discarded or overlooked due to the secularist perspective on scientific research and investigation that require apparent proofs and evidences. This kind of reasoning in itself can be considered as biases that need to be overcome in investigative research work.

According to the various readings on and by al-Ghazāli,[8] Allåh (s.w.t.) wanting to reveal to men the idea of inspiration has given them a kind of glimpse of it in sleep and visions. In fact, man perceives whilst asleep the things of the unseen world either clearly discernible or as metaphors to be subsequently interpreted by spiritual insights. To a skeptic whom has never experienced this kind of dreams, he may attribute them as hallucinations in a state of lethargy or reclusion where the extreme effects of fast and complete suspension of the senses (like sight and hearing) in which a man can see the things of the unseen world. The skeptic would argue that the sensitive faculties are the causes of perception, and whence suspended, real perception becomes impossible.

However, al-Ghazāli rebukes such falsity of argument by claiming that the proofs are in evidence and experience. To him, in the same way as reason constitutes a particular phase of existence in which intellectual concepts are perceived that are hidden from the senses, similarly, inspiration is a special state in which the inner eye discovers mysteries out of the reach of reason. To prove the possibility of inspiration is to prove that it belongs to a category of branches of knowledge that cannot be attained by reason. It is the same with medical science and astronomy. Al-Ghazāli points out that he

[8]The readings include 'The Revival of the Religious Sciences' and 'Incoherence of the Philosophers' as well as those written about him in 'The Many Faces of Philosophy: Reflections from Plato to Arendt' edited by Amelie Oksenberg Rorty.

who studies them is obliged to recognize that they are derived solely from the revelation and special grace of God. Some astronomical phenomena only occur once in a thousand years; how then can we know them by experience?

This is the same for divine inspiration, being one of the branches of intuitive knowledge. The characteristic of inspiration mentioned here is only one of its many attributes, a drop in the vast ocean of knowledge,[9] and it is mentioned here because people experience what is analogous to it in dreams and in the sciences of medicine and astronomy. These branches of knowledge belong to the domain of prophetic miracles, and reason cannot access it without Allåh's (s.w.t.) permission (i.e. through spiritual efforts).

As to the other characteristics of inspiration, they are only revealed to adepts in Sufism and in a state of ecstatic experience. There is a condition of the person initiated in this kind of ecstasy that builds a degree of certitude and conviction that cannot be attained by reason. This single fact is sufficient to make us believe in inspiration. Experiential evidence results in comprehending such ephemeral occurrences and consequently believing in it, for conviction results from comprehension.

Al-Ghazāli believes that when we have ascertained the real nature of inspiration and proceed to the serious study of the Qur'ān and the Sunnah, we will ascertain that Muhammad ﷺ is the greatest of prophets. After that, he urges us to fortify our faith by verifying the truth of the Prophet's preaching and its effects upon the soul. Some examples given to verify through experience the truth of sentences from the following Hadiths (sayings of the Prophet ﷺ): "He who makes his conduct accord with his knowledge receives from God more knowledge" and "Whosoever when rising in the morning has only one anxiety (to please God), God will preserve him from all anxiety in this world and the next". When we have verified these sayings in experience thousands of times, al-Ghazāli believes that only then can we be in possession of a certitude on which doubt cannot hold. Such is the path we must traverse in order to realize the truth of inspiration.

[9]In the Qur'ān, there is a story (in Surah Kahf 18:60–82) of Prophet Moses (a.s.) meeting Khidr (a.s.). In Sufi literature, the parable of this meeting is that of the Spiritual Seeker (Moses) meeting with a Higher Knower (Khidr) where the two rivers meet: the river from human knowledge and river from divine knowledge. Of course, rivers lead to the ocean, and our knowledge is but a drop in that ocean. In Sufi theology, divine knowledge is of two types: first, the knowledge that takes its legitimacy from the study of religion (*'ilm*) and secondly the knowledge (*irfan*) that comes from God through prayer and contemplation. In other words, these two types of knowledge are outwardly gained and inwardly gained.

3.2.4.1 Revelation in the Scriptures

The al-Qur'ān mentions three principal names of the book revealed: 'the mother of the book' (*umm al-kitab*) as the eternal prototype of the Qur'ān, 'the recitation' (*al-Qur'ān*) as the auditory revelation, and 'the criterion' (*al-furqan*) as the sacred law. According to Al-Jili (Burckhardt, 2000), the 'mother of the book' corresponds to the unfathomable depths of the divinity and maternal source of the universe. 'The recitation' analogically corresponds to the state of how the message descended into the Prophet and how the divine knowledge in the scripture was transferred. 'The criterion' as a symbol of the divine qualities translated into the sacred law for humanity and in it lies the prescribed and proscribed behaviours.

There are nonterrestrial aspects of the Qur'ān that concerns the order of the universe and on a more spiritual sense, parables of stories narrated in its chapters that derived lessons suited for a particular time or circumstance. From a chronological perspective, the Qur'ān follows after three other divine scriptures: *Zabur* or Psalms (descended upon Dawud a.s. or David p.b.u.h.), *Taurat* or Torah (descended upon Musa a.s. or Moses p.b.u.h.), and *Injeel* or Holy Bible (descended upon Isa a.s. or Jesus p.b.u.h.). Al-Jili believes that each revelation is necessarily limited in its form – not its essence – to be compensated by another. As the final revelation to mankind, the Qur'ān will appear as a synthesis to Judaic and Christian beliefs and re-establishes the original unifying message of Allåh (s.w.t.).

The divine qualities in rational terms remain incomprehensible as they are attempted to be conceived based on traces of intellect, reason, memory, and mental frames. They appear as abstracts of concrete fathomable things in our minds as we attempt to conceive them in our heads. Instead, Al-Jili likens them more accurately to the colours contained in white light of the Sun – where they are not directly perceptible – manifesting themselves in some form of matter that filters them and reflects them. Hence, for our understanding, the glimpses of these qualities or in the same sense, inspiration, are like the vision (dream) of the rainbow and the image of the white light (the Sun) through the falling scattering veil of the rain.

3.2.4.2 Morality and Practical Decision-Making

In Islam, there is no contradiction between reason and revelation. Deep sincerity and a persevering attitude in looking for answers will definitely lead to the truth being revealed. In sources of revelation, the divine law clearly states that the intellect is a necessity for rational decision-making and its well-being must be preserved. Alcohol, for instance, nullifies the ability for rationality, and it impedes proper decision-making, condemning it to prohibition in the eyes of *Sharī'ah*. It says in the Qur'ān, 'They ask thee concerning wine and gambling'. *Say:* "In them is great sin, and some profit, for men; but the sin is greater than the profit..." (Qur'ān 2:219). Since alcohol can possibly cause harm that inflicts injury on all – society, family, and especially to the own individual – the prohibition has been stated clearly and agrees with simple reasoning that requires no skill in deeper interpretation. The danger and social ills of intoxicants are well documented and apparent.

However, there are limitations to reason. Although it draws similarity in the verse by acknowledging benefit and warning of the harm, however, reason is limited to its methodology – which is either deductive or inductive. Since deductive reasoning cannot predict the future, we refer to inductive reasoning. Without prior knowledge, to understand benefit and harm is by experience and, by this, through investigation, research, 'trial-and-error' experimentation, and drawing lessons from similar historical events. Society then decides what is appropriate whilst considering other aspects like encroachment into the freedom of choice, freedom of beliefs, etc. It becomes a logical fallacy[10] when a harm cannot be legislated due to other reasons not attributed to its harmful effects. Here, we find limitations to our collective reasoning.

However, there are other evidences to show inherent morality, whether it is inborn in the young or through religion or secular institutions. In his book *Big Gods: How Religion Transformed Cooperation and Conflict*, Norenzayan (2013) showed that, amongst other things, when belief in God was distilled into belief in a *mean* God (i.e. vengeful and punishing) versus belief in a *nice* God (i.e. compassionate and forgiving), participants endorsing a mean-God concept were less likely to cheat relative to nice-God supporters. Thus, there appears to be evidence that "mean Gods make good people" (p. 44). So, having a God that people both love and fear helps motivate people to behave in desirable, prosocial, and cooperative ways. Norenzayan also addresses a potential problem facing many religious groups: that some people might feign their religiousness to be part of the in-group and reap rewards in a selfish, free-rider manner. With tough practices associated with a religion, however, religious hypocrites have a harder time faking their religious commitments. Proscription of certain dietary practices and adherence to strict marital and sexual practices, for example, helps to monitor religious adherents. As Norenzayan (2013) suggests, such strict religious behaviours keep possible free-riders at check, which ultimately helps to maintain group solidarity.

[10]In this case, it is the logical fallacy of false cause. False cause fallacy is the presumption that a real or perceived relationship between things means that one is the cause of the other.

In *Just Babies: The Origins of Good and Evil*, Bloom (2013) argues that humans are in fact hard-wired with a sense of morality. Drawing on his research at Yale, Bloom demonstrates that, even before they can speak or walk, babies judge the goodness and vileness of others' actions; feel empathy and compassion; act to soothe those in distress; and have a rudimentary sense of justice. One set of researchers, for example, asked kids ages 6–8 to help decide how to divide up an uneven number of rewards to two imaginary characters who cleaned up their room. When given the option, participants tended to choose to throw the extra reward away rather than give it to one of the characters and thus generate an unfair distribution. Similarly, children as young as 16 months old prefer a character who divides goods equally amongst the other characters and are surprised at unequal distributions (based on looking times). Still, he contends that this innate morality is countered by its duality evident in hostility towards strangers, tendency to parochialism, bigotry, and base desires. Broadly, internal and external influences on behaviours make practical moral decision-making complex and rarely straightforward.

3.2.4.3 Moral Dilemmas: The Case of the Abandoned Ship

There was an instance that was attributed to al-Ghazāli who presented this case study to his students, in his book on the principles of Islamic jurisprudence called 'al-Mustasfa min 'ilm al-Usul' or 'On Legal Theory of Islamic Jurisprudence' (Al-Allaf, 2003). It went like this:

> *Three hundred people were in a boat sailing on the sea. They realized that their safety was at risk, and the lives of the majority could only be saved by throwing 10 people overboard. Would it be morally right to kill 10 people in order to save 290?*

This case cleverly highlights a unique moral dilemma situation. Following the different dimensions (viz. individualistic, social, and mental frames) of decision-making discussed in Sections 3.2.1–3.2.3, this case study in moral dilemma reveals that another more crucial dimension is required in decision-making when it involves the decision of who lives and who does not for the benefit of the whole.

According to al-Ghazāli and on the basis of *Sharī'ah* (in this case, specifically rulings derived directly from the Qur'ān and Sunnah), it is morally wrong to kill some people in order to save others. Al-Ghazāli gave three reasons against the justification of killing in this case of the abandoned ship:

1. *Certainty*: it is not certain that killing some people will save the rest. What if they killed them and still faced problems, should they kill another 10

people to save the rest? This is morally unjustifiable and becomes a slippery slope.[11]

2. *Necessity*: the benefit of those people on the boat is not necessary to a degree to break another necessity[12] and kill human beings.
3. *Universality*: the benefit of people, in this case the majority, is not a universal benefit; it is only the interest of small community who are going to use others as means to their end.

In Islam, the life of every single human is precious; it is one of the five necessities in the objectives of the *Sharī'ah* that must be preserved and protected. Allåh (s.w.t.) commanded Muslims in the Qur'ān that killing is prohibited, and to kill one soul is as if you have killed the entire human race and to save one soul is as if you saved the entire human race (Qur'ān 5:32). From the reasoning given by al-Ghazāli, we can deduce two moral rules in the domain of Islamic ethics. Firstly, the consequences, no matter how good and no matter how much, do not justify any immoral act. Secondly, the ends, no matter how noble, do not justify the means.

In a strictly Islamic jurisprudence perspective, the justification of moral and legal actions in Islam is not sufficient (and cannot only) be based on personal reflection or personal desires or even solely for the benefits of the majority – only justice in objectively carrying out the letter of the law. In the face of a moral dilemma, one can use either rational/logical faculties or faith in the scriptures of religion – both of which can lead to moral outcomes. One does not even need to contemplate that one is more dependable; in real life, we have both for use and reference. For al-Ghazāli "…the noblest knowledge is where reason and tradition are coupled, where a rational opinion and the Sharī'ah are in association" (1322–1324 I:103; tr. 303).

[11]A slippery slope is a logical fallacy where arguments falsely assume that one thing must lead to another. They begin by suggesting that if we do one thing, then that will lead to salvation, but end up doing something that we do not want to do. It is presumptuous to assume certainty in a highly unpredictable situation.

[12]The necessity here refers to one of the tenets of the *Maqasid Al-Shari'ah*, which Al-Ghazāli himself summarized to five key tenets, that is, protection of life (*nafs*), religion (*deen*), mind (*'aql*), progeny (*nasl*), and property (*mal*). The necessity he refers to in his explanation is the protection of life, of course.

CHAPTER 4

Markets and Investment Behaviour

I can calculate the motions of heavenly bodies, but not the madness of people.
Isaac Newton (1720)

4.1 PROSPECT THEORY AND LOSS AVERSION

In the late 1970s, an experimental psychologist named Amos Tversky began to find evidence that investors and gamblers might not behave in a manner consistent with maximizing utility. Tversky, in collaboration with others, and Daniel Kahneman (who earned the Nobel Prize in Economics in 2002 for his work on prospect theory; Tversky died in 1996; otherwise, he may have shared the prize with Kahneman) have conducted numerous experiments on subjects testing decision-making characteristics. Generally, the results of these experiments question the empirical validity of the neoclassical rationality axioms. They have also written on applications of their results to financial decision-making, suggesting that investors may actually be quite different from the theoretical rational economic man. Kahneman and Tversky were particularly interested in how people made decisions when faced with uncertainty. They called their new viewpoint *Prospect Theory*. The fundamental challenge of prospect theory is that, although expected utility might be linear in the probabilities, those probabilities do not necessarily add up to unity, and they are distorted (overestimated and underestimated) at low and high values, respectively.

Using an argument based on Kahneman and Tversky's (1979) prospect theory, Shefrin and Statman (1985) predicted that individual investors will have a greater propensity to sell stock trading at a gain relative to purchase price, rather than stock trading at a loss. They provide some evidence for it using records of investor trading. Contrary to the common adage to 'let your profits run and cut your losses', individual investors in the financial markets often follow the impulse to sell winning stocks but are reluctant to sell losing ones. This is *loss aversion*, where decision makers tend to weight

Belief and Rule Compliance
https://doi.org/10.1016/B978-0-12-813809-0.00004-7

losses more heavily than gains. More detailed evidence for the effect can be found in Odean (1998a,b), who analyses the trading activity, from 1987 to 1993, of 10,000 households with accounts at a large discount brokerage firm. The phenomenon has now been replicated in several other large databases of trading behaviour.

Behavioural finance, largely rooted in *Prospect Theory*, is concerned with the impact of human emotions and cognitive impairments on investment decision-making. Economists have used expected utility maximization for over two centuries as the presumed objective of the rational investor. Expected utility maximization has served and still serves as the industry standard for modelling investor behaviour. In this section, we review a number of studies concerning individual and investor rationality. Many of these studies were conducted by experimental psychologists, whilst most of the remainder are based on statistical analyses of financial data. The case for assuming capital market efficiency when developing financial models is strong. Models based on rationality tend to be simple, and one can argue that rational investors generate market prices despite a large contingent of irrational investors. However, regardless of their intuitive appeal, theoretical models cannot and should not be accepted without consideration for empirical evidence.

4.2 BEHAVIOURAL BIASES IN INVESTING

Coincidentally, the beginning of this psychologically based financial analysis began with the start of many empirical findings (starting with the small firm effect) that raised doubts about some of the key foundations in standard finance: the efficient market hypothesis (EMH) and the capital asset pricing model (CAPM) (Baker and Nofsinger, 2010), derived from the seminal work of Black-Scholes theorem. A fundamental observation concerning the actual behaviour of stock markets is that markets are *far more volatile* than the standard efficient market theorem would predict (Fama, 1965). The earliest identified violations of market efficiency are apparent in calendar patterns. Researchers report that average returns seem to differ systematically within the calendar year. For example, whilst Banz (1981) documented that small-capitalization firms listed on the New York Stock Exchange (NYSE) earned significantly higher returns than those predicted by the CAPM, Reinganum (1983) showed that much of the abnormal return to small firms occurs during the first 2 weeks in January (the January effect). Cooper et al. (2006) showed that January returns have predictive power for market returns over the next 11 months of the year (the other January effect). French (1980) documents that the average return to the Standard & Poor's (S&P) composite portfolio was significantly negative over weekends in the period 1953–77 (the weekend effect). McConnell and Xu (2008) found that over the period 1926–2005 in 31 out of 35 countries, investors on average received no reward for bearing market risk except at turns of the month. Other examples of market inefficiency include investor reactions to other corporate news events. Ritter (1991) uncovered that initial public offerings (IPOs) significantly underperform relative to a set of comparable firms matched on size and industry. By investing in a sample of IPOs, investors would have earned around 17% less than investors in matching firms. Loughran and Ritter (1995) extended these results to seasoned equity offerings (SEOs). They discovered that investors investing $1 in each IPO or SEO immediately following the event would earn, at the end of 5 years, about 70% of the amount they would have earned had they invested in a sample of stocks matched to the IPOs and SEOs on size.

Results from the growing field of behavioural finance, which applies psychology to economic models, seem to indicate that neither investors are rational nor markets are efficient (at least in the sense of prices' rationality). The importance of socio-psychological factors in economic interactions is also revealed in the experimental economists' work on financial markets. Vernon Smith (2000) showed, using experimental methods, that the behaviour of individuals participating in trust games is sensitive to reciprocity. This means that traders tend to accept a reciprocal exchange even if this is not economically rational for them to do so. The early anomaly studies examined security prices and found either that markets were not as efficient as once purported or that the asset pricing models were inadequate (Froot and Dabora, 1999; Shiller, 2000; Shleifer, 2000). However, later studies cut to the potential root of the problem and examined the behaviour and decisions of market participants. Mantel et al. (2006) classified previous studies on behavioural decision-making into three major classes of effects: task, context, and personal characteristics of the decision maker. They claim that task effects relate to any change in complexity as perceived by the individual or the presentation of the task to the human decision maker. These include the number of alternatives considered, time pressures, information formality, and presentation or the type of response needed. Context effects concern the way in which the task relates to itself or to the environment.

The long-standing puzzle of finance such as market inefficiency and the equity premium puzzle (EPP) continues to challenge efficient market theory, and theories that relax the assumptions of the expected utility paradigm (e.g. incorporating nonexpected utility preferences, rank-dependent utility, and subadditive probability weighting) seem to fare better in explaining EPP according to Erbaş and Mirakhor (2013). They argue that ambiguity aversion may be instrumental in explaining the observed equity premium, which seems too large under expected utility theory. Without a formal portfolio model, they propose that uncertainty can be modelled using cumulative prospect theory, according to which equity premium can be decomposed into two conceptual parts, risk premium and ambiguity premium. Thus, when ambiguity aversion is taken into account, a significant part of the premium can be attributed to unquantifiable uncertainty or ambiguity.

Needless to say due to the rapid growing field of behavioural finance, the current research literature has to be organized in a coherent manner to be systematically analysed, and we attempt to do so, by discussing them within four key contexts: emotions (moods, intuition, and the weather), framing (information presentation including how the media shapes markets), heuristics (mental shortcuts), and market forces (which includes the overwhelming influence of institutional investors).

4.2.1 Emotions

Behavioural finance adds a crucial emotional dimension to the incomplete rational underpinnings of efficient market theory. It draws on the psychoanalytic understanding of the human mind and dynamic mental states explained originally by Sigmund Freud (and developed by later psychoanalytic thinkers such as Melanie Klein and Wilfred Bion) to describe how unconscious processes can drive investment decisions and financial activity. People's emotions and associated universal human unconscious wants, fantasies, greed, and fears drive many of their decisions. This aspect of behavioural finance recognizes the role of 'animal spirits' in explaining investor choices and thus shaping financial markets (Akerlof and Shiller, 2010). The underlying premise is that the subtle and complex way our feelings determine psychic reality affect investment judgments and may explain how markets periodically break down. Being aware of the emotional and psychological traps can give both the financial experts and investors a clearer picture of the risk-return potential of investments and guide their expectations. Behavioural finance can help client managers identify investors' weaknesses and biases and allow them to calibrate their investment approach accordingly.

4.2.1.1 Affects and Animal Spirits

The relevance of human behaviour to financial markets and economic affairs is not a new idea. Keynes (1936) observed over eight decades ago that economic decisions were due more to 'animal spirits' than carefully weighed probabilities and that financial markets operated more like subjective judgment calls than efficient price-discovery platforms. One of the few positive consequences of the recent financial crisis is the realization that the current approach to measuring and managing systemic risk in the financial system is inadequate and that policymakers need a broader intellectual framework.

Freudian psychoanalysis postulates that the feelings created by thoughts are ultimately of two types: pleasurable (exciting) or unpleasurable (painful, anxiety generating, or loss provoking) (Freud, 1911). Mental functioning reflects the outcome of a developmental struggle between the *pleasure principle* and the ability to acknowledge reality, the *reality principle*, the capacity to sense reality as it is, however painful, rather than how people might wish it to be.

All judgments are made within states of mind. Klein (1935) describes two alternating basic mental states that people experience throughout life. In the depressive (D) state of mind, people see themselves and others more or less as they are – complex with attractive and unattractive characteristics, good and bad, ultimately frail, inherently separate, and distinct individuals. In the paranoid-schizoid (PS) state of mind, they operate in a black-and-white world where good feelings are kept separate from bad ones. Schizoid refers to the splitting and projection process where the good or bad experiences are disowned and attributed to others who are then either idealized or feared and hated. Paranoid refers to the outcome of the splitting when one feels persecuted by the now hated other. Tuckett and Taffler (2008, p. 400) summarize the distinction[1] between D and PS senses of reality: "…a D state involves giving up the feeling that one is all-powerful and all-knowing, … feeling a certain amount of regret about the consequences of past actions, and a potential anticipatory feeling of depressive anxiety or

[1]This distinction is remarkably similar to the 'dual-process' frameworks advanced by psychologists and what Adam Smith conceived as motivation for behaviours. In *The Theory of Moral Sentiments*, Adam Smith argued that behaviour was determined by the struggle between what he termed as the 'passions' and the 'impartial spectator'. The passions included drives such as hunger and sex, emotions such as fear and anger, and motivational feeling states such as pain. Smith viewed behaviour as under the direct control of the passions but believed that people could override passion-driven behaviour by viewing their own behaviour from the perspective of an outsider – the impartial spectator.

guilt when contemplating potentially repeating past actions which led to failure or suffering. In a PS state, all such feelings are evaded by evacuating them from awareness…". This psychological affect facilitates fast and frugal decision-making (Gigerenzer, 2004) that feels good but removes the balancing sense of regret that would curb prohibitive behaviours. Here, the D state is a comparative equal to the Allåh-consciousness state where *insaf* embodies the regret and guilt notion. In the PS state of mind, the psychic pain of dealing with undesirable reality is avoided by mentally splitting of the good from the bad. This may be akin to losing grip of reality by focusing only on what is desirable and subsequently delude oneself to claim power over an unpredictable outcome. It is therefore important to understand properly the role of emotions in investment decision-making. We will see later how these PS and D state of mind concepts can be used to explain the 2008 financial crisis that spread and became a global financial crisis.

4.2.1.2 Hubris and Irrationality

Masini and Menichetti (2012) state that as opposed to efficient market theory, behavioural economics and finance theory argue that individuals are not fully rational, as demonstrated by Barberis and Thaler (2003). They also argue that people do not deviate from rationality randomly, but rather, mostly do so in similar ways. In their work, they studied the impact of behavioural factors on the renewable energy investment decision-making process. They conclude that those agents are not fully rational and that behavioural factors can strongly affect human decisions.

Managerial optimism is one of the most documented biases in economic literature, and in recent years, there has been a wave of papers that investigate its effect on firms' decisions (Heaton, 2002; Lin et al., 2005; Huang et al., 2011). Odean (1998a,b) examines how the overconfidence (as a psychological bias) of different managers affects markets differently. Kent et al. (1998) develop models in which, due to a self-attribution bias, overconfidence increases with success. Empirical studies in psychology have shown that individuals tend to overestimate their capabilities and the accuracy of their knowledge. Optimism is an unrealistic overestimation regarding future events related to personal skills, whilst excess of confidence reflects an overestimation of the latter. Formally, in the modelling of these two biases, optimism is seen as a mean error (overestimation) and excess of confidence as underestimation of the variance, but both terms are frequently used interchangeably (Aggarwal, 2014). Most religious people believe that hubris causes one not to think deeply and thoroughly about his/her inner self and actual ability and results in not only behavioural repulsiveness but also critical judgment errors. Hubris is Greek for pride (or arrogance) that is the primary trait of Satan and regarded as a deadly sin. In Islam, the intelligence seen in people is not an independent ability; it is given to them. The real owner of intelligence and all knowledge is the Almighty, the Creator of man. Allåh is the Owner of an infinite and boundless intelligence, and He grants this blessing to the one He wishes according to his faithfulness. To counter hubris is to practice humility: They said, "Glory be to You! We have no knowledge except what You have taught us. You are the All-Knowing, the All-Wise" (Qur'ān 2:32). In the midst of Knightian uncertainty and unquantifiable risk, it is clearly imprudent to approach *anything* with hubris.

Tyszka and Zielonka (2002) argued that financial experts make use of clinical judgment or of a combination of clinical and actuarial methods, which may result in being highly confident and committing errors at the same time. In their study, they asked financial analysts to forecast the value of the Warsaw Stock Exchange Index at the end of 2000, one and a half months in the future. Additionally, the analysts' task was to rate on a nine-point scale their general confidence in their ability to correctly assess future stock returns and, in particular, the forecast of the Warsaw Stock Exchange Index they were asked to make. The results showed that, on average, financial analysts rated their knowledge as being relatively high. Mean self-evaluation was equal to six (on a nine-point scale). However, a positive self-evaluation and high confidence in the forecast was not reflected in the correctness of the stock exchange index prediction; only one-third of the analysts were correct in their forecasts.

Heaton (2002) demonstrates that managerial optimism can affect corporate policy. More specifically, optimistic managers will exhibit investment cash flow sensitivity, and they will overinvest when internal cash flow is ample and underinvest if transport firms run short of cash. In this case, optimism is a personal characteristic and describes a manager's subjective belief that a firm's future performance is rosier than it actually is. We propose that managerial optimism can affect all other corporate decisions including resource allocation, optimal production, and the use of technology. According to behavioural economics, an optimistic manager will not invest and make decisions in a rational way. For example, he will never purchase new technology if he does not have sufficient internal liquidity available to finance an investment that can affect the firms' technical efficiency. The argument here is that optimistic CEOs will perceive that markets and investors are undervaluing their firms' shares, and external financing will be perceived as very costly.

4.2.1.3 Mood and Investment Decisions

Weather seems to be important in predicting returns to ordinary stocks as well, even though it is unrelated to fundamental firm activity. Hirshleifer and Shumway (2003) examine the relationship between morning sunshine in the city of a country's leading stock exchange and daily market index returns across 26 countries from 1982 to 1997. They find a strong and significant correlation between sunshine and stock returns and confirm the intuition that sunny weather is associated with upbeat moods, and this generally translates to higher stock returns. Kamstra et al. (2003) argue that stock market returns exhibit seasonal patterns consistent with the influence of seasonal affective disorder on investor risk aversion. Factors other than the weather may also affect investor 'mood' and hence affect prices. Edmans et al. (2007) use international soccer results as a mood variable and find evidence of significant market declines after soccer losses. A loss in the World Cup elimination stage, for example, leads to a next-day abnormal stock return of −49 basis points. These and other findings indicate that cognition and emotion are two sides of the same coin, and in order to have an intelligible grasp of financial markets, they need to be considered together as they are intertwined in all investment activity.

4.2.1.4 Neuroeconomics and Neurofinance

The idea that our moods and emotions underlie all financial decisions is also the main lesson from neuroeconomics and neurofinance. Although we cannot observe our emotional state during a typical workday, we can monitor subtle signs of that biology such as feelings or emotions. The nascent field of neuroeconomics and neurofinance may be able to identify the point at which the biological influences impact decisions, often through understanding one's mood and feelings to improve self-awareness. Without self-awareness, biological and emotional influences on financial decisions cannot be systematically addressed. As people become aware of the biological influences that impact their financial decisions, whether through scientific means[2] (genetic or blood samples) or a daily practice of decision monitoring and emotional self-awareness, a plan for minimizing vulnerabilities and maximizing strengths can be implemented.

[2]These genetic and blood samples test for biological influences like medications, drugs of abuse, hormones, dietary additions, and restrictions. These are separated from psychological influences like recent events (gains and losses), early life events, and the framing of decision options.

According to Peterson (2010), in order to improve the emotional balance in financial decision-making, three techniques are recommended:

1. Practitioners can observe and acknowledge both well-made and nonoptimal decisions in the course of their work. For this purpose, keeping a decision journal is highly recommended.
2. Meditation (or the Islamic equivalent of *dzikr*), peaceful reflection (*tafakkur*), and contemplation (*tadabbur*) are disciplines used to improve self-awareness. Beyond genetic and blood tests, such practices can hone awareness of emotions like impulsivity and irritability that impact decision-making. Patterns and unseen relationships between their feelings, beliefs, and actions can be identified during such self-reflection.
3. A behavioural plan for minimizing identified mistakes can be generated by first noticing one's emotional reactions to an event and developing a plan to deal with destructive reactions. For example, a long-term investor may feel strong emotional reactions (and engage in maladaptive trading behaviours) whilst watching ticker prices moving intraday. As a result, that investor should limit price checking and commit to price observations only at necessary and prescheduled intervals to maintain non-judgmental beliefs and flexible expectations.

However, there have been some acute criticisms on neuroeconomics and neurofinance due to the lack of experimental replication of many early findings and limited sample sizes and composition. This field of research uses functional magnetic resonance imaging (fMRI) that allows researchers to visualize changes in oxygenated blood flow, synapse, and other neuroconnections as a proxy for brain activity during decision points. fMRI and other techniques are expensive, and many such studies use small samples of 20 test subjects or less. The subjects in these studies are typically students where results found on young samples may not be confirmed for older individuals due to substrate lifespan variance. In addition, student samples may not reflect accurately the learning and experience of 'real-world' decision makers. Still, there are numerous findings emerging on the various biological factors (e.g. Frydman et al., 2014; De Martino et al., 2013; Lo, 2011; Ballard and Knutson, 2009) that can predict individual economic decision-making in economic contexts. For practitioners, working to improve one's own financial decisions remains a huge challenge that would require research in all related fields.

Given the determining role these emotional fallibilities can have on financial and investment decisions, establishing strict procedures, such as a rigorous, rule-based investment system that includes strict technical guidelines and profit-taking targets, can help investors and fund managers avoid behavioural traps and keep emotional turbulence in check. In this way, the Islamic practices of prayer-worship at specific times throughout the day help to keep faith and remain patient by maintaining connection with the Almighty. Although prayer is the second pillar of the religion, it is the most regular compulsory action in a Muslim's way of life. Fasting is obligatory just 1 month a year, *Zakat* or obligatory alms (different from *sadaqah* or ordinary charity) are given once a year, and Hajj is performed only once in a lifetime. However, prayer is the one act that must be fulfilled at least five times a day regardless of circumstance:

'Attend constantly to prayers…

But if you are in danger, then (say your prayers) on foot or horseback…'

(Qur'ān 2:238–239)

And the Prophet ﷺ used to say: "The first of his deeds for which a man will be called to account on the Day of Resurrection will be the prayers. If it is found to be perfect, he will be safe and successful. But if it is defective, he will be unfortunate and a loser". The strict regiment of prayer itself may provide a safeguard against behavioural traps and emotional turbulence.

In addition, if substantial changes in wealth or personal circumstances have occurred, investors should go back to the drawing board to ascertain the appropriate asset allocation rather than simply making marginal adjustments (*status quo* bias[3]). Conversely, taking positions against the *status quo* like a major trend (or even a bubble) can be highly risky as the market can be wrong for longer than investors can stay liquid. The systematic use of technical analysis, quantitative models, and fund-flow data can help investors assess not only how long it may be worth 'going with the wisdom of crowds' but also when a contrarian stance looks more promising and hedging may become appropriate. Finally, stop-loss rules enforce selling discipline, thereby minimizing the loss aversion created through emotional attachments to certain positions and preventing individuals from holding on to losing stocks for too long.

[3]The status quo bias is the tendency for individuals to do nothing or maintain their current/previous decision.

The 2008 Financial Crisis – A Psycho-Analytic Perspective

Although the underlying reasons for the 2008 financial crisis are highly complex, formal analysis of the contributory role unconscious phantasies[4] play in all market behaviour and financial activities can be helpful in understanding what went wrong. Taffler and Tuckett (2010) believes that the degree of the contagious excitement seemingly dominating financial markets until recently, which encouraged investors to expect exceptional returns in an environment of low yields – return without risk, may be inadequately recognized. Governments, central bankers, and regulators became caught up with investment banks and other market participants in a basic assumption group euphoria that implicitly suggested that there was no downside to speculation. Taffler and Tuckett believed that those involved seemed to deny and repress the associated uncertainty and anxiety. They posit that the divided state of mind then dominating mortgage-backed securities (MBSs) and related financial products became represented in investor psychic reality as unconscious phantastic objects with the speculative loans 'safely' split off and securitized into complex investment vehicles such as collateralized debt obligations (CDOs). The fear that property prices might ever fall was 'denied' and the risk of lending to subprime borrowers rendered invisible through the 'spread-transfer' or avoidance of ownership of risk. (This is incongruent to the Islamic finance concept of risk sharing.)

Taffler and Tuckett pointed out that the comforting cover story of 'new millennium finance' was rationalized around the idea of a further phantasy – 'rocket scientists' with PhDs in mathematics and nuclear physics have managed to vanquish risk and uncertainty forever with their complex and opaque derivatives products. What was good (the excitement) was kept conscious, and what was bad (the potential loss) was repressed and split off. Inevitably, the euphoric bubble had to burst. What people had always known could no longer be defended against and ignored (Tuckett, 2009). Bankruptcies of major financial institutions, government bailouts, and the inevitable panic and contagion to other markets with investors now unable to distinguish between 'good' and 'bad' followed. Disintegration of

[4]Phantasy or phantastic is a technical term that psychoanalysts use to describe an individual's unconscious beliefs and wishes, which, it teaches, are derived from the earliest stages of an infant's mental development. Thus, a phantastic object is a mental representation of something (or someone or an idea) that fulfils the individual's deepest (and earliest infantile) desires to have exactly what they want and exactly when they want it. As Tuckett and Taffler (2008, p. 396) point out, phantastic objects are exciting and transformational; "... (they) appear to break the usual rules of life and turn aspects of 'normal' reality on its head".

trust in the debt markets leading to paranoia meant that banks refused to lend to each other. Clearly, the time needed for economic activity to recover is likely to be many years. Not surprisingly, those arraigned take no responsibility with blame and shifting of responsibility onto others to avoid personal 'guilt' or regret. Lehman Brothers' former CEO Dick Fuld's reaction at a congressional hearing is illustrative of this phenomenon. He blamed Lehman's collapse on a plague of short selling and US regulators for not arranging a federal bailout as they did for AIG (Kirchgaessner and Farrell, 2008). Fuld even saw himself as the victim, not playing a major role in the Lehman collapse, which was the largest bankruptcy in recent years. The unravelling of the euphoric idea of a phantastic desire for continued exceptional returns without complementary risks led to market panic, which quickly turned to blame. Those in the firing line included the government, the Federal Reserve System, the Securities and Exchange Commission and other regulators, credit rating agencies, hedge funds and short sellers, bankers and investment bankers, accountants, and the financial media. Similarly, market participants doing the blaming were equally caught up in the divided market state of mind themselves even though it did not occur to them.

The insights of emotions in behavioural finance suggest that to prevent such financial crises in the future, governments, financial regulators, and investors need to understand the inherent instability of a market where a paranoid-schizoid (PS) state of mind is allowed to dominate. Markets need an integrated (or depressive, D) sense of reality to function appropriately, one in which their inherent uncertainties can be properly acknowledged and inform the decision-making of market participants.

The 2008 Financial Crisis – An Islamic Finance Perspective

The more common view of the financial crisis was how economic agents and regulators were fooled by those who had asymmetric information. The ruse was executed, as Erbaş and Mirakhor (2013) note "through creative bookkeeping to mask off-balance sheet liabilities; collusion between the rated and rating agencies; oblivious indifference of regulators to fulfilling their public fiduciary responsibilities and mandated duties; outright fraud; and, last but not least, the outright failure of market professionals and their sophisticated methodologies to assess derivative risks associated with complex financial products and their reckless marketing, taking advantage of investors' trust". The fundamental cause then, to them and most economists, of the 2008 financial crisis was the negligent, immoral, and even criminal behaviour of some actors. This is a breach of the social contract implicit in fiduciary responsibility and trust, bore disastrous consequences, and is not compatible with the commonly shared morals that guide economic behaviour across many cultures and faiths. The main themes to financial reform following the aftermath were basically to encourage greater responsibility after (ex post) and accountability for risks taken prior (ex ante), in the form of not bailing out the bankruptcies, limiting the increasing complexity of financial instruments, transparency, and answerability for derivative trading to prevent investment managers from making enormous bets with other peoples' money, amongst other reforms.

Here, the fundamental principal of Islamic risk sharing becomes important because of the acknowledgement of such temptations and human penchants as well as uncertainty. Erbaş and Mirakhor (2013) emphasize that Islamic risk sharing does not permit washing one's hands off of the liability once a loan is made *ex ante*, but one must remain a party to it until risks are realized *ex post*. Thus, it is not permitted to create derivatives of derivatives (exotics, toxics, etc.) and other highly complex products, and it becomes possible to know who owes what to whom for an *ex post* settlement of claims and liabilities. The extended set of rules derived from the Qur'ān and Sunnah earlier in Chapter 2 and the concept of the *khalifah* support this commitment to fiduciary and personal accountability, building and maintaining trust and dispensing and upholding justice. Furthermore, the availability of *khiyar* or options in Islamic contracts gives investors the option of continuing or halting or abandoning an investment to hedge against uncertainty over time, and decision makers may be willing to pay for such contractual flexibility. An early discussion of economically significant benefits from flexibility is by Marschak and Nelson (1962). They argue that flexibility comes at a cost, such as the cost of accepting lower payoffs or the cost of delaying some payoffs into the future. They propose a measure of flexibility in decision-making according to which the more the decision maker expects to learn from each decision outcome, the more he/she values flexibility. Sequential decision programs are ambiguous over time and more so as the time horizon becomes longer. Erbas and Mirakhor note that splitting multistage investments or implementing them as segmented decisions over time, as opposed to once-and-for-all decisions with an *ex ante* commitment for the entire time horizon, gives investors the option of continuing or halting or abandoning an investment to hedge against uncertainty over time, and decision makers may be willing to pay for such flexibility.

4.2.2 Framing

People's perceptions of the choices they have are strongly influenced by how these choices are framed. In other words, people often make different choices when the question is framed in a different way, even though the objective facts remain constant or frame dependence.

Glaser et al. (2007) wanted to know if investors expect trend continuation or mean reversion in their investments. They note that the vast majority of studies that ask for future price levels find mean reverting expectations, whereas studies that ask directly for returns usually find a belief in trend continuation. But all these studies ask either for future price levels or returns. Furthermore, they differ in some other dimensions such as subject pool, time series to be forecasted, or forecast horizon that cannot be ruled out as potential explanations for the observed differences. In their study, they present analyses on whether individual expectations of stock returns are influenced by the specific elicitation mode. Their results show that investor forecasts of the stock market vary depending on whether they are given and asked to forecast future prices or future returns. Volatility estimates are lower (indicating a stronger overconfidence bias) when subjects are asked for returns compared with price forecasts. They also found that education improved performance – the observed framing effect and the overconfidence bias are less pronounced for subjects with higher financial education.

Standard economic theory predicts that automatic enrollment should not influence the employee's saving decision, because automatic enrollment does not change the economic fundamentals of the planning problem. However, Choi et al. (2004) show that pension fund enrollment is heavily dependent on how the choices and processes are framed. Default options have an enormous impact on household 'choices'. Such effects are documented in the literature on 401(k) plans (Madrian and Shea, 2001). Default options affect 401(k) participation, savings rates, rollovers, and asset allocation by framing choices for immediate action. For example, when employees are automatically enrolled in their 401(k) plan, only a tiny fraction opt out, producing nearly 100% enrollment as opposed to less than half enrollment on their own during their first year of employment. Choi et al. noted that default options matter for three key reasons: Opting out of a default can be costly, other option values will need to be generated that will vary over time, and people are susceptible to procrastination – even if they want to make a change, they have a tendency to delay that change longer than they should. These effects imply that the choice of defaults can have significant welfare consequences.

Thaler and Sunstein's (2008) book, *Nudge*, is largely about framing important decisions in such a way to as 'nudge' people towards better choices. They use everyday examples to illustrate that in many situations, a planner must make choices that will affect the behaviour of others. The authors make three main claims: First, the architecture of choice greatly influences how people make choices; second, choice architecture is unavoidable (so why not design in ways that improve well-being); and third, libertarian paternalism is not an oxymoron: paternalists can nudge whilst preserving freedom of choice. Thaler and Sunstein note that our brains are dichotomous, as discussed earlier, and that too often, our impulsive, myopic, unreflective animalistic self seizes the levers of choice from our resolute, farsighted, thoughtful human half. The self as such fails systematically, but he can be allowed to make better decisions by savvy architects of choice.

4.2.2.1 Shaping the Markets

The influence of media on people's opinions and subsequent behaviour underlies the global marketing industry. But its effect on investment behaviour is less well understood although the ability of various media to highlight events and colour them emotionally affects people's financial decision-making (Davis, 2005) that cannot be refuted.

From the behavioural finance perspective, the function of the media would appear primarily to be that of disseminating information, like details of company fundamentals and the recommendations of analysts. By the time financial information reaches investors via the media, it is usually already out of date. By the time it is fixed in print in the morning newspaper or prerecorded for TV broadcast, big investors have already acted on this information, obtained from other sources. By this measure, the media's effect on investors as means of spreading information is not especially compelling. But the media do more than just disseminate financial information. Media coverage, through newspapers, magazines, TV, radio, and now the Internet in all of its manifestations (webcasts, RSS feeds, Facebook, Twitter, and blogs), also brings financial issues to the attention of investors, accentuating certain perspectives and information about a development and de-emphasizing others. Movements of companies or fundamentals may be described in terms of losses or gains, a selective framing. In interpreting, framing, and describing events, the media arguably affect investment decisions. But here, investors are generally not reacting to relevant financial information but to 'background information' or supposed 'market sentiment', and the choices they make are accordingly based less on reason than on feelings (Tetlock, 2007).

Perspectives on issues presented by news media may constitute the basis for judgments about a company, industry, or region targeted for investment. A media that focus on a company's losses as opposed to its gains or vice versa can sway the decisions investors make about whether to buy that company's stocks or bonds or those of the industry in which that company operates. In the process, investors may ignore other information that might be relevant but that has not been picked up by the media. This human tendency to choose differently based on how a certain piece of information is presented is one of the basic principles of prospect theory discussed earlier. Although Kahneman and Tversky did not explicitly discuss media effects, we believe that media coverage should be taken into account in considering the influence of framing on investment decisions. Media coverage also highlights specific issues or 'angles'. This kind of selective attention increases the perceived importance of a given issue, which subsequently also influences investors' judgments. To some extent, the media control the accessibility of information by deciding what is newsworthy.

Priming mechanisms are especially obvious when different media highlight the same information or perspectives on an issue (Roskos-Ewoldsen et al., 2009). If investors are given consistent information from different media, they weight the information more heavily, a phenomenon known in behavioural finance as the 'information sources effect'. Furthermore, cumulative coverage in a single medium that people tend to go back to because they find it highly credible – *The Economist* and *The Wall Street Journal*, for example – compounds the information sources effect. Apart from selecting information and perspectives, journalists also provide context and reduce complexity in reporting developments. Illustrating global events with examples of individual companies, for instance, helps to increase the vividness of a story and makes it more interesting. In addition, people read newspapers and watch TV for information and for entertainment. Consequently, dramatic or hot events are often given an emotional spin in order to sell newspapers or TV channel subscriptions.

4.2.3 Heuristics

A heuristic and bias framework can be envisioned as a counterpart to standard finance theory's asset pricing model. When faced with huge amounts of data and information and an array of decision problems, people are incapable of doing the complex optimization calculations that are expected of them under standard finance theory. Instead, they rely on a limited number of cognitive strategies or heuristics that simplify the complex scenarios faced by them in making decisions. Heuristics are information processing (mental) shortcuts that mainly result from one's experiences in a field of work. Of course, such simplifying shortcuts are productive and allow humans to function in daily life. By nature, heuristics are imperfect and consequently will result in biases and errors.

Hence, Read and Taleb (2014) view religion as a set of interdicts upon action. They provide heuristics that are divine, coming as the word of God, that are sacred and not open to 'rationalization' – "what we cannot presently understand is not necessarily irrational, and it might have reasons that can be probed only across generations of experience and experimentation". In fact, the three main Abrahamic religions are mostly heuristics, laws, and regulatory frameworks. They believe that religion supplies powerful secrets to mitigate people's natural epistemic arrogance and overconfidence about the future. 'I don't know' is something hard for humans to accept and say; this is made easier in the Arabic language, as the typical traditional expression is 'only God knows'.

4.2.3.1 Heterogeneous Beliefs

Our belief formation process allows us to not only react quickly to cues or changes in the environment that are important for survival but also influence behaviour by changing risk preferences. In effect, predictions based on risk preferences and survival concerns form an important part of everyday economic life. Economists are constantly making predictions about inflation, economic growth, the length of the current recession, etc.; analysts are making predictions about a particular stock or an entire market. Here, it is important to point out that the people who are making predictions are very often *not* the same people who are making decisions based on those predictions. These differences (or diversity) in beliefs, perceptions, and perspectives can and sometimes result in behaviours that result in speculative bubbles and volatility. To take one example, analysts studying individual stocks are, in principle, independent from the traders and brokers who are acting on their research.

Our beliefs or mental models about certain events affect our ability to predict the outcome that culminates from those events (Costa-Gomes and Weizsäcker, 2008). The difference that makes some people better at making predictions than others comes from the rootedness of those beliefs in reality. Understanding belief formation requires the understanding of how the belief formation process works, which includes the initial beliefs, the updating rules to the belief system, and its level of sophistication (Haruvy, 2002;

Nyarko and Schotter, 2002). People also update their beliefs according to what they observe and the different types of information they receive (e.g. historical actions data and/or payoffs) (Palfrey and Wang, 2009).

In a market in which agents disagree (having differing beliefs or perceptions) about an asset's fundamental and short sales are constrained, an asset owner is willing to pay a price higher than his own expectation of the asset's fundamental because he expects to resell the asset to a future optimist at an even higher price. Such speculative behaviour leads to a bubble component in asset prices. This approach does not require a substantial amount of aggregate belief distortions to generate a significant price bubble. Instead, the bubble component builds on the fluctuations of investors' heterogeneous beliefs. Even when investors' aggregate beliefs are unbiased, intensive fluctuations of their heterogeneous beliefs can lead to a significant price bubble through frenzied trading (Scheinkman and Xiong, 2003).

The biggest bubble of the twentieth century was undoubtedly the Internet bubble in the late 1990s. Precipitated by the rapid development of the Internet, a wave of new Internet firms went public. These firms included household names such as Yahoo and Amazon, as well as many other firms that eventually disappeared. The new Internet technology provided these firms with the promise of revolutionizing the way we obtained information, purchased goods, and received services. According to Ofek and Richardson (2003), an index tracking the performance of Internet stocks experienced an extraordinary growth of nearly 1000% from October 1998 to February 2000. At the peak in February 2000, the Internet sector had roughly 400 companies and was largely profitless but commanded an astonishing capitalization of about 6% of the entire US stock market. This sector contributed an even higher fraction – 20% of the publicly traded volume of the US stock market, which directly speaks to the frenzy of trading Internet stocks. Taken together, the Internet bubble shared many common characteristics with the previous bubbles: highly inflated market prices accompanied by speculative frenzies, short sale constraints in preventing arbitrage, the lack of favourable economic news, and the largely increased asset float in eventually crashing the prices.

The effects of belief and mental models are wide enough to incorporate several important aspects of bubbles and crises, such as overinvestment and crashes (Abreu and Brunnermeier, 2003). Abreu and Brunnermeier used a generalized notion of heterogeneous beliefs to model the synchronization problem of rational arbitrageurs in coordinating their selling strategies during a bubble. In their model, a bubble caused by irrational investors emerges at a random time and then grows at an exogenous speed. The model focuses on a group of rational arbitrageurs who are allowed to short sell the bubble. The bubble will eventually burst under sufficient selling pressure from arbitrageurs. Arbitrageurs are privately informed of the presence of the bubble at different times, and he faces the uncertainty that other arbitrageurs may not yet be informed. The heterogeneity in the times that arbitrageurs get informed leads to heterogeneous beliefs about the presence of the bubble at a given time, which, in turn, makes it difficult for arbitrageurs to coordinate their short selling of the bubble. As riding the bubble before it crashes is profitable, it is rational for each arbitrageur to initially ride on the bubble rather than short sell. Thus, the bubble may persist for a substantial time even though arbitrageurs are well informed.

Heterogeneous beliefs can also lead to credit cycles (Geanakoplos, 2010). The speculation induced by heterogeneous beliefs also leads to endogenous wealth fluctuations and endogenous risk in general equilibrium settings without short-sale constraint (Detemple and Murthy, 1994; Kurz, 1996), which can help explain various phenomena such as excess volatility, time-varying risk premium, and high equity premium.

4.2.3.2 Confirmation and Hindsight Bias

Confirmation and hindsight biases are a subset of self-serving biases showing that people tend to arrive at judgments of what is fair or right that are biased towards their own self-interests. Confirmation bias refers to the selective gathering of (or the giving of undue weight to) information in order to support a previously held belief (Nickerson, 1998) and to the neglect (or discounting) of information that does not support those previously held beliefs. It arises when individuals restrict their attention to a single hypothesis and fail to actively consider alternatives (Fischhoff and Beyth-Marom, 1983). Once a particular hypothesis has been accepted, individuals selectively look for information to support it (Wason, 1960; Wetherick, 1962). Confirmation bias may surface from a deep-seated inclination of human beings to use reason for the function of convincing others and winning arguments (Mercier and Sperber, 2011).

Hindsight bias, on the other hand, is the tendency to view the past as having been more predictable than it actually was. When test subjects were instructed to give reasons for why outcomes other than the one that actually occurred could have occurred, the bias reduced (Slovic and Fischhoff, 1977). These biases result from the tendency to neglect contradicting evidence and that calibration may be improved by making such evidence more salient. Research on other biases has produced similar debiasing success stories when subjects are instructed to 'consider the opposite' (Lord et al., 1984; Anderson, 1982). These self-serving biases are important in evaluating oneself especially when one is supposed to be the reformer or expert responsible for policy or effecting how other people behave (see Section 7.1).

4.2.4 Market Forces

Zooming out from the cognitive errors and biases of individuals, we next examine how groups of people with these emotional fallibilities and cognitive biases can affect markets and market prices. Indeed, part of the original attraction for a budding behavioural finance field was that the market was not efficient, and prices did not appear to be fair. Standard finance argues that investor mistakes would not affect market prices because when prices deviate from fundamental value, rational traders would exploit the mispricing for their own profit (arbitrage).

Hence, trying to measure how information diffuses from one investor to another seems important for financial economists interested in decision-making determined by social interactions. Shiller and Pound (1989) used a questionnaire to survey institutional and individual investors. They found that direct interpersonal communication is very important in one's investment decision-making process. Unfortunately, there have been relatively few papers since that provide further understanding of information diffusion. The difficulty in measuring information diffusion arises because investors' information sets are unobservable. At present, there is almost no way to ascertain the information to which an investor has been exposed. And as the world gets more connected, the trend for less direct and personal communication becomes more pervasive with internet and wireless technology. Their access to information and their connectivity mean that they will be able to pick up and learn subjects on their own, which is quite a departure from those of us who relied on formal education to acquire knowledge. People who have information and can use it well will be 'better off' than people who do not, because information is what enables arbitrage, market control, and speculation.

Consider, on the other hand, a hypothetical (rational, well-equipped, and well-coordinated) market where professional analysts and competing investors are attempting to secure and employ all information that would enable them to evaluate stocks more accurately. However, none of the analysts have perfect information and cannot know with certainty what the values of stocks are. Each analyst may have some information (or method for analysing this information) not available to other analysts, and information sets available to different analysts are not perfectly correlated. Given a reasonably large number of analysts, one might expect their errors to offset or cancel to some extent and that their average or consensus projections to outperform any given analyst's forecasts. In this scenario, the market prices generated by the large number of analysts and investors may be closer to the true security prices estimated by any individual analyst or investor. It would be very difficult for the individual investor to outperform the market in this scenario.

Surowiecki (2004) described the popular TV show *Who Wants to be a Millionaire?* to demonstrate the 'wisdom of crowds' relative to individual decision makers. In this show, a contestant was asked multiple-choice questions, which, if answered correctly, could result in innings of as much as US$1 million. The contestant had the option (called lifelines) of seeking each of three types of assistance should he require it. The contestant could request to have two of three incorrect answers eliminated from the answer set, call a friend or relative to ask for help or poll the studio audience who would vote on the correct answer. Eliminating incorrect answers should produce correct answers at least 50% of the time. Phone calls to friends or relatives produced the correct answer almost 65% of the time. However, the studio polls produced the correct answers 91% of the time, suggesting that the crowd wisdom did seem superior to individual opinions, even the potentially expert opinions offered by the phone calls. Surowiecki proposed conditions under which collective wisdom works well, including diversity, independence, and aggregation. For example, investors have diverse decision rules and may well make investment decisions independently of one another. They absorb information from their environments, combine it with their own interactions with their environments, and then formulate decision rules. Their effective decision rules survive, adapt, and are maintained. Security markets provide the mechanism for aggregating the diverse rules and opinions of investors.

So, in view of the decision biases discussed earlier, at least in the short run, market failures and volatility are imminent. New product or asset information dissemination throughout markets may take time, and in an environment of imperfect information, it is possible to persuade speculators who are not well informed about the odds (at least for a substantial period of time). For example, it is possible to sell worthless real estate securities, derivatives betting on defaults, and derivatives of derivatives, until all or most market participants have more or less the same information through the market dissemination process. The fact is that such phenomena are observed in the form of outright fraud (usually, Ponzi schemes) and also made possible by other cognitive forces such as herd behaviour.

4.2.4.1 Peer Effects and Herd Mentality

Herd mentality and peer effects are cognitive forces that can be manipulated or make possible of fraudulent financial undertaking. Stock markets are one of the key mechanisms for allocating economic resources for society, and they function without formal leadership or hierarchies. Some observers have compared stock markets with swarms of bees and ant colonies (Miller, 2007). Each ant has a sliver of information that is communicated in a very rudimentary fashion to other ants, but no ant comes close to understanding the 'big picture', and no ant can direct the activities of the colony as a whole. Similarly, individual traders, each with a tiny subset of relevant information, communicate bids and offers. Most traders do not reveal their rationale for their quotations, only their quotes. Through this process, the market collectively sets prices and allocates productive resources throughout the economy. All of this is accomplished without formal leadership or without anyone really understanding exactly why stock prices behave as they do. Ivković and Weisbenner (2007) find evidence of herding in an examination of 35,000 brokerage accounts detailing investor zip codes. They found that investors were substantially more likely to invest in securities if their neighbours had already done so.

The sequential decision process in which each decision maker bases his decision on those made by his neighbour or previous decision makers was made by following what their predecessors did rather than using their own information. This information cascading may form the basis for herd behaviour, where decision makers pursue the same action without collaborative planning. In an information cascade, decision makers earlier in the queue have information relevant to subsequent decision makers, so this herding might be rational. However, herd behaviour need not be the result of sequential decision-making. Instead, herding behaviour may seem consistent with collective irrationality.

Psychoanalytic theory also provides another important potential contribution to the understanding of financial markets in terms of the relations between the individual investor and the group. Drawing on Freud (1921), Bion (1952) distinguishes between work groups and basic assumption groups, which function in quite different ways. The work group generally defines its task and is clear about its purpose and hence promotes its members' cooperation. On the other hand, when a basic assumption group is operating, individuals do not think for themselves but engage collectively in groupthink (Janis, 1982). Groupthink provides comfort and good feelings to the group members through the unconscious defences the group as a whole adopt against anxiety, rather than creative group reality-based thinking and functioning. This keeps the 'discontent' of alternative views in check whilst maintaining the 'safety' of being with the herd.

4.2.4.2 The Influence of Institutional Investors

Collective effects of large groups of individual investors and traders on financial decision-making have been reviewed to grasp the understanding of what constitutes as market forces. Here, we review the effects of a smaller group of investors but whom have large abilities to influence the markets – the institutional investors. They are the best candidates for keeping markets efficient because they have the capabilities in knowledge and capital required to move markets.

There are two obvious differences between institutional investors and individuals (ignoring exceptional cases). First, the level of wealth controlled by institutional investors is per capita higher than that controlled by individual investors. Second, decisions are taken in some structured fashion by institutions, which may or may not be the case for individual investors. There is an assumption that institutional investors attempt to arbitrage apparent market inefficiencies in the process of making returns for their investors. However, there are many situations in which institutional investors (or arbitrageurs more generally) have incentives to 'ride' rather than trade against mispricings. For example, if they expect mispricing to increase over the short run, arbitrageurs have an incentive to jump on the bandwagon rather than trade against the mispricing. Brunnermeier and Nagel (2004) document just such an effect during the technology bubble before the NASDAQ crash of 2000. They find that hedge funds were long technology stocks on the way up but reduced their positions in stocks that were falling in value, thus managing to avoid much of the downturn. Evidence of Griffin et al. (2003), who find that institutional investors trend-chased NASDAQ-100 stocks at high frequencies over the period of the NASDAQ bubble, support this finding.

Edison and Warnock (2008) find that cross-border flows follow the trend in dividend yields, not just equity returns, suggesting that the trend chasing of international flows may be related to expectations of fundamentals rather than simply positive feedback trading or bubble-riding behaviour. Brunnermeier and Pedersen (2009) describe another class of situations in which institutional investors act to exacerbate the deviation between prices and fundamentals. These authors study 'predatory trading' occurring on the back of other investors' needs to reduce their positions. In particular, if some investors have knowledge of other investors' needs to liquidate positions, strong incentives exist for these investors to sell and subsequently repurchase the same assets. This leads to greater deviations of prices from fundamentals and greater illiquidity at precisely those moments when liquidity is sought by traders.

Where researchers have sought to answer whether institutional investors have detectable and consistently superior investment ability and whether institutional investors act as if to discipline prices in financial markets, Ramadorai (2010) found that some institutions possess superior investment ability, but it is hard to detect and short-lived. He notes the evidence on the trading behaviour of institutions strongly suggests that they are well informed about the direction of cash flow-relevant news, and this can be seen as a stabilizing behaviour. Yet, whilst institutional investors may well be informed, they do not have complete discretion over their trading decisions because their financing comes from outside investors. The fluctuations of capital flows to institutions impose significant constraints on their discretion when investing (Coval and Stafford, 2007). Sudden withdrawals of capital may force their predictable trading behaviour and affect institutional investors' incentives to act as arbitrageurs. Finally, several situations exist in which institutional investors have strong incentives to engage in positive feedback[5] or predatory trading, both of which have potentially destabilizing influences on prices.

4.3 RISK PREFERENCES

Human behaviour shows some very interesting biases in weighing losses and gains and as such demonstrates irrational risk preferences. Consider a slightly modified version of an experiment conducted by Kahneman and Tversky, 1979 – suppose you are offered two investment opportunities, A and B:

A yields a sure profit of RM 4.5 million.

B yields RM 10 million with a 50% probability and RM 0 with 50% probability.

So, which would you choose, A or B?

[5]Positive feedback investors are those who buy securities when prices rise and sell when prices fall. Many forms of behaviour common in financial markets can be described as positive feedback trading. It can result from extrapolative expectations about prices or trend-chasing (De Long et al., 1990).

Whilst investment B has an expected value of RM 5 million that is higher than A's payoff, most people would not care because they would perceive it as receiving either RM 10 million or nothing at all, not the expected value in probability terms. There is no right or wrong choice here; it is simply a matter of personal preference. Faced with this choice, most subjects prefer the sure profit (A), to the possibility of winning considerably more (B). This example can be interpreted as risk aversion. Now, suppose you are faced with another two choices, C and D:

C yields a sure loss of RM 450,000.

D yields RM 0 with 50% probability and loss of RM 1 million with 50% probability.

Which would you prefer?

This situation may not be as improbable as it may seem because many financial decisions involve choosing between the lesser of two evils. In this case, most test subjects choose D, despite the fact that D is more risky than C. When faced with two choices that both involve losses, individuals seem to behave in exactly the opposite way – they are risk seeking in this case, not risk averse as in the case of A versus B. The fact that individuals tend to be risk averse in the face of gains and risk seeking in the face of losses – which Kahneman and Tversky (1979) called 'aversion to sure loss' – can lead to some very poor financial decisions. To see why, observe that the combination of the most popular choices, A and D, is equivalent to yielding RM 4.5 million with 100% probability and – RM 1 million with 50% probability, whereas the combination of the least popular choices, B and C, is equivalent to yielding RM 10 million with 50% probability and – RM 450,000 with 100% probability. If the B and C combination has the same probabilities of gains and losses, the gain would be RM 500,000 higher, and the loss is RM 50,000 lower. In light of this analysis, would you still prefer A and D?

Aversion to risk seems nearly universal amongst all living organisms, most likely a close corollary of the survival instinct. In fact, in a simple evolutionary model of behaviour, Brennan and Lo (2011) have shown that when there are systematic environmental risks to fertility, the forces of natural selection will favour those individuals that are risk averse. The reason is simple: if one course of action leads to three offspring with certainty and a second course of action leads to a 50/50 gamble of two or four offspring, it can be shown that the first course of action leads to much faster population growth.

In fact, aversion to sure loss is a very real problem that lies at the heart of one of the biggest potential exposures of every major financial institution – the rogue trader. The cases of Nick Leeson (Barings, 1995, £827 million loss), Yasuo Hamanaka (Sumitomo, 1996, US$2.6 billion loss), John Rusnak (Allied Irish Banks, 2002, US$691 million loss), Chen Jiulin (China Aviation Oil, 2005, US$550 million), Jerome Kerviel (Societe Generale, 2006–08, €4.9 billion loss), Boris Picano-Nacci (Caisse d'Epargne, 2008, €751 million loss), and most recently Kweku Adoboli (UBS, 2011, US$2.3 billion loss) are all too familiar: a trader loses more than he expected but hides it and increases his bet, hoping to make it up on the next trade, after which all might be forgiven. This advice applies not only to traders and investors but also to regulators. Whilst we still have much to learn about the behaviour of bank supervisors in the years leading up to the recent financial crisis, some economists claim that regulatory forbearance – the tacit or active cooperation of regulators in overvaluing bank assets to avoid violating minimum capital requirements – is partly responsible for the crisis (Huizinga and Laeven, 2010; Brown and Dinc, 2011). Although there are elaborate explanations for why regulatory forbearance might occur, including global competition amongst regulatory agencies and the political economy of regulation, a more ordinary explanation is aversion to sure loss. When a bank supervisor first identifies an undercapitalized bank, he must decide whether to require the bank to raise additional capital or to wait and see whether the bank's assets will rebound. Requiring a bank to raise capital is costly to the supervisor in terms of the bank's invariably negative response and the potential risk that this action may cause a loss of confidence amongst the bank's customer base, possibly triggering a bank run. Furthermore, the regulatory action may seem unwarranted, causing a loss of confidence in the regulator's competence. Far worse consequences result when the regulator chooses to wait for the bank's assets to rebound that is as devastating as the rogue trader hoping to make it up on the next trade.

The asymmetry between our reactions to monetary gains and losses has a neurophysiological explanation. Kuhnen and Knutson (2005) ran fMRI experiments involving a computer game they developed – the Behavioural Investment Allocation Strategy (BIAS) task – whilst being scanned in the MRI. The players had a choice between three investment options, a 'safe' bond or one of two stocks, which moved randomly. Unknown to the players, one of the stocks was a 'good' stock, which was gained in the long run, and the other a 'bad' stock, which declined in the long run. Additionally, the 'good' stock gave a larger long-run reward than the 'safe' bond, on average $2.50 per turn versus a consistent $1.

Kuhnen and Knutson discovered a very interesting pattern. When players made a risk-seeking mistake (i.e. choosing the 'bad' stock over the 'good' stock), their *nucleus accumbens*[6] (feel-good response) was activated before they made their decision. In contrast, before players made a risk-averse mistake (i.e. choosing the 'safe' bond over the 'good' stock), a completely different part of the brain was activated, the *anterior insula*[7] (feel-disgust response). It seems risk-averse investors process the risk of monetary loss similar to viscerally disgusting things, whilst risk-seeking investors process the risky potential gain similarly to a cocaine high.

4.3.1 Gender and Investment Decisions

Research consistently shows that women exhibit lower levels of satisfaction, confidence and optimism than men when it comes to investing. This negativity, it seems, has little to do with innate biological differences and a lot to do with a lack of experience and good advice. Döbeli and Vanini (2010) reported that if an investment opportunity lacks clarity and transparency, women are less willing to take a risk than men. Moreover, a 2007 survey by the ShareBuilder Securities Corporation concluded that women are generally less confident than men when it comes to making investment decisions, despite the fact that, more often than not, they oversee the family budget and are responsible for paying the bills.

A Credit Suisse Global Investor Report (2011) found that women revise their investment decisions more often than men after learning how financial markets behave. In other words, they appear to be more adaptive than men and therefore profit more from this kind of information. Moreover, a Merrill Lynch survey (Frank and Bishop Tiller, 2005) found that women learned from their investment mistakes and were much less likely than men to repeat them. Evidence thus indicates that women make good and profitable investment decisions when they have the confidence to do so. In evaluating women's investment decisions prior to experience simulations, Frank and Bishop Tiller realized that they showed a stronger aversion to loss than men, preferring to avoid losses rather than make gains. From a behavioural point of view, it may be men are simply too 'risk hungry'. The literature

[6]The *nucleus accumbens* is the same part of the reward circuit that is activated in response to cocaine and monetary gain.

[7]This part of the brain is not associated with any reward pathways at all; rather, it seems to be associated with disgust, whether due to an unpleasant odour, expressions of reacting to an unpleasantness, or seeing graphic pictures of contamination or bodily mutilation (Wicker et al., 2003; Wright et al., 2004).

suggests that they fall prey to a behavioural trait known as 'overconfidence', which often leads to more aggressive and active trading (Deaves et al., 2009). The notion that men appear to have a higher risk appetite[8] and women are more risk averse is increasingly important for the financial service industry in light of the rising wealth and economic freedom of women globally. Demographic trends in the developed world point to a growing number of wealthy female clients in the coming decade, with the 'new female wealth' rising, as is the number of female executives.

Outside of investments decision-making, gender (like class, race, or nation) represents a form of collective identity that is conducive to coalition formation. Its outcomes are determined not only by exogenous factors but also by non-cooperative outcomes and endogenously determined social institutions (Folbre, 2006). Individual men and women bargain over the terms of their collaboration as parents. Coalitions of men and women bargain over the establishment of marriage rules that influence more general rules of political governance. Groups with different rules of political governance compete with one another for resources. Thus, small initial differences in gendered endowments and preferences may be amplified by the development of social institutions and the process of group selection.

4.3.2 Culture, Religion and Economic Choice

Individual preferences with respect to risk taking play an important role in financial economic behaviour and, hence, in financial markets. Shin and Hanna (2014) investigated risky asset ownership after the financial crisis by race/ethnicity using the 2010 Survey of Consumer Finances (SCF) datasets. The results indicate that 65% of White, 38% of Black, 31% of Hispanic, and 61% of Asian/other households own one or more risky high-return assets such as stock, business assets, and investment real estate. Their analysis suggests that Black, Hispanic, and Asian/other households are less likely to hold risky assets than White households, even after controlling for income, risk tolerance, education, and other factors.

[8]Coates and Herbert (2008) sampled, under real working conditions, endogenous steroids from a group of male London traders in the City of London. They found that a trader's morning testosterone level predicts his day's trading profitability. More specifically, they found that on mornings when testosterone levels were high, 14 of the 17 traders in their study realized higher trading profits. They also found that a trader's cortisol rises with both the variance of his trading results and the volatility of the market. Thus, Coates and Herbert found that higher testosterone levels seem to contribute to trading returns, whilst cortisol levels increased as risk and risk-taking increase.

In terms of religious values, Leon and Pfeifer (2013) argue that individual religiosity is a determinant of household willingness to take risks, since it shapes relevant individual values and norms. Their study (in the German society) found that Protestants, Catholics, and Muslims are less risk-tolerant in general, but not in financial concerns, and that further religious involvement is associated with higher risk aversion. Several authors such as Iqbal and Mirakhor (2011) and Schoon and Nuri (2012) also argue that religion is indeed a determinant at the firm's level of the interplay between financial and investing decisions. For instance, the three monotheistic religions – Judaism, Christianity, and Islam – together with Buddhism and Hinduism, forbid the use of interest. Furthermore, individuals who claim to be religious also claim to behave differently from those who are not. Porter and Steen claim that 79% of American investors describe themselves as religious or spiritual and 62% of them keep in mind their faith when they make financial and investing decisions. The non-religious and agnostic investors amount to about 33% and use personal values in their decisions.

McCleary and Barro (2006) emphasized how religion matters to economic and other outcomes. From a religious perspective, some motivators influence human behaviour such as salvation, damnation, and nirvana. Perhaps, these compensators spur religious individuals to behave in a given manner, that is, to be risk averse and to promote growth whilst protecting available resources.

4.3.3 Fear, Trauma and Countercyclical Risk Aversion

Fear of the unknown is also one of the most powerful motivating forces of our conscious and subconscious minds. Neuroscientists have demonstrated with remarkable detail that our fear circuitry is highly refined, in some cases reacting much faster than we can perceive. In his book, *The Gift of Fear*, public safety expert De Becker (1997) points out that we can detect and process subtle cues of impending danger far faster than our conscious minds realize. For example, when the hairs on the back of your neck stand up, it is your fear instinct kicking in, and you should prepare for immediate action. But when removed from of its apposite perspective, our fear circuitry can be counterproductive and, in some cases, fatal. For example, a familiar error amongst inexperienced pilots is the propensity to pull back on an airplane's control wheel to prevent the plane from crashing during a stall.[9] Pulling

[9]A stall is when the engines of an airplane 'dies' due to, in this case, increasing altitude too quickly due to pulling back on the controls 'instinctively'.

back on the wheel causes the airplane to point upwards, and in the face of a life-threatening situation, it is no surprise that our instinctive reaction is to direct the plane towards the sky and away from the ground.

Traumatic experiences during the critical stages (from birth to early adolescence) where major structural central nervous system changes may have a determining effect on brain structural development and sympathetic nervous system responsiveness and the hypothalamic pituitary adrenal axis[10] (Lipschitz et al., 1998). Therefore, traumas experienced early in life could reasonably affect adults' risk-taking behaviour. Several papers from psychology and neuroscience suggest that risk aversion has a specific neural basis and an important emotional component (e.g. Frank, 1988; Kuhnen and Knutson, 2005; Lo, 2011). Others focused on noneconomic traumas, in particular the exposure to natural disasters – as causes of change in people risk attitudes. For example, Cameron and Shah (2012) found that individuals, who recently suffered a flood or an earthquake in Indonesia over the lapse of the previous 3 years, exhibit higher risk aversion than similar individuals living in villages in the same area not touched by the disasters. Furthermore, as an immediate reaction to a natural disaster, individuals tend to become less risk averse (Eckel et al., 2009; Page et al., 2012).

One of the major puzzles in financial economics is the fact that risk premiums of many asset classes vary strongly and systematically over time. In particular, the equity risk premium seems to be higher during recessions than in business cycle peaks. Over the past decades, a high price-dividend ratio of US stocks preceded several years of low returns and vice versa (Shiller, 1981; Cochrane, 2011). To account for this pervasive pattern, asset pricing models have evolved that assume investors exhibit countercyclical risk aversion. In these models, investors are less risk averse during financial booms compared with busts. Cohn et al. (2015) primed financial professionals with either a boom or a bust scenario and by subsequently measuring their risk aversion in two experimental investment tasks with real monetary stakes. Subjects who were primed with a financial bust were substantially more risk averse than those who were primed with a boom. Subjects were also more fearful in the bust than in the boom condition, and their fear is negatively related to investments in the risky asset, suggesting that fear may play an important role in countercyclical risk aversion. The same logic

[10]The sympathetic nervous system (one of three major parts of the autonomic nervous system) is responsible for mobilizing the body's nervous system fight-or-flight response. The fight-or-flight response is a physiological reaction that occurs in response to a perceived harmful event, attack, or threat to survival.

applies to financial risk management, economic policy, and regulation and crisis response. In each of these contexts, fear can play a productive role if properly balanced against other considerations. The fear of losing money will rationally cause investors to manage their risks actively and in proportion to their expected reward; extreme fear, however, can cause investors to quickly sell all their risky assets at fire-sale prices in favour of government bonds and cash, which may not serve their longer-term objectives if they maintain these holdings for too long. On a wider dimension, if we allow our fear impulses to steer our reaction to financial crises, we may eventually regret the policy responses produced by our amygdalas. This applies not only to investors but also to regulators and policymakers, whose response to fear may have considerably larger consequences.

4.3.4 Recency and Uncertainty

Apart from how experience (fear, trauma, lucky streaks, and boom/bust cycles) can affect risk-taking behaviour, there are two other factors that are also worth mentioning. The first is how insurance (risk avoiding) behaviour can change depending on the proximity (how close or far removed one is) from a natural disaster with respect to time. For example, it has been observed (International Insurance Institute) that, after large earthquakes in California, homeowners tend to buy more earthquake insurance but, over time, they tend to drop their insurance policies, and the number of households covered declines as time passes. Evidently, it matters in the decision makers' minds that the memory of a disaster is still strong, more recent memories being more salient or also termed as recency bias.

The second factor (closely related to and supported by evidence from neurology and neuroeconomics) is the extent to which decision makers can confidently assess probabilities of various events (prospects) they are facing. In real life, event probabilities are not precisely known. This fact distinguishes risk (known probability distributions) from uncertainty (unknown probability distributions).[11] For example, when faced with uncertainty, decision makers behave as if they are *more* risk averse and *more* loss averse. This is demonstrated in Daniel Ellsberg's two-colour problem (1962): there are two urns with 100 black and red balls in each. Urn 1 contains exactly 50 black and 50 red balls; Urn 2 also contains 100 balls but the number of black or red balls varies from 0 to 100. The experiment requires a bet on a colour of

[11]Kahnemann and Tversky and other researchers have provided ample evidence on how uncertainty affects risk behaviour.

choice; if the colour of choice is drawn, one wins $100 and, otherwise, gains or lose nothing (it is a pure gain prospect). So the question is which urn would you pick from, Urn 1 or Urn 2? The probability of winning for Urn 1 is exactly 50%, and the probability of winning for Urn 2 varies from zero to one. Repeated experiments show that most subjects prefer Urn 1 (known probability) to Urn 2 (unknown probability). Likewise, stock markets and other investment behaviours are greatly influenced by uncertainty.[12]

Behavioural finance actually equips finance professionals with a set of new lenses, which allows them to understand and overcome many proven psychological traps that are present involving human cognition and emotions. This includes corporate boards and managers, individual and institutional investors, portfolio managers, analysts, advisors, and even policy makers. Behavioural traps exist and occur across all decision spectrums because of the psychological phenomena of heuristics and biases. These phenomena and factors are systematic in nature and can move markets for prolonged periods.

[12]See Advances in Behavioural Finance I (1993) and II (2005), edited by Richard Thaler.

CHAPTER 5
Game Theory and Testing for Rule Compliance

Far be it from me to say that we ever shall have the means of measuring directly the feelings of the human heart. A unit of pleasure or of pain is difficult even to conceive; but it is the amount of these feelings which is continually prompting us to buying and selling, borrowing and lending, labouring and resting, producing and consuming; and it is from the quantitative effects of the feelings that we must estimate their comparative amounts.

William Stanley Jevons (1871)

5.1 THE RULES OF THE GAME

Game theory provides the conceptual and procedural tools for studying social interaction, including the characteristics of the players, the rules of the game, the informational structure, and the payoffs associated with particular strategic interactions (Camerer, 2003). The essential elements of a game are players, actions, payoffs, and information (PAPI). These are collectively known as the rules of the game, and the experimenter's objective is to describe a situation in terms of the rules of a game so as to explain what will happen in that situation. Trying to maximize their payoffs, the players will devise plans known as *strategies* that pick actions depending on the information that has arrived at each moment. The combination of strategies chosen by each player is known as the equilibrium. Given an equilibrium, the experimenter can see what actions come out of the conjunction of all the players' plans, and this tells him the outcome of the game. It facilitates cross-disciplinary information exchange and provides a unified analytical framework (Davis and Holt, 1993) to assess this research's investigation in testing for Islamic rules of behaviour between the two groups.

Until the mid-1970s, game theory remained an autonomous field with little relevance to mainstream economics, important exceptions being Schelling's book, *The Strategy of Conflict* (1960), which introduced the focal point, and a series of papers that showed the relationship of the core of a

Belief and Rule Compliance
https://doi.org/10.1016/B978-0-12-813809-0.00005-9

game to the general equilibrium of an economy. In the 1970s, information became the focus of many models as economists started to put emphasis on individuals who act rationally but with limited information. When attention was given to individual agents, the chronological order of their actions began to be specifically incorporated. With this addition, games had enough structure to reach interesting and non-obvious results (Rasmusen, 2006).

Game theory has been successful in recent years because it fits so well into the new methodology of economics. In the past, macroeconomists started with broad behavioural relationships like the consumption function, and micro-economists often started with precise but irrational behavioural assumptions such as sales maximization. Now, all economists start with primitive assumptions about the utility functions, production functions, and endowments of the players in the models (to which the available information must often be added). The reason is that it is usually easier to judge whether primitive assumptions are sensible than to evaluate high-level assumptions about behaviour. Having accepted the primitive assumptions, the game designer (experimenter) figures out what happens when the actors maximize their utility subject to the constraints imposed by their information, endowments, and production functions (Rasmusen, 2006). Consequently, this trend moved towards primitive assumptions and maximizing behaviour towards simplicity but not compromising in its search for behavioural meaning, first termed 'exemplary theory' by Fisher (1989). The experimenter then uses the model to come up with precise propositions, whose proofs may tell him still more about the idea. After the proofs, he goes back, trying to understand more than whether the proofs are mathematically correct, according to Rasmusen. However, we believe that these days, more experimenters are keen to observe the outcomes of the games and connect them with broad-based real-world data *and then* posit theories, models, and recommendations. Taking a long hard look at what the real-world data (be it history, behavioural outcomes, etc.) tells us before beginning to theorize with economic models and accounting for all of the assumptions, records, and circumstances. This allows to explain current behaviours and with that find their solutions or craft policies to fine-tune outdated models and institutions.

Similarly at the micro level, people who generally try to win games also try to 'win' or achieve their interests or goals in competitive situations. And both in games and in real life, we generally follow a set of rules to do this. Some games, like some real situations, are 'winner-take-all'. These games are by their nature very competitive, as only one person can win (e.g. most board games and single-player digital/video games). Other games, however, require cooperation to win. Many of the newer multiplayer digital/video games, for example, require cooperative strategies amongst multiple players in order for any single player to advance. In the real world, even during times of hostility, rivals generally have common interests and must cooperate to some degree[1] (Schelling, 1960). This set of rules that people rely on to make decisions may be influenced or even determined by religious beliefs, where religious prescriptions and proscriptions provide a moral framework to aid beneficial decision-making.

5.1.1 Motivation for Our Games

Consequently, one of the main motivations for running these experimental games in the context of Islamic behavioural expectation was to understand why Muslim countries are such overwhelming underperformers whilst Islam provides the institutional scaffolding (according to NIE) needed for far stronger performances. In 2010, the Islamicity Index study conducted by Prof Hossein Askari and Dr. Scheherazade S. Rehman (2010) examined 208 countries and determined that those with the greatest economic and social success by the criteria they say are spelt out in the Qur'ān were Ireland (1), Denmark (2), Luxembourg (3), and Sweden (4). Malaysia is the Muslim country highest on the list, at a distant 33, and the only other Muslim majority country in the top 50 is Kuwait at 42, whilst Saudi Arabia ranks number 91 and the largest Muslim population, Indonesia, ranks 104. Singapore, a religion-ambivalent secular state, ranks at 7. The index was meant to be a benchmark to assess the degree of rule compliance termed as 'Islamicity'. It set out to obtain an indicator of political, social, and economic performance within Muslim nations against tenets of justice, freedom, poverty, opulence, equal opportunity, sharing of God's bounty, etc., and clearly, Muslim countries across the board performed much poorer than their non-Muslim counterparts. In essence, we wanted to investigate further why such macrobehaviours were captured and postulate if microbehaviours could be a contribution to these ranked outcomes.

5.1.2 Games We Play(ed)

In order for us to carry out such investigations, we had to select appropriate well-documented games that could account and test for the rules that we

[1] Even during the Cold War, despite an intense standoff, Moscow and Washington cooperated to achieve their common goal of averting a nuclear war.

want to investigate. We chose them so that we would have sufficient historical data to observe for predicted (or previously observed data) behavioural outcomes as a benchmark. However, there was no appropriate game for the capstone rule, that is, the 'rule of affirming rule compliance and discouraging non-compliance', and we had to create an original game – the rowing game – to give a more accurate test for the rule. Even so, this game is a variant of the documented stag hunt game whose own observations were used to provide some kind of benchmark for our newly created rowing game.

For simplicity, Table 5.1 describes the selected documented games that we will be playing in order to test for these rules. The games were chosen from a historical list of documented games within the game theory branch of economics with expected outcomes and suitability (see Table 5.2) from previous game-theoretical experiments. The justifications for choosing those games to test the corresponding rules are in the references of published materials in the game descriptions in Section 5.2 and in Table 5.2.

We have reduced the extracted nine rules of Islamic behaviours (from Section 2.4) to seven (tested in six games[2]) as we have dropped testing for behaviours with asymmetric and symmetric information (rule of free flow of information) and testing for consultation (rule of consultation). We believe that our focus on seven out of the nine extracted rules is sufficient in testing the adherence to the principles of Islamic behaviours, taking into consideration the size, scope, schedule, and resources available to us.

Table 5.1 Games to be played

Institutional rules (Formal Rules)	Game theory (games to test compliance of rules[a])
Affirming rule compliance and discouraging non-compliance (Capstone Rule)	Rowing game (*original variant of Stag Hunt*)
Cooperation	Prisoner's dilemma game
Contract	Ultimatum game
Property rights	Cake-cutting game
Right not to be harmed and the obligation not to harm (Golden Rule)	Volunteer's dilemma
Trust and reciprocity	Trust game

[a] See Section 5.2 – Methodology (game design) for detailed descriptions of the games to be played.

[2]The test for rule of trust and rule of reciprocity is combined in a single game – game 6 (the trust game). The first move by player 1 indicates trust, while the subsequent decision by player 2 indicates trustworthiness and an act of reciprocity. See also Table 5.2.

Table 5.2 Summary of games' decision rules, payoffs, and sample sizes

Game	Decision rules	Payoffs	SG size	MY size	Total size
Game 1 – Test for Capstone Rule (rowing game)	Player 1 and player 2 decide how fast they want to row	If rowing effort matches, a matching premium is paid accordingly	18 non-Muslims (11 primed), 12 Muslims (7 primed)	20 non-Muslims (11 primed), 20 Muslims (9 primed)	38 non-Muslims (22 primed), 32 Muslim (16 primed)
Game 2 – Test for Cooperation (prisoner's dilemma)	Player 1 and player 2 indicate their choices with red or black cards	Payoff for a red card is S$5/RM5, but a black card gets the other player S$10/RM10	18 non-Muslims (11 primed), 12 Muslims (7 primed)	20 non-Muslims (11 primed), 20 Muslims (9 primed)	38 non-Muslims (22 primed), 32 Muslims (16 primed)
Game 3 – Test for Contract Rule (ultimatum game)	Player 1 makes an offer in which player 2 can decide to accept or reject	If player 2 accepts the offer, both players keep the money If player 2 rejects, then both players lose all the money	18 non-Muslims (11 primed), – 8 offerers (6 primed), – 10 responders (5 primed) 12 Muslims (7 primed), – 7 offerers (3 primed), – 5 responders (4 primed)	20 non-Muslims (11 primed), – 11 offerers (5 primed), – 9 responders (6 primed) 20 Muslims (9 primed), – 9 offerers (4 primed), – 11 responders (5 primed)	38 non-Muslims (22 primed), – 19 offerers (11 primed), – 19 responders (11 primed) 32 Muslims (16 primed), – 16 offerers (7 primed), – 16 responders (9 primed)
Game 4 – Test for Property Rights Rule (cake-cutting game)	Player 1 cuts a piece of cake; then, player 2 chooses which piece for himself/herself	Player 1 and player 2 indicate fairness of 'cutting' and 'choosing' through rewarding S$10/RM20	18 non-Muslims (11 primed), – 8 cutters (4 primed), – 10 choosers (7 primed) 12 Muslims (7 primed), – 6 cutters (3 primed), – 6 choosers (4 primed)	20 non-Muslims (11 primed), – 10 cutters (6 primed), – 10 choosers (5 primed) 20 Muslims (9 primed), – 10 cutters (4 primed), – 10 choosers (5 primed)	38 non-Muslims (22 primed), – 18 cutters (10 primed), – 20 choosers (12 primed) 32 Muslims (16 primed), – 16 cutters (7 primed), – 16 choosers (9 primed)

Continued

Table 5.2 Summary of games' decision rules, payoffs, and sample sizes—cont'd

Game	Decision rules	Payoffs	SG size	MY size	Total size
Game 5 – Test for Golden Rule (volunteer's dilemma)	Starts with pairs then progressively increased by pairs to 10 players. Player volunteers but loses S$1/RM1 in the process	As long as one player volunteers, everyone in the group gets S$2/RM2. If there are no volunteers, the group gets nothing	18 non-Muslims (11 primed), 12 Muslims (7 primed)	20 non-Muslims (11 primed), 20 Muslims (9 primed)	38 non-Muslims (22 primed), 32 Muslims (16 primed)
Game 6 – Test for Trust and Reciprocity (trust game)	Player 1 starts with S$40/RM40 and decides how much to invest in player 2 Moderator decides that investment has tripled. Player 2 now decides how much to give back to player 1	Player 1 retains uninvested amount plus what player 2 returns Player 2 keeps what is not returned	18 non-Muslims (11 primed), – 9 investors (5 primed), – 9 trustees (6 primed) 12 Muslims (7 primed), – 6 investors (4 primed), – 6 trustees (3 primed)	20 non-Muslims (11 primed), – 8 investors (4 primed), – 12 trustees (7 primed) 20 Muslims (9 primed), – 12 investors (6 primed), – 8 trustees (3 primed)	38 non-Muslims (22 primed), – 17 investors (9 primed), – 21 trustees (13 primed) 32 Muslims (16 primed), – 18 investors (10 primed), – 14 trustees (6 primed)

In Section 5.2, we describe briefly why the games were appropriate for the test of the corresponding rule and also a brief background and history of the games played in order to provide some familiarity to the reader.

5.2 GAMES DESIGN

The methodology of this study aims to assess the behaviour of the subject pool (players representative of the Muslims and non-Muslims) in six different scenarios (games). The same games will be played by the two groups. For our purposes, all the games will have the following:

i. There is a set of participants, whom we call the players. There will be two players in each game, except for game 5 that will have an incremental number of players.

ii. Each player has a set of options for how to behave, which are the player's possible strategies.

iii. For each choice of strategies, each player receives a payoff that can depend on the strategies selected by everyone. The payoffs will generally be incentives for playing the game, with the assumption that each player preferring larger payoffs to smaller payoffs.

The instructions in a session will be read stage by stage. Neutral terminology was used to avoid any potential bias (see Annex 4). The test subjects do not know what is being tested for in each game to obtain neutrality and objectiveness in our outcomes. This allows us to extract actual behavioural responses as they would behave naturally in real life. The test subjects only know the boundaries of the scenarios (games) we set, not the rules that we are testing.

At the end of each scenario, the data are tabulated for analysis to examine the decisions made in different situations. Also, we will focus on simple, one-off games: games in which the players simultaneously and independently choose their actions, and they do so only once.

5.2.1 Game 1: Rowing Game (Test for Capstone Rule)

The rowing game was created to test for the capstone rule that is 'to enjoin good and forbid evil'. It is derived from the original stag hunt dilemma presented by Jean-Jacque Rousseau in 'A Discourse on Inequality' (1755) to illustrate how 'mutual undertakings' create a tension between individual rationality and group benefit. The rowing game is an original game that is a variant of the documented stag hunt game. The game is a prototype of a social contract where the hunters have the choice of hunting hare or hunting deer. The chances of getting a hare are independent of what others do. There is no chance of bagging a deer by oneself, but the chances of a successful deer hunt go up sharply with the number of hunters. A deer is much more valuable than a hare.

Similarly, David Hume (1739) provides the example where two individuals who must row a boat. If both choose to row, they can successfully move the boat and get to where they want to go (social utopia as described by Qur'ān and Sunnah). However, if one rower does not, the other wastes his effort, and they go round in circles, not getting anywhere. In order to achieve maximum mutual benefit, both rowers are required to match their efforts so that the boat travels straight to the destination or goal, but the results from stag hunt games show that although payoff levels do not affect strategic decisions, monetary payoffs can affect behaviour (Feltovich et al., 2012).

In this research, the game is played with cash to indicate effort of rowing – S$10/RM10 for maximum rowing effort, S$5/RM7 medium effort, and S$2/RM5 for low effort. In reality, the rowers only get to where they want to go if their efforts match; any mismatch however slight will result in straying off. A matching bonus is paid out to both players if their premiums match; S$10/RM10 is paid for matching maximum premiums, S$5/RM7 is paid for matching medium premiums, etc. Results are tabulated based on premium placed and difference in their contributions.

5.2.2 Game 2: Prisoner's Dilemma Game (Test for Rule of Cooperation)

In the prisoner's dilemma game, the two players are suspects supposedly apprehended by the police and are being interrogated in separate rooms. Each of the suspects was given these options:

i. Confess, and if your partner does not confess, then you will get a reduced sentence and your partner will be charged with the crime. Your confession will be sufficient to convict the other player of the robbery and imprisoned for 5 years.

ii. If both players confess, then both will be convicted of the robbery. (Sentence will be less – 2 years only – because of guilty plea.)

iii. If neither confesses, then no conviction can be made, so the police have to release them.

iv. Both players are offered the same deal.

In the traditional version of the game, the police have arrested two suspects and are interrogating them in separate rooms. Each can either confess, thereby implicating the other, or keep silent. No matter what the other suspect does, each can improve his own position (self-interest) by confessing. If the other confesses, then one had better do the same to avoid a poorer outcome by holding out. If the other keeps silent, then one can obtain the favourable treatment accorded a state's witness by confessing. However, the best outcome is if both do not confess (cooperate), as there would be no crime to charge them with. Based on our earlier discussion in Chapter 2, the rule of cooperation encouraged in Islamic scriptures requires mankind to cooperate, especially in shared resources; hence, we would expect more Muslims to not confess. The concept of the prisoners' dilemma was developed by RAND Corporation scientists Merrill Flood and Melvin Dresher and was formalized by Albert W. Tucker, a Princeton mathematician.

In this research, the game is played with a deck of cards (diamonds and hearts are red, whilst club and spades are black). The players indicate their choice through the red or black cards (Holt and Capra, 2000). The payoffs for red are S$5/RM5, and black indicates no change, but the player's partner earns S$10/RM10.

The prisoner's dilemma is a typical example in game theory that shows why two purely 'rational' individuals might not cooperate, even if it appears that it is in their best interests. The interesting part of this result is that pursuing individual reward logically leads both of the prisoners to betray, when they would get a better reward if they both cooperated.

5.2.3 Game 3: Ultimatum Game (Test for Rule of Contract)

The ultimatum game is played between two parties, and the first player is referred to as the 'offerer', and the second player will be called 'responder'. The two parties will be playing for S$20/RM20. Player 1 (offerer) makes an offer to player 2 (responder) of S$/RMxx from a total of S$/RM20. If responder accepts the offer, then offerer is paid S$/RM(20 − xx), and responder receives S$/RMxx. If responder rejects the offer, the game ends with both players getting nothing.

Under a strictly utilitarian view of economics, player 1 would give player 2 the lowest possible amount. In this case of 20 dollar/ringgit bills, an offer of a dollar would suffice. Since it is found money, player 2 should accept the dollar. It may appear that player 1 was cheap; economically, player 2 made a dollar out of it. However, this strictly utilitarian view does not translate to how people actually behave when faced with this decision. In experiments based on the ultimatum game, test subjects on the receiving end routinely reject offers they find too low, and subjects who must choose how much to give often offer more than the lowest amount. This unlikely behaviour provides some unique insight into the human mind and how we function as social animals.

The ultimatum game is also important from a sociological perspective, because it illustrates the human unwillingness to accept injustice. Faithfulness to the terms of all contracts entered into, establishing justice, reward for rule compliance and punishment for rule violation is linked to the fulfilment of obligations incurred under the stipulation of terms and conditions of a contract. The tendency to refuse small offers may also be seen as relevant to the concept of honour.

5.2.4 Game 4: Cake-Cutting Game (Test for Rule of Property Rights)

The cake-cutting game is a kind of fair division game. The problem involves a divisible and heterogeneous resource, in this case, an actual cake to be divided between two players so that each of them feels they got a fair share. For this study, one person would cut the cake into two pieces, after which the other person gets to choose which piece he/she wants. This obviously gives the first person great incentive to carefully cut the cake into equal halves; otherwise, he/she will get stuck with the smaller one. However, the resource has to be divided amongst partners who have different preferences over different parts of the cake, that is, some people prefer the chocolate toppings, some prefer the cherries, and some just want as large a piece as possible. The division should be subjectively fair, that is, each person should receive a piece that he/she believes to be a fair share. This game tests the respect for property rights and just allocations on perceived value.

In this research, we will be using envy-freeness and proportionality to tabulate agreeableness on equitability. Envy-freeness and proportionality are equivalent when there are only two players, that is, the existence of one property implies the existence of the other (Brams et al., 2006). Thus, if each player receives what he or she thinks is at least half the cake (proportionality), neither thinks the other player received more (envyfreeness). After 'cut and choose', player 2 (chooser) indicates fairness by rewarding player 1 (cutter) with S$10/RM20. Similarly, player 1 (cutter) indicates fairness by rewarding player 2 (chooser) with S$10/RM20. The existence of envy-free feelings allows the players to exchange the money and is an indication of fair division. No exchange of cash or one-sided exchange indicates unfairness.

5.2.5 Game 5: Volunteer's Dilemma (Test for Golden Rule)

The rule of the 'right not to be harmed and the obligation not to harm' is known as the Golden Rule as it is akin to 'do unto others as you would have them do unto you'. The game is a multiplayer version of the chicken game,[3] where 'volunteering' is akin to swerving. If no one volunteers, the worst possible outcome is obtained. If any one person elects to volunteer, the rest benefit by not doing so. In this research, the game is played in a symmetric payoff design, the benefit to every member of the group if at least one person volunteered was S$2/RM2, and the individual cost of volunteering was S$1/RM1. If there were no volunteers in the group, each participant earned nothing. The game will be played with 2, 4, 6, 8, and 10 players where everyone starts with S$2/RM2.

A public good is only produced if at least one person volunteers. In this game, bystanders decide independently on whether to sacrifice something for the benefit of the group. Because it will cost the volunteer to ensure mutual benefit, there is a greater incentive for free-riding. The social phenomena of the bystander effect[4] and diffusion of responsibility[5] heavily relate to the volunteer's dilemma (Poundstone, 1993).

The story of Kitty Genovese is often used as a classic example of the volunteer's dilemma. Genovese was stabbed to death in an alley where various residential apartments overlooked the assault. Although many people were aware of the assault at the time (even though they may not have been aware of the exact scope and nature of the assault), only one person contacted the police. It was assumed that people did not get involved because they thought others would contact the police and people did not want to incur the costs of getting involved in the dispute (Takooshian, 2014). The apparent lack of reaction by numerous neighbours purported to have watched the scene or to have heard Genovese's cries for help,

[3]A game in which two drivers drive towards each other on a collision course: one must swerve, or both may die in the crash, but if one driver swerves and the other does not, the one who swerved will be called a 'chicken', meaning a coward. The chicken game, also known as the hawk-dove game, is an influential model of conflict of personal gain and mutual benefit for two players in game theory.

[4]The bystander effect is a social psychological phenomenon in which individuals do not offer any means of help to a victim when other people are present. The greater the number of bystanders, the less likely it is that any one of them will help.

[5]Diffusion of responsibility is a sociopsychological phenomenon whereby a person is less likely to take responsibility for action or inaction when others are present. Considered a form of attribution, the individual assumes that others either are responsible for taking action or have already done so.

although erroneously reported, prompted research into diffusion of responsibility and the bystander effect. Social psychologists John M. Darley and Bibb Latané started this line of research, showing that contrary to common expectations, larger numbers of bystanders decrease the likelihood that someone will step forward and help a victim (Zimbardo, 2014). The reasons include the fact that onlookers see that others are not helping either, that onlookers believe others will know better how to help, and that onlookers feel uncertain about helping whilst others are watching. The Kitty Genovese case thus became a classic feature of social psychology textbooks.

5.2.6 Game 6: Trust Game (Test for the Rules of Trust & Reciprocity)

In the final game, the trust game, the first player (investor) decides how much money he is given (S$40/RM40) to keep and how much to give to player 2 (trustee) as an investment. This first stage of the game is a test of trust (of player 1) and trustworthiness (of player 2). The amount invested earns a certain return (triple of the amount invested). Player 2 must now decide how much to give back to player 1. Ultimately, both players are better off with the investment, but player 1 takes a risk with investing in player 2 and counting on that he/she is trustworthy. This game underscores the value of trust as a social capital that makes social interactions more efficient.

The trust game was designed by Berg et al. (1995) and also called the 'investment game'. It was an experiment in decision-making to measure trust in economic decisions and to demonstrate that trust is as basic to economic transactions as self-interest. As 'trust is not intrinsically part of mainstream economics', the success of this experiment in demonstrating the primacy of trust is problematic for basic assumptions of standard economics, which tend to ignore trust. Under standard economic assumptions of rational self-interest, the predicted actions of the first player in the trust game will be that he will choose to invest nothing. However, in the original Berg et al. experiment, 30 out of 32 game trials resulted in a violation of the results predicted by standard economic theory. In these 30 cases, first players sent money that averaged slightly over 50% of their original endowment.

Table 5.2 is a summary of the decision rules, payoffs, and sample sizes.

For a quick understanding, we have collated the observations from the literature and present them below, against fundamental economic theory. Table 5.3 also serves as the expected outcomes for the experimental games:

Table 5.3 Established behavioural outcomes

Games	According to economic theory	Real-world observations
Game 1 (Rowing game – *original variant of stag hunt*)	Rational choice theory suggests that an individual acts as if balancing costs against benefits to arrive at action that maximizes personal advantage	In order to achieve maximum mutual benefit, both rowers are required to match their efforts so that boat travels straight to the destination or goal, but the results from *Stag Hunt* games show that **i.** although payoff levels does not affect strategic decisions, monetary payoffs can affect behaviour; **ii.** loss avoidance are real factors in decision-making; **iii.** cognitive ability and risk-aversion has no statistically significant bearing on any aspect of behaviour or outcomes. *From Skryms (2001), Feltovich* et al. *(2012)*
Game 2 (Prisoner's dilemma)	In pursuit of self-interest, the players will rat each other out, even though it is actually in their best interest to cooperate	**i.** Increased gain from defection from \$2 to \$8 caused the rate of cooperation to fall from 22% to 11% **ii.** Seventeen percent cooperative choices in one-off games, 58% cooperative choices in repeated pairings *From Axelrod (1984), Holt and Capra (2000), Capraro (2013), Kaznatcheev (2015)*
Game 3 (Ultimatum game)	In an anonymous one-time transaction, the offer will be minimalist; variation of large sums should not matter	**i.** Median/mode offers in 40% range. Mean varies 30%–40%. **ii.** Offers of 20% or below are typically rejected. Rarely are offers ≥40% rejected **iii.** If 20% offers are rejected, then it is rational to offer more; conflicts with payoff maximizing behaviour **iv.** Offers in the ultimatum game appear to have some mix of strategic play (fear of rejection) and some degree of altruism/fairness *From Kahneman et al. (1986), Gale et al. (1995), Camerer (2003), Sanfey et al. (2003), Alvard (2004)*

Continued

Table 5.3 Established behavioural outcomes—cont'd

Games	According to economic theory	Real-world observations
Game 4 (Cake-cutting game)	The cutter will cut the cake to maximize his/her utility, and the chooser will choose the piece that maximizes his/her utility	The cutter knowing that the choice is not up to him/her after cutting the cake will cut it as equitably as he/she perceives it The chooser chooses the piece according to his/her preference, although it may not seem equitable in terms of division (50/50) Fairness needs to consider preferences to understand perception of value and equity *From Barbanel and Taylor (1995), Brams and Taylor (1995), Moulin (2003), Brams et al. (2006)*
Game 5 (Volunteer's dilemma)	In line with self-regard, if there is a possibility that someone else will pay for the call, then players will wait for others to make the call	**i.** The results show that as the group size gets bigger (from group 2–10) the cost/utility ratio approaches 0.10 from 0.50 **ii.** The likelihood of someone volunteering to call reduces by three times when group size is increased from 2 to 5. *From Diekmann (1986, 1993), Poundstone (1993), Franzen (1995), Takooshian (2014), Zimbardo (2014)*
Game 6 (Trust game)	Theoretically, player 1 (investor) would be better off if he kept all the money to himself and invest nothing in player 2	**i.** On average, about 50% is invested; around 95% of investment is returned **ii.** There is wide dispersion, with half returning nothing or only a token amount **iii.** More indirect repayment or larger group tends to reduce investment, fall off in trust. **iv.** Social pressure – 'image' – can increase investment and repayment rate *From Berg et al. (1995), Henrich et al. (2004), Cesarini et al. (2008), Bourgeois-Gironde and Corcos (2011)*

5.2.7 Priming Instrument

The experimental results will be tested for significance, in particular, for the significance of possible differences between Muslim and non-Muslim subjects. In order to statistically control for religious effects, we use a priming instrument used by Shariff and Norenzayan (2007) to segregate the Islamic salient subjects within the Muslim group and the religious salient subjects within the non-Muslim group via sentence-unscrambling task (see Annex 3). The sentences vary depending on whether the subject is in the Islamic salient condition or the control condition. Five of the sentences unscrambled by Islamic salient subjects contain religious content. None of the control subjects' sentences contain religious content. An advantage of this priming instrument is that it is subtle; compared with blatant primes, subtle primes more reliably cause behaviour to conform to norms (Wheeler and Petty, 2001), which aids in interpreting our results within our theoretical framework of self-categorization.[6] The basic idea is that priming a social category temporarily increases the strength of affiliation with that category. Stronger affiliation with a category causes behaviour to shift towards that category's norms, so comparing primed and unprimed behaviour allows us to infer something about what the category's norms are and how they affect steady-state behaviour.

5.3 SAMPLE

Friedman and Cassar (2004) found that students (undergraduates) were a good choice for the subject pool for several reasons. Firstly, if the experiment were done at a university facility, the subject pool is readily accessible, making it convenient to recruit. Secondly, most students have a low opportunity cost. Thirdly, students tend to have a steep learning curve and could be easily taught on how to follow the instructions of the game, and lastly, they seldom know much about the hypotheses of the study. By contrast, PhD students and faculty members are unreliable subjects. Often, they get interested in what is being done and respond to their understanding of the topic rather than according to the incentives constructed.The results can be disastrous from Friedman and Cassar (1984:395–396, agent 5).

[6]A framework inspired by Akerlof and Kranton (2000) and developed by Benjamin et al. (2010).

However, in our study, we feel that having only students as a sample group is not representative of a society. Hence, we have chosen to take an accurate snapshot of society in our experiments by recruiting players for the games coming from various age groups (grouped as 20s, 30s, and 40s), male/female (games were played with a relatively equal gender distribution, including mixed pairs), and varied education background and income levels (instead of limiting our study to students who may be unrepresentative). Our sample is however limited by size as we were limited by the amount of funding available.[7] The resources made available to us could only afford a sample size of 30 for experiments run in Singapore, and 40 for the experiments carried out in Malaysia. We feel that the diversity in the sample size and being able to run in two separate countries with different Muslim denominations (majority and minority) push the boundaries of such experimental behavioural research as this has not been done prior.

5.4 GAME MATRIX AND GROUP SELECTION

This study's data and variables will come from the diverse group of people that it can attract (and needs to in order to remain unbiased) for the game play in order to record and extract the required data for analysis.

The table reflects a list of player information required for the subject pool. This is to be used when analysing the outcomes of the games once they have been played. The list of game iterations also describes the constraints/limits to the games we will be playing to give focus to this research. At the end of the session of all the games and after payoffs had been calculated, accounted for, and disbursed, test subjects completed a questionnaire that collected information about their demographic characteristics, beliefs, how they view themselves, and the level of influence social media play in their lives. We include the actual questionnaire in Annex 5. We discuss responses to the relevant questions in further detail in Section 6.2.1 (Table 5.4).

[7]After significant delays and unsuccessful attempts to acquire the required funding, we decided to proceed with a scaled down version of the experiments, in terms of sample sizes.

Table 5.4 Game and subject variables.

Subject information required[a]	Game iterations
Course of study Income group (household income) Nationality Hometown (urbanized? rural?) Gender Age Race Religion and religiosity Parents' occupation Number of siblings and position (eldest? youngest?) Confidante Social media influence	The games are run with mixed subject profiles, and after each run, the results are tabulated according to interactional outcome (e.g. acceptance and rejection rates) and payouts Unlike previous games in other studies, the results are scrutinized firstly based on religiosity, that is, Muslims versus non-Muslim, and subsequently analysed for the subjects' background (on top of the games' outcomes) to explain the findings The games are one-off, anonymous and non-anonymous, and repeated for consistency

[a] See Annex for the details and actual questions asked in the participant particular form.

5.5 BACKGROUND OF CITIES WHERE GAMES ARE PLAYED

In order to make sense of the games results, we need to also understand the demographics of the two cities where the experiments were carried out. Here, we provide some social and institutional structure background information for both countries. Albeit not extensive, this section is meant to provide some information in order to give relevant perspective in interpreting the behavioural outcomes observed, which is done in Chapter 6.

First of all, Singapore and Malaysia share the main cultural traditions that are Malay, Indian, Chinese, and to some extent Western (British). The different communities do not regard themselves as sharing a culture; instead, they consider themselves parts of a whole. Singapore and Malaysia made up Malaya, but Singapore became independent of the Federation of Malaysia in 1965. Singapore has a population of about 5.54 million, 3.9 million of whom are citizens and permanent residents. The other 1.6 million are mainly expatriate, foreign workers, and non-residents. The Chinese constitute about 78%, the Malays constitute 14%, the Indians constitute 7%, and others comprise 1% of the population (Yearbook of Statistics Singapore, 2015). Malaysia has a population of about 30.27 million, 27.2 million of whom are citizens and permanent residents. The other 3.1 million are mainly expatriate, foreign workers, and non-residents. The Malays constitute about 50.4%, other native tribes constitute 11.8%, the Chinese constitute 21.8%, the Indians constitute 6.5%, and others comprise 0.87% of the population (Department of Statistics, Malaysia, 2014).

In addition, we use the critical behaviour thresholds of the two cities based on WEF's Global Competitiveness Index 2015–16 as a means to provide some kind of social and institutional performance information for both countries. For public institutional performance indices like property rights, ethics and corruption (including diversion of public funds and irregular payments and bribes), public trust in politicians, undue influence (judicial independence and favouritism in decisions of government officials), and wastefulness of government spending, we note that Singapore was ranked higher (out of a study of 144 countries) at 3 (6.2 out of a scale of 0–7), 1 (6.3), 1 (6.3), 10 (5.5), and 3 (5.9), respectively. Malaysia ranked 27 (5.4 out of a scale of 0–7), 26 (4.8), 14 (4.8), 25 (4.8), and 8 (4.9), respectively.

As for performances in their respective private institutions, Singapore ranked 4 (6.1 out of 7) for ethical behaviour of firms, 4 (5.9) for corporate accountability (such as efficacy of corporate boards), 9 (82.7%) for tertiary education enrollment rate (gross percentage), 1 (6.1) for quality of education (which includes quality of the education system, quality of math and science education, quality of management schools, and internet access in schools), 3 (6.0) for cooperation in labour-employer relations, and 4 (5.9) for trustworthiness and confidence (as in soundness of banks, regulation of securities exchanges, and legal rights index). Malaysia ranked 23 (5.2), 10 (5.5), 29 (37.2%), 13 (5.4), 11 (5.5), and 21 (5.1), respectively. These behavioural parameters act as control variables (see Summary on Annex 2), and such information will be useful to understand the experimental results.

CHAPTER 6

Rule-compliance and Institutional Quality

Every fact is related on one side to sensation, and, on the other, to morals. The game of thought is, on the appearance of one of these two sides, to find the other: given the upper, to find the underside.

Ralph Waldo Emerson (1836)

From the description of the methodology detailed in Chapter 5, we use behavioural game theory as the study of how people actually behave in strategic situations where the individual's outcome depends on the choices of all players, which can often contrast considerably to theoretical predictions (Camerer, 2003). In doing so, theories predicting behaviour can be verified and modified, and new ones are created through experimental testing, most commonly in a controlled environment, where people are invited to make decisions in strategic situations and receive proper economic payment accordingly.

6.1 MAIN EXPERIMENTAL RESULTS

6.1.1 Details of Test Subjects

As mentioned, we carried out our tests in two different cities – Singapore and Kuala Lumpur. Our sample size was 30 in Singapore and 40 in Malaysia due to resource constraints in procuring a larger sample. Still, we had a good spread of demographics based on their age, education, gender, and income (see Annex 1).

The Singaporean sample consisted of 12 Muslims and 18 non-Muslims – 6 Buddhists, 3 Catholics, 1 Christian (non-Catholic), 1 Atheist, 5 free-thinkers, 1 Hindu, and 1 Taoist. There is less variation in the Muslim community in Singapore and Kuala Lumpur that is predominantly Sunni and follows the Shafi'i school of thought. We are not aware of existing hypotheses in the literature regarding how atheism or agnosticism might affect economic behaviour. Of the sample, 17 were males and 13 females. Out of the 30 test

Belief and Rule Compliance
https://doi.org/10.1016/B978-0-12-813809-0.00006-0

subjects, 18 were primed, and 12 were unprimed. Of the 18 primed samples, 7 were Muslims, and 11 were non-Muslims. 5 Muslims and 7 non-Muslims were unprimed.

The Malaysian sample comprised 20 Muslims and 20 non-Muslims – 10 Buddhists, 1 Catholics, 3 Christian (non-Catholic), 3 free-thinkers, and 3 Hindus. Of the sample, 20 were males and 20 females. Out of the 40 test subjects, 20 were primed, and 20 were unprimed. Of the 20 primed samples, 9 were Muslims, and 11 were non-Muslims. 11 Muslims and 9 non-Muslims were unprimed.

As mentioned in Section 5.2, the games were administered by trained gamemasters using neutral terminology to avoid any potential bias (see Annex 4 again). The test subjects do not know what is being tested for in each game to obtain neutrality and objectiveness in the outcomes. This allows us to extract actual behavioural responses as they would behave naturally in real life.

6.1.2 Results of Game 1: Rowing Game (Test for Capstone Rule)

For the rowing game, both rowers needed to match their effort and speed (in tandem) in order to move in a straight line that is the shortest distance and will enable the rowers to reach their destination more efficiently. This illustrates the need for all parties involved to acknowledge mutual goals and decide to achieve them together by making choices that are aligned to achieving them. When one party does not match the same effort to strive for those goals, the outcome will result in veering away from those goals. In 'affirming rule compliance and discouraging non-compliance', we expect outcomes to match at the highest value amount of S$/RM10.

In this game, the sample distribution in Singapore is 18 non-Muslims (11 primed) and 12 Muslims (7 primed), whilst in Malaysia, it was 20 non-Muslims (11 primed) and 20 Muslims (9 primed); in total, there were 38 non-Muslims (22 primed) and 32 Muslims (16 primed) (Table 6.1).

In the Singapore experimental run, almost every pair had their decisions matched and bonuses paid out accordingly except for one pair that did not match (unprimed non-Muslim pair). When the pair later realized that there was no bonus paid out to them, they wanted to change their minds in order to match. In the Malaysian run, two pairs did not match, one of which only realized after no payout was given to them that they could have discussed to match their choices and obtain some kind of payout. All four players did not even discuss, and one pair (both unprimed Muslims) had hidden their choices from each other.

Table 6.1 Rowing efforts in the rowing game

Game 1	Singapore				Malaysia			
Effort	**$2**	**$5**	**$10**	**Total**	**RM5**	**RM7**	**RM10**	**Total**
Muslim	**0**	**2**	**10**	**12**	**5**	**3**	**12**	**20**
Primed	0	2	5	**7**	2	2	5	**9**
Unprimed	0	0	5	**5**	3	1	7	**11**
Did not match				***0***				***3***
Non-Muslim	**0**	**3**	**15**	**18**	**6**	**2**	**12**	**20**
Primed	0	2	9	**11**	2	2	7	**11**
Unprimed	0	1	6	**7**	4	0	5	**9**
Did not match				***1***				***1***
Ratios (%)								
Muslim	**0%**	**17%**	**83%**	100%	**25%**	**15%**	**60%**	**100%**
Primed	0%	29%	71%	**58%**	22%	22%	56%	**45%**
Unprimed	0%	0%	100%	**42%**	27%	9%	64%	**55%**
Did not match				***0%***				***15%***
Non-Muslim	**0%**	**17%**	**83%**	100%	**30%**	**10%**	**60%**	**100%**
Primed	0%	18%	82%	**61%**	18%	18%	64%	**55%**
Unprimed	0%	14%	86%	**39%**	44%	0%	56%	**45%**
Did not match				***6%***				***5%***

83% of both the Muslim and non-Muslim groups in SG and 60% of both groups in MY chose the maximum payout matching bonus. These results seem to indicate that both Muslim and non-Muslim groups in both countries equally want the same objectives and are willing to work together to achieve those goals (maximize payoffs) together. However, upon closer scrutiny of the maximum payoff, the priming seems to be negative for the Muslim group, both in SG (71% primed vs 100% unprimed) and MY (56% primed vs 64% unprimed) (Table 6.2).

When the data are combined, the negative priming effects still persist – Muslims 63% primed versus 75% unprimed as compared with non-Muslims

Table 6.2 Rowing efforts in the rowing game (combined SG and MY data)

Game 1		Combined SG and MY		
Effort	**S$2/RM5**	**S$5/RM7**	**S$10/RM10**	**Total**
Muslim	**5**	**5**	**22**	**32**
Primed	2	4	10	**16**
Unprimed	3	1	12	**16**
Did not match				***3***
Non-Muslim	6	5	27	38
Primed	2	4	16	**22**
Unprimed	4	1	11	**16**
Did not match				***2***
Ratios (%)				
Muslim	**16%**	**16%**	**69%**	**100%**
Primed	13%	25%	63%	**50%**
Unprimed	19%	6%	75%	**50%**
Did not match				***9%***
Non-Muslim	**16%**	**13%**	**71%**	100%
Primed	9%	18%	73%	**58%**
Unprimed	25%	6%	69%	**42%**
Did not match				***5%***
Combined	**11**	**10**	**49**	**70**
Primed	4	8	26	**38**
Unprimed	7	2	23	**32**
Did not match				***5***
Ratios (%)				
Combined	**16%**	**14%**	**70%**	**100%**
Primed	11%	21%	68%	**54%**
Unprimed	22%	6%	72%	**46%**
Did not match				***7%***

73% primed and 69% unprimed. This seems to indicate that this group of primed Muslims would 'command right and forbid wrong' more at a lower-to-moderate pace rather than at the highest level. This may appear to be a skewed understanding of the mutually beneficial goals (or of moderation), especially when trying to maximize one's goals (payoffs). It could also be interpreted that when viewed in terms of payoffs alone, primed Muslims were less economically driven to maximize them than non-Muslims.

6.1.3 Results of Game 2: Prisoner's Dilemma Game (Test for Rule of Cooperation)

The 'dilemma' faced by the prisoners in the game scenario is that, whatever the other does, it seems that each is better off confessing than remaining silent. But the best outcome obtained would be when both did not confess and had remained silent. A common view is that the puzzle illustrates a conflict between individual and group rationality. A group whose members pursue rational self-interest may all end up worse off than a group whose members cooperate to obtain the best outcome together. Based on our earlier discussion in Chapter 2, the rule of cooperation encouraged in Islamic scriptures requires mankind to cooperate, especially in shared resources (e.g. fire, water, and pastures); hence, we would expect more Muslims not to confess. The act of choosing cooperation over self-interest will also prevent the tragedy of the commons as can be seen in the destructive effects of overfarming and overfishing.

In both countries, the percentages of confession and nonconfessions were about the same in the Muslim group – 28% for confessions and 22% for nonconfessions, with no noticeable priming effect. But for the non-Muslim group, there was a noticeable *positive priming effect in the Singapore sample* (primed nonconfession was higher at 22% vs 17% of confession, and unprimed nonconfession was higher at 44% vs 17%) but a *negative priming effect for the Malaysian sample* (primed nonconfession was at 15% vs 40%, and unprimed nonconfession was higher at 30% vs 15%). When we combined the Muslim and non-Muslim groups together and evaluated solely on the priming effects, the Singapore sample showed some positive effects between primed (23% confession vs 23% nonconfession) and unprimed (37% confession vs 17% nonconfession). But in the Malaysian sample, negative effects were observed, primed (33% confession vs 18% nonconfession) and unprimed (23% confession vs 28% nonconfession). In a generally more modern and open society like (Table 6.3).

Table 6.3 Confessions in the prisoner's dilemma game (breakdown)

Game 2	Singapore	Malaysia	SG and MY
Muslim	**12**	**20**	**32**
Primed	**7**	**9**	**16**
Confess	4	5	9
Did not confess	3	4	7
Unprimed	**5**	**11**	**16**
Confess	3	6	9
Did not confess	2	5	7
Non-Muslim	**18**	**20**	**38**
Primed	**7**	**11**	**18**
Confess	3	8	11
Did not confess	4	3	7
Unprimed	**11**	**9**	**20**
Confess	8	3	11
Did not confess	3	6	9
Combined (M and nM)	30	40	70
Primed	14	20	34
Confess	7	13	20
Did not confess	7	7	14
Unprimed	16	20	36
Confess	11	9	20
Did not confess	5	11	16
Combined (P and uP)			
Muslim	**12**	**20**	**32**
Confess	7	11	18
Did not confess	5	9	14
Non-Muslim	**18**	**20**	**38**
Confess	11	11	22
Did not confess	7	9	16
Combined (M and nM)	**30**	**40**	**70**
Confess	18	22	40
Did not confess	12	18	30

Singapore, the priming effects appear to work as it was designed, in this case to foster cooperation by not confessing to achieve better outcomes for both partners. However, it may appear in Malaysia, which is generally more conservative; they are willing to admit to mistakes (or confess) to preserve amicability when primed (Table 6.4).

When the data were combined, we note that there were no significant differences between Muslims versus non-Muslims and primed versus unprimed groups.

Table 6.4 Confessions in the prisoner's dilemma game (breakdown in ratio %)

Game 2/ratios (%)	Singapore	Malaysia	SG and MY
Muslim	**100%**	**100%**	**100%**
Primed	**58%**	**45%**	**50%**
Confess	33%	25%	28%
Did not confess	25%	20%	22%
Unprimed	**42%**	**55%**	**50%**
Confess	25%	30%	28%
Did not confess	17%	25%	22%
Non-Muslim	**100%**	**100%**	**100%**
Primed	**39%**	**55%**	**47%**
Confess	17%	40%	29%
Did not confess	22%	15%	18%
Unprimed	**61%**	**45%**	**53%**
Confess	44%	15%	29%
Did not confess	17%	30%	24%
Combined (M and nM)	**100%**	**100%**	**100%**
Primed	**47%**	**50%**	**49%**
Confess	23%	33%	29%
Did not confess	23%	18%	20%
Unprimed	**53%**	**50%**	**51%**
Confess	37%	23%	29%
Did not confess	17%	28%	23%
Combined (P and uP)			
Muslim	**100%**	**100%**	**100%**
Confess	58%	55%	56%
Did not confess	42%	45%	44%
Non-Muslim	**100%**	**100%**	**100%**
Confess	61%	55%	58%
Did not confess	39%	45%	42%
Combined (M and nM)	**100%**	**100%**	**100%**
Confess	60%	55%	57%
Did not confess	40%	45%	43%

6.1.4 Results of Game 3: Ultimatum Game (Test for Rule of Contract)

In this popular economics experiment known as the ultimatum game, one player (the offerer) makes a monetary offer to another player. The second player chooses whether to accept or reject. If the second player rejects, both get nothing. If he accepts, they keep their portions as proposed. The ultimatum game has a unique aspect to it that comes from the fear that the offer will be rejected. In past experiments, the average accepted offers were about 50% of the original value made to the second player. Not surprisingly, lower offers are more likely to be rejected, whilst higher offers were more likely to be accepted (from Kahneman et al., 1986; Camerer, 2003; etc.). Assuming that both players are rational, forward-looking, and motivated by some monetary payoff, then the subgame-perfect equilibrium prediction involves player A offering the smallest monetary unit possible to player B and player B accepting that offer. So any amount offered >0 is better than 0, so rationally, player B's response should be to accept. Consequently, no player has anything to gain by unilaterally changing strategy on their own. But experiments often do not lead to this Nash payoff outcome: players do not always maximize payoffs in this way. Instead, their behaviour is consistent with taking additional, intangible, nonpecuniary factors into account, such as honour, custom, and fairness, even when they cannot bargain with one another and the game is not repeated. In our study, we use this game to measure faithfulness and generosity in contractual obligations.

In this game, the test subjects were grouped as offerers and responders. There were as follows:

Muslim offerers – 7 (SG) + 9 (MY) = 16 (7 are primed)
Non-Muslim offerers – 8 (SG) + 11 (MY) = 19 (12 are primed)
Muslim responders – 5 (SG) + 11 (MY) = 16 (9 are primed)
Non-Muslim responders – 10 (SG) + 9 (MY) = 19 (10 are primed)

which makes 35 offerers and 35 responders of 70 in total of which 38 are primed.

In both countries, the results of other documented ultimatum games were replicated with >50% of the offers gravitating to the 50% value of S$20 at S$10 regardless of priming effects. However, lower offers of S$4 and S$6 were not rejected in our sample as expected (typically offers of <20% are rejected although our lower offers were between 20% and 30%). Conventional economic theory predicts that any dollar amount (no matter how small) will make the second player economically better off, and so, he should accept it, and no rejection lower than 50% offers by our test subjects seems to adhere to that theory (Table 6.5).

We focus on the 50% offers (i.e. S$10 and RM10) because it is more or less representative of the ultimatum game outcomes (about 50% offers seem to be the norm) and it is regarded as the 'fair' sharing outcome.

When the data of the Muslim and non-Muslims were combined, the results seem to indicate that the primed and unprimed segments were almost equally disposed to make a fair offer (i.e. about 80% of all offerers made the 50% offer). However, the priming effects seemed more positive for Muslim subjects (86% primed vs 67% unprimed) compared with non-Muslims who showed negative priming effects (75% primed vs 100% unprimed). For the

Table 6.5 Breakdown of offerers and 50% offers by numbers and ratios
Game 3

Total number of offerers	Singapore	Malaysia	SG and MY
Muslim	7	9	16
Primed	3	4	7
Unprimed	4	5	9
Non-Muslim	8	11	19
Primed	6	6	12
Unprimed	2	5	7
Combined (M and nM)	15	20	35
Primed	9	10	19
Unprimed	6	10	16
Subjects who made 50% offers (i.e. S$10 or RM10)			
Muslim	6	6	12
Primed	3	3	6
Unprimed	3	3	6
Non-Muslim	6	10	16
Primed	4	5	9
Unprimed	2	5	7
Combined (M and nM)	12	16	28
Primed	7	8	15
Unprimed	5	8	13
Ratio of subjects who made 50% offers (i.e. S$10 or RM10)			
Muslim	86%	67%	75%
Primed	100%	75%	86%
Unprimed	75%	60%	67%
Non-Muslim	75%	91%	84%
Primed	67%	83%	75%
Unprimed	100%	100%	100%
Combined (M and nM)	80%	80%	80%
Primed	78%	80%	79%
Unprimed	83%	80%	81%

Muslims, the primes did in fact nudge Islamic subjects to honour fairness and make more fair offers (86% primed Muslims vs 79% of all primed subjects). But the negative results for the non-Muslim group seem puzzling; no co-relations with the subject profiles[1] nor country characteristics could explain this. It seems to indicate that when religiously primed, non-Muslims seem to act less fairly but made 100% fair offers when not primed.

[1] Subject profiles include age, education level, gender, income, marital status, parental occupation, religiosity, siblings, and position as previously mentioned in Table 5.6 in Chapter 5.

Interestingly, the one offer that was rejected was a fair one at RM10, but the responder (a primed Muslim) rejected it due to personal reasons. When prodded why she rejected it after the session, she said that she will not accept any money without having to work for it. This rejection indicates that there are other moral considerations at play, albeit it was 1 respondent out of 35. This notion of other moral considerations seems also substantiated by the two maximum offers (S$20 and RM20) and two 75% offers (RM15) by offerers who 'wanted the best for others' and 'wanted to be generous'.

6.1.5 Results of Game 4: Cake-Cutting Game (Test for Rule of Property Rights)

Cake cutting is a game-theoretic problem of fair division. It consists in dividing a heterogeneous good so that all parties believe that they have received a fair share. Beyond the metaphor of cutting a cake, fair divisions are advised in a wide variety of situations: to determine the borders in an international dispute, to divide goods in an inheritance, or to split the costs of building a shared road amongst the different users (Mawet et al., 2010). The problem is interesting when players value the parts of the cake differently. This potentially allows the players to receive more than the value of the cake according to their own preferences. Fairness needs to consider preferences to understand perception of value and equity.

There are three parts to the analysis of this game: the cutter, the chooser, and the reward. The first part analyses how a player cuts the cake (to measure fair division in property rights), the second which portion does a player chooses to indicate his/her preference/perception of value (Barbanel and Taylor, 1995), and finally if there was a reward awarded to indicate envy-freeness (Brams and Taylor, 1995). There are as follows:

Muslim cutters – 7 (SG) + 10 (MY) = 17 (9 are primed)
Non-Muslim cutters – 8 (SG) + 10 (MY) = 18 (10 are primed)
Muslim choosers – 5 (SG) + 10 (MY) = 15 (7 are primed)
Non-Muslim choosers – 10 (SG) + 10 (MY) = 20 (12 are primed)
which makes 35 cutters and 35 choosers of 70 in total of which 38 are primed.

The results of the experimental run in Singapore showed that almost all of the cakes were cut in equal portions (60/40, 55/45, and 50/50). Of the 15 pairs, two of the pairs cut 10/90 and 20/80 because the cutters did not understand or had misunderstood the instructions. When they were asked after the game ended, how they would have cut the cake according to the instructions, they responded with 50/50. However, the misunderstanding

Table 6.6 Cutter actions in the cake-cutting game of fair division
Game 4

	60–40, 55–45, 50–50		30–70, 20–80, 10–90		
Cutter	**Count**	**Ratio %**	**Count**	**Ratio %**	**Total**
Muslim	13	76%	4	24%	17
Primed	5	63%	3	38%	8
Unprimed	8	89%	1	11%	9
Non-Muslim	18	100%	0	0%	18
Primed	10	100%	0	0%	10
Unprimed	8	100%	0	0%	8
Combined (M and nM)	31	89%	4	11%	35
Primed	15	83%	3	17%	18
Unprimed	16	94%	1	6%	17

of the two players did not disqualify the observations that followed in the choice of the chooser and rewards given.

We grouped the choices from the choosers into three categories: smaller, same, and bigger. The choices from the 60–40/55–45/50–50 cuts were grouped as all the same, whilst the smaller and bigger categories were reserved for choices from distinct cuts of 30–70/20–80/10–90 splits (Table 6.6).

When the rounds of sessions were over, the test subjects that made unfair cuts were asked why they did so. All four replies noted that they had misunderstood the instructions and thought that they were required to cut a slice of cake to serve the chooser – they did not view the act of cutting as apportioning the cake between each other. When asked if they were to play the game again, all four indicated that they would have cut it in half for just distribution. In those four instances, however, only one person did not reward the cutter. This subject chose the bigger slice and commented that he did not want to reward because the cutter had cut unfairly (Table 6.7).

In general, the results showed that choosers agreed with the cutters that the cuts were fair and were evenly so across the Muslim/non-Muslim and primed/unprimed groups. The choice of bigger pieces may have been a result of indicating resentment towards unfair cuts and showing a sense of retaliation/retribution by choosing the bigger piece for themselves (Table 6.8) (Brams and Taylor, 1995).

The small number of no reward given seems to point towards the perception of equity in fairness division by the primed subjects from both groups. Those who issued no reward (of which mostly were primed and Muslim) cited that choices, particularly in business, are made and need not be rewarded. They seem to indicate that making fair or unfair cuts

Table 6.7 Chooser responses in the cake-cutting game of fair division
Game 4

	Smaller		Same		Bigger		
Chooser	**Count**	**Ratio %**	**Count**	**Ratio %**	**Count**	**Ratio %**	**Total**
Muslim	1	7%	14	93%	0	0%	15
Primed	1	13%	7	88%	0	0%	8
Unprimed	0	0%	7	100%	0	0%	7
Non-Muslim	1	5%	17	85%	2	10%	20
Primed	0	0%	10	83%	2	17%	12
Unprimed	1	13%	7	88%	0	0%	8
Combined (M and nM)	2	6%	31	89%	2	6%	35
Primed	1	5%	17	85%	2	10%	20
Unprimed	1	7%	14	93%	0	0%	15

Table 6.8 Reward responses in the cake-cutting game of fair division
Game 4

	Yes		No		
Reward	**Count**	**Ratio %**	**Count**	**Ratio %**	**Total**
Muslim	28	88%	4	13%	32
Primed	13	81%	3	19%	16
Unprimed	15	94%	1	6%	16
Non-Muslim	36	95%	2	5%	38
Primed	20	91%	2	9%	22
Unprimed	16	100%	0	0%	16
Combined (M and nM)	64	91%	6	9%	70
Primed	33	87%	5	13%	38
Unprimed	31	97%	1	3%	32

and subsequent choices either way are accepted and allude that decisions and choices should be respected as they are, hence need not be rewarded. Further, it can be also interpreted that the question of rewards may be up to God and not up to them.

6.1.6 Results of Game 5: Volunteer's Dilemma (Test for Golden Rule)

The volunteer's dilemma is a binary-choice game in which a single contributor (volunteer) is all that is needed for a given benefit to be enjoyed by all players. Larger external examples include casting a politically costly veto or attempting an emergency rescue, but in our experiment, the scenario involves volunteering to call the power company in a blackout in order to test for the Golden Rule. The contribution decision is costly (in our case, half of the money given out). Previous finding showed that the probability of volunteering is a decreasing function of the number of players (Diekmann, 1993). We use this game to measure the adherence to the Golden Rule of 'doing unto others as you would have done unto you'.

In order to get all subjects to participate in this experiment, three sessions were conducted in Singapore (for 30 players) and four in Malaysia (for 40 players). Table 6.9 contains the number of volunteers as the group gets progressively bigger (increasing number of pairs) in the respective sessions, with the average percentage of volunteers as the group size increases in Fig. 6.1.

Table 6.9 and Fig. 6.1 validate the results of previous findings that the likelihood of someone volunteering reduces when group size is increased (Table 6.10) (from Diekmann, 1986, 1993, and Franzen, 1995).

In analysing for Muslim versus non-Muslim behaviours, the Muslims were more likely to volunteer as compared with their non-Muslim counterparts (88% vs 68%). The primed Muslims were also more likely to volunteer as compared with their primed non-Muslim counterparts (69% vs 55%). In terms of priming only, the primed subjects were overwhelmingly (61% vs 31%) likely to volunteer. Overall, the results indicate that Muslims 'outperform' non-Muslims and primed subjects 'outperform' the unprimed subjects in the Golden Rule of 'do unto others as they would have done unto them'.

6.1.7 Results of Game 6: Trust Game (Test for Rule of Trust & Reciprocity)

The trust game, designed by Berg et al. (1995), is a popular experiment used to measure trust in economic decisions (Brulhart, 2012). The experiment is designed to demonstrate that trust is basic to economic transactions but standard assumptions of conventional economics tend to ignore trust. The first round of play requires the first player (with the capital) to invest in a second player to test the rule of trust. In the second round of play, the gamemaster deems that the investment has tripled, and the second player decides how much to share the proceeds (to test reciprocity).

In terms of trust, we may view subjects who invested S$/RM20–40 had higher levels of trust. In those terms, Muslims performed better than non-Muslims (94% vs 82%). Primed and unprimed subjects performed almost exactly the same at 89% versus 88% (Table 6.11).

Table 6.9 Number of volunteers as group size increases from 2 to 10

	Game 5										
No. of players	**2**		**4**		**6**		**8**		**10**		
SG volunteers	**Count**	**Ratio %**	**Count**	**Ratio %**	**Count**	**Ratio %**	**Count**	**Ratio %**	**Count**	**Ratio %**	**Total**
Session 1	2	100%	2	50%	4	67%	4	50%	1	10%	13
Session 2	2	100%	4	100%	1	17%	2	25%	2	20%	11
Session 3	2	100%	2	50%	2	33%	2	25%	1	10%	9
MY volunteers	**Count**	**Ratio %**	**Count**	**Ratio %**	**Count**	**Ratio %**	**Count**	**Ratio %**	**Count**	**Ratio %**	**Total**
Session 1	2	100%	3	75%	4	67%	5	63%	5	50%	19
Session 2	1	50%	2	50%	1	17%	1	13%	4	40%	9
Session 3	2	100%	1	25%	2	33%	1	13%	2	20%	8
Session 4	1	50%	2	50%	1	17%	2	25%	1	10%	7
Combined volunteers	**Count**	**Ratio %**	**Count**	**Ratio %**	**Count**	**Ratio %**	**Count**	**Ratio %**	**Count**	**Ratio %**	**Total**
Overall	12		16		15		17		16		76
Average	1.71	86%	2.29	57%	2.14	36%	2.43	30%	2.29	23%	10.86

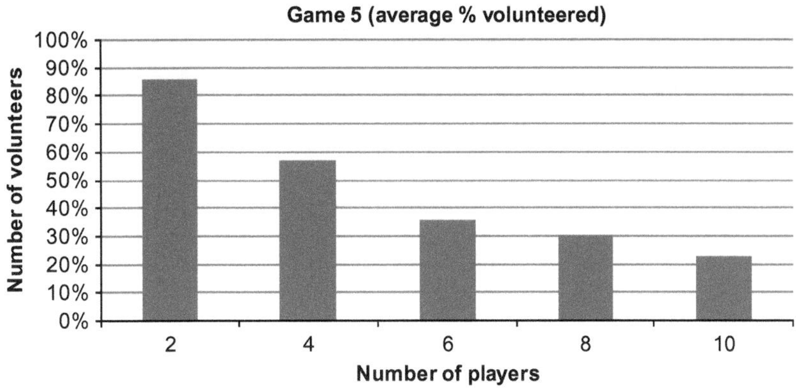

Fig. 6.1 Average percentage of volunteers decreases as group size increases from 2 to 10.

Table 6.10 Breakdown of likelihood of volunteering between sample groups

Game 5

	Yes		No		
Volunteered?	**Count**	**Ratio %**	**Count**	**Ratio %**	**Total**
Muslim	28	88%	4	13%	32
Primed	11	69%	5	31%	16
Unprimed	4	25%	12	75%	16
Non-Muslim	26	68%	12	32%	38
Primed	12	55%	10	45%	22
Unprimed	6	38%	10	63%	16
Combined (M and nM)	54	77%	16	23%	70
Primed	23	61%	15	39%	38
Unprimed	10	31%	22	69%	32

Table 6.11 Breakdown of responses for trust in the game of trust

Game 6	**Trust**				
	S$/RM0–15		S$/RM20–40		
Invest	**Count**	**Ratio %**	**Count**	**Ratio %**	**Total**
Muslim	1	6%	17	94%	18
Primed	1	10%	9	90%	10
Unprimed	0	0%	8	100%	8
Non-Muslim	3	18%	14	82%	17
Primed	1	11%	8	89%	9
Unprimed	2	25%	6	75%	8
Combined (M and nM)	4	11%	31	89%	35
Primed	2	11%	17	89%	19
Unprimed	2	13%	14	88%	16

Table 6.12 Breakdown of responses for reciprocity in the game of trust

Game 6	Reciprocity								
	Less		Equal		S$/RM5–15		>S$/RM20		
Net returns	Count	Ratio %	Count	Ratio %	Count	Ratio %	Count	Ratio %	Total
Muslim	0	0%	3	23%	5	38%	5	38%	13
Primed	0	0%	0	0%	3	50%	3	50%	6
Unprimed	0	0%	3	43%	2	29%	2	29%	7
Non-Muslim	3	14%	4	18%	5	23%	10	45%	22
Primed	2	15%	3	23%	2	15%	6	46%	13
Unprimed	1	11%	1	11%	3	33%	4	44%	9
Combined (M and nM)	3	9%	7	20%	10	29%	15	43%	35
Primed	2	11%	3	16%	5	26%	9	47%	19
Unprimed	1	6%	4	25%	5	31%	6	38%	16

In terms of reciprocity, the reciprocity value is calculated based on returned amount subtracted by the initial amount invested (returned-invested) or *net returns*. The responses were in Table 6.12.

We understand that reciprocity is giving back (net returns) equal or more to what was received. So upon combining the ratios for equal, S$/RM5–15, and >S$/RM20 categories, we find that Muslims performed better (100%) versus non-Muslims (86%). Primed and unprimed subjects performed about the same (89% vs 94%) although primed subjects tend to reciprocate at higher amounts (i.e. >S$/RM20).

6.2 STATISTICAL ANALYSES OF ALL EXPERIMENTAL GAMES

A set of non-parametric comparisons were developed to test the hypothesis of differences between Muslims versus non-Muslims (see Table 6.13) and primed versus unprimed groups regarding their adherence to several rules (see Table 6.14). Due to the small sample sizes, non-parametric tests were

Table 6.13 Mann-Whitney *U* tests for religion (Muslim or non-Muslim)

		Religion (Muslim or non-Muslim)			
Game	**Rules**	***N***	**Mann-Whitney U**	**Standard error**	**Sig. (two-sided test)**
1	Capstone rule	70	600.5	68.112	0.912
2	Cooperation	70	554	73.435	0.462
3	Contract	35	158.5	14.649	0.832
4	Property rights	35	135	12.186	0.944
5	Golden rule	70	656.5	83.481	0.561
6	Trust	35	171.5	16.703	0.546
6	Reciprocity	34	139	13.689	0.568

Table 6.14 Mann-Whitney *U* tests for priming (primed or unprimed)

		Priming (primed or unprimed)			
Game	**Rules**	***N***	**Mann-Whitney *U***	**Standard error**	**Sig. (two-sided test)**
1	Capstone rule	70	599	68.112	0.895
2	Cooperation	70	592	73.435	0.828
3	Contract	35	145.5	14.649	0.832
4	Property rights	35	136	12.186	0.59
5	Golden rule	70	758.5	83.481	0.071
6	Trust	35	155	16.649	0.935
6	Reciprocity	34	137	14.17	0.864

carried out to adequately analyse the data. Mann-Whitney *U* tests[2] were employed for its versatility to conduct the two-sided test of significance. There were three main reasons why we selected the Mann-Whitney U method to test the differences amongst groups based on religion and priming with regard to rule compliance:

1. *Level of measurement of the dependent variable*: The measurement level of 'rule compliance' is determined as an interval, which allows the calculation of the median (not mean) of each group in this variable and tests the differences between them. If the level of measurement had been 'nominal', then we would have had to use a different test such as the chi-square test.
2. *Number of groups based on independent variable*: For each independent variable (games), there are two main groups and four subgroups (i.e. main group 1, religion, with subgroups of Muslim and non-Muslim, and main group 2, priming, with subgroups of primed and unprimed). We chose the Mann-Whitney *U* test as our non-parametric test method to evaluate differences between two groups. Another method used to evaluate differences between two groups is the Wilcoxon signed-rank test but did not fit our use (see the next paragraph). There are other tests that deal with more than two groups, and that is the case of Kruskal-Wallis and Friedman test, but we do not require these.
3. *Relation between the groups*: Mann-Whitney *U* test was used to assess differences between independent groups. Independent measures involve using two separate groups of participants, each containing different individuals, where each participant only takes part in each condition once. In Wilcoxon signed-rank test, the comparison is made amongst related groups, matched samples, or repeated measurements on a single sample.

The statistical analyses seem to indicate that generally, the null hypothesis was accepted (due to sig>0.10), which implies that there was no detectable difference between the groups regarding their medians of adherence

[2]The test was initially designed in 1945 by Wilcoxon for two samples of the same size and was further developed in 1947 by Mann and Whitney to cover different sample sizes. Thus, the test is also called Mann-Whitney-Wilcoxon (MWW), Wilcoxon rank-sum test, Wilcoxon-Mann-Whitney test, or Wilcoxon two-sample test. The *U* test is a non-parametric test, in contrast to the *t*-test; it does not compare mean scores but median scores of two samples. Thus, it is much more robust against outliers and heavy tail distributions. Because the Mann-Whitney *U* test is a non-parametric test, it does not require a special distribution of the dependent variable in the analysis. Therefore, it is an appropriate test to compare groups when the dependent variable is not normally distributed and at least of ordinal scale.

to the capstone rule, cooperation, contract, property rights, Golden Rule, trust, and reciprocity.

Due to significance level being >0.10, we accept the null hypothesis and can only interpret the statistics for this model as not significant for all the games, except for one game (the Golden Rule) and that too only for the priming data set.

In Table 6.14, under game 5, we note that the significance for priming data set for the Golden Rule is 0.071 < 0.100, the only marginally significant datapoint in all the data sets. This corresponds to the large difference in performance found in Table 6.10 where primed subjects volunteered 61% versus 31% of unprimed subjects.

In general, we would conclude that there is no statistically detectable evidence that rule compliance is different for Muslim and non-Muslim and prime and unprimed groups. Subtle nuances are observed when primary data are analysed in its percentage form in Section 6.1.

Also, a regression was developed to test the linear joint effect of religion and priming on rule compliance. The model ($F = 0.013$ $P = .987$) (see Table 6.15) and individual effects were not significant ($\beta_{\text{religion}} = -0.002$; $P = .964$; $\beta_{\text{priming}} = 0.008$; $P = .882$) (see Table 6.16), which implies that rule compliance is not detectable by the regression analysis through the dummy variables of religion and priming.

Table 6.15 Model summary[a] of linear regression to predict rule compliance based on priming and religion

Model	*N*	*F*	Sig.	*R*	*R* square	Adjusted *R* square	Std. error of estimate
1	349	0.013	0.987[a]	0.009[b]	0	−0.006	0.43456

[a]Dependent variable: rule compliance.
[b]Predictors: (constant), priming, religion.

Table 6.16 Regression coefficients[a] of linear regression to predict rule compliance based on priming and religion

Model	Unstandardized coefficients		Standardized coefficients		
	B	Std. error	Beta	*t*	Sig.
(Constant)	1.684	0.042		40.329	0
Religion	−0.002	0.047	−0.002	−0.045	0.964
Priming	0.007	0.047	0.008	0.149	0.882

[a]Dependent variable: rule compliance.

6.3 OVERALL PERFORMANCE IN THE TESTS FOR ALL THE RULES

In Table 6.17, we attempted to summarize the performance of the two test groups in both cities to grasp an overall understanding of adherence to the rules we set out to test and the priming effects on the test subjects. Since the statistical analyses could not detect any significance, we refer to our primary percentage values.

Overall, it can be observed that the Muslim group performed better in four out of the seven games, namely, in the tests of cooperation, Golden Rule, trust, and reciprocity. The non-Muslim group performed better in two out of the seven games: the tests of contract and property rights. Both groups performed the same for the capstone rule. Also, the priming effects had no effect on the test for the rule of trust but negative effects on the combined sample groups (Muslims and non-Muslims combined) for the test of cooperation, contract, property rights, and reciprocity and positive effects for the capstone and Golden Rules. Specifically, for the Muslims, the priming had no effect on cooperation and reciprocity and positive effects in the rules of contract and Golden Rule but negative effects for the rules of the capstone rule, property rights, and trust.

As for the non-Muslims, the priming had positive effects in the capstone rule, property rights, Golden Rule, and trust but negative effects for the rules of cooperation, contract, and reciprocity.

It may well appear that priming only affects five out of the seven game outcomes in the Muslim group as compared with the non-Muslims where they had an influence in *all* the games. This could mean that Islamic values captured in the rules of cooperation and reciprocity were significantly embedded in the lives of the Muslim group that even when primed, it had no significant impact on the behavioural outcomes. Interestingly, where we have expected positive effects of religious saliency in both groups, we noted significant negative effects from triggering the religious identity in both of them in rules of cooperation and reciprocity. This may indicate a reactionary behaviour towards their religious identity. For example, a poorer performance by both primed groups of Muslims and non-Muslims in cooperation and reciprocity may indicate the perceived mistrust towards their religious identity and the reactionary poorer performance in turn by them in those tests. The negative effect of primes in both groups for the respective tests may have triggered an adversarial view of others and that their game partners were outside of their social network (particularly shared values) based on their religious identity.

Table 6.17 Overall performance for all tests in both cities (Islamic and priming effects)

	Game 1	Game 2	Game 3	Game 4	Game 5	Game 6	
Summary	**Capstone rule**	**Rule of cooperation**	**Rule of contract**	**Rule of property rights**	**Golden Rule**	**Rule of trust**	**Rule of reciprocity**
Muslim							
Priming effects	P < UnP	P = UnP	P > UnP	P < UnP	P > UnP	P < UnP	P = UnP
Non-Muslim							
Priming effects	P > UnP	P < UnP	P < UnP	P > UnP	P > UnP	P > UnP	P < UnP
Combined (M and nM)							
Priming effects	P > UnP	P < UnP	P < UnP	P < UnP	P > UnP	P = UnP	P < UnP
Muslim versus non-Muslim	M = nonM	M > nonM	M < nonM	M < nonM	M > nonM	M > nonM	M > nonM

P, primed; UnP, unprimed subjects; M, Muslim; and nonM, non-Muslim participants > means performs better, and < means conversely according to the primary criteria of the experimental game.

6.4 OVERALL ANALYSIS BASED ON THE PERFORMANCE OF THE TESTS IN BOTH CITIES

Standard economics assumes that people are perfectly informed (know all of the alternatives) and that they act on the basis of pure logical calculus. However, human actions are also influenced by a certain belief system (learned or unlearned) that determines what incentive structure is fair and just. For Muslims, the rules of prescribed conduct to attain maximum reward (hence utility) have been defined in broad terms (through the Qur'ān and Sunnah), but the extent of the expected outcomes may be limited due to the non-compliance with these rules – knowingly or unknowingly.

The results provided unique[3] observable transactional data the way Muslims and non-Muslims behave within their communities and towards each other. In some respects, Muslims behaved similarly to non-Muslims, but in others, they behaved quite differently. Also, we observed that non-Muslims of Singapore did not behave the same as non-Muslims in Malaysia. However, the Muslims in Singapore and Muslims in Malaysia did perform the best in the experiments ran in both their respective countries, although they did not behave consistently with what was expected from the priming instrument. So why then do Muslim countries perform so poorly in the Islamicity indices of Rehman and Askari (2010, 2013)? How do we reconcile the better behavioural Muslim performance in Singapore and Malaysia as compared with the poorer performance in the Islamicity indices?

First of all, both Singapore and Malaysia are ranked relatively high in the various global Islamicity indices ranking by Rehman and Askari (2010). In the economic Islamicity index (EI^2) rankings by economy, Singapore ranked 7, whilst Malaysia ranked 33; the highest for a predominantly Muslim country, as compared with the closest Muslim country, Kuwait, which ranked at 42, followed by Kazakhstan at 54 and Brunei Darussalam at 55. In the overall Islamicity index ranked by economy (which included the economic, legal and governance, human and political rights, and international relation Islamicity indices together), Singapore and Malaysia placed at 37 and 38, respectively, whilst the next closest Muslim countries were Kuwait (48), Bahrain (64), and Brunei Darussalam (65). The better than expected performance by the Muslims in Singapore and Malaysia may be attributed to the better overall performance by the nations themselves. In turn, their

3The testing of adherence to Islamic rules of conduct through game theory and behavioural economics experiments has not been done in Singapore and Malaysia or anywhere in the world for that matter.

better performance as nations could be ascribed to the better quality of institutions and civil service that govern, rule, and enforce laws, rights, and civility amongst its citizens. Table 6.18 indicates the various performances of OECD, OIC, and Persian Gulf countries and the different levels of income all over the world to understand their ranking in the different Islamicity indices. The countries that performed better in the individual indices and in the overall ranking were the more developed nations, with more developed institutions that govern these areas.

Secondly, the higher performance by the Muslims in Singapore and Malaysia simply indicates that the rules we tested in our experiments were familiar values to them (particularly values captured in the rules of cooperation, Golden Rule, trust, and reciprocity), through the social and mental frame dimensions, values espoused by their religion and reinforced in their social, racial, or cultural identity. These values could also have been instilled

Table 6.18 Summary results of the Islamicity index (I2) by country subgroup (the lower the ranking, the better the adherence to Islamic precepts (Rehman and Askari, 2013))

Subgroups (no. of countries)	EI^2	LGI^2	HPI^2	IRI^2	Overall I^2 rank
OECD[a] (30)	24	28	29	37	25
High income[b] (60)	60	40	84	40	60
Upper middle income[c] (41)	83	84	88	87	85
All countries (208)	104	96	104	75	104
Non-OECD, non-OIC (123)	111	101	110	89	108
Persian Gulf (7)	94	104	138	109	112
Non-OECD (178)	118	112	116	99	118
Lower middle income[d] (55)	116	124	115	112	122
OIC[e] (56)	133	136	130	115	139
Low income[f] (54)	170	154	126	107	153

Note: EI^2 = economic Islamicity index; LGI^2 = legal and governance Islamicity index; HPI^2 = human and political rights Islamicity index; IRI^2 = international relations Islamicity index; I^2 = Islamicity index = $EI^2 + LGI^2 + HPI^2 + IRI^2$.

[a]The 30 OECD countries are Australia, Austria, Belgium, Canada, the Czech Republic, Denmark, Finland, France, Germany, Greece, Hungary, Iceland, Ireland, Italy, Japan, the Republic of Korea, Luxembourg, Mexico, the Netherlands, New Zealand, Norway, Poland, Portugal, the Slovak Republic, Spain, Sweden, Switzerland, Turkey, the United Kingdom, and the United States.

[b]Economies are divided according to 2011 GNI per capita, calculated using the World Bank Atlas method. High-income countries are classified as having a GNI per capita of US$12,476 or more.

[c]Upper-middle-income countries are classified as having a GNI per capita of US$4036–12,475.

[d]Lower-middle-income countries are classified as having a GNI per capita of US$1026–4035.

[e]Only 56 out of the 57 OIC countries are included in this data set. Significant data on the West Bank and Gaza were not available and thus were not included.

[f]Low-income countries are classified as having a GNI per capita of US$1025 or less as per the World Bank.

Source: Rehman and Askari, 2013.

in them via their upbringing, affirmed through their social circles or become ingrained as part of their identity – be it as part of their cultural evolution or racial identity. This is because people in unfamiliar or complex situations (like the scenarios in our experiments) rely on a limited number of cognitive strategies or heuristics that simplify the unfamiliar or complex scenarios faced by them in making decisions. These information-processing mental shortcuts that mainly result from one's experiences (and subsequently form their identity) reflect their choices and better performance that we infer is based on their own understanding of their religious values. Earlier, we had hypothesized that Muslims would be more adherent to these rules as they were extracted from the Qur'ān and Sunnah, and it seems in the case of Singapore and Malaysia that this hypothesis was true. This should not be viewed as representative of all other Muslims in other countries. In order to verify this, we need to repeat these experiments in those respective nations. Looking closer, the better performance for unprimed test subjects may indicate that based on our limited sample size, for effective behavioural intervention in the rules tested (possibly for policy implementation), it may be a good idea to be religion-neutral and not invoke any religious salient values.

CHAPTER 7

Economic and Institutional Applications

> *The economy is governed spiritually and intellectually by technical and organisational ideas and institutions. New techniques, new organisations, new combinations are expressions of the spirit.*
>
> ***Hjalmar Schact (1967)***

Whilst the results in Chapter 6 provided some insights into actual human behaviour and shed light into the performance of the existing economies of Singapore and Malaysia, it is also evident that the influence of behavioural factors can be mediated by the ability of institutions (such as governing bodies and competitive markets) to contain and reduce aggregate results of human idiosyncrasies. It seems that the performance of Muslim countries can be improved by improving the quality of the governing institutions and civil service.

We believe that the behavioural outcomes of individuals, Muslim or otherwise, can be further strengthened by these universal Qur'ānic rules that can be applied to existing policy. Laws, rules, norms, and beliefs inherited from the past[1] constrain the introduction of new institutions because various groups have vested interests in the old rules. Improving institutional performance requires clear understanding of social norms, like the accepted behaviours of a particular society and social rules of conduct according to the Qur'ān and Sunnah. Improvements happen on the margins by modifying the institutional 'rules of the game'. Furthermore, underperforming institutions do not just disappear the way undesirable genetic traits disappear in evolutionary species. They do not go 'quietly into the night' but instead need to be removed or modified. The four-dimensional framework (individualistic, social, mental frames, and divine dimensions) discussed earlier in Chapter 3 points to new tools for achieving development objectives and

[1]Former Malaya (Singapore and Malaysia) inherited much of its institutions from British rule and administration since the early nineteenth century.

Belief and Rule Compliance
https://doi.org/10.1016/B978-0-12-813809-0.00007-2

new means of increasing the effectiveness of existing interventions. It provides more entry points for policy and new tools that practitioners can draw on in their efforts to reduce, for instance, disparate poverty and increase shared prosperity. The framework shows how impediments to people's ability to process information and the ways societies shape mindsets not only can be sources of development disadvantage but also can be changed. Adherence to the prescribed rules of behaviour and the regard for the rule of law regardless of religiosity ensures a social order that results in an organized, cohesive, just, and prosperous social system.

The interplay of institutions and individuals is more complex than is often recognized; yet, the potential for temporary interventions and changes in institutions to alter long-standing patterns is greater than has been acknowledged. For instance, the Behavioural Insights Team in the United Kingdom (BIT,[2] also known as the 'Nudge Unit') was created in 2010 with the objective of applying insights from academic research in behavioural economics and psychology to public policy and services. It was created at a time of economic and financial crisis and resource scarcity, when psychological and socially informed interventions seemed a viable alternative to legislation. Similarly, Islamic tenets can be interpreted as institutional nudges for Islamic finance and, to a larger extent, applications of these tenets to revivify ineffective legislative, political, and economic institutions to improve socio-economic equality, justice, and performance outcomes.

7.1 KEY ASPECTS AND RECOMMENDATIONS FOR INSTITUTIONAL DEVELOPMENT AND REFORM

Although social problems are more than an accumulation of individual woes, they will not be solved through an accumulation of individual solutions. We recommend that social solutions take into account how our economic, legal, and political systems really work in practice, not only in theory. This means taking into account our own individual behaviours as measured against the rules of behaviours clearly spelt out in the divine revelation of the Qur'ān and the exemplary actions of the Sunnah. The application of game-theoretic concept to the design of policies for institutional reform in Muslim countries starts from the following four aspects of implementation.

[2]Applying behavioural insights to reduce fraud, error, and debt. London: Cabinet Office, Behavioural Insights Team.

7.1.1 Aspect 1: Broad Principles and Core Values

For economic development and institutional reform, broad principles and subsequently the core values of the institution need to be defined and implemented. The major problem for implementing effective 'principles' and 'core values' remains that no law or code will be of much value if individuals lack the technical competence to recognize an ethic, moral, or behavioural problem for what it is or if they do not know what standards their organization (institution) expects of them. Even worse, they consider it to be not in their interests, personally or professionally, to take a stand for integrity and against immorality. Here, we undertake two tasks; the first primes the individual to act according to the 'principles' and 'core values' of the institution. The second is to create a buy-in such that the individual behaves according to a code. These can be done not only through monetary incentives but also through social inclusion and identity – associating with ethics and morality or success and status. For example, the 'code of ethics' is best regarded as a general statement of 'core values' that define the professional role of the civil service institution. In general, modern civil service codes of ethics set out broad high-level principles such as integrity, accountability, responsibility, and trustworthiness. Similarly, companies can draw upon intrinsic motivational forces of their corporate agents by structuring compliance standards and systems accordingly. By structuring regulation around core values, agents can gain incentives in a way that effectively induces social norms even in a corporate setting. Recognizing the organizational psychology of intrafirm dynamics, behavioural science provides well-established lessons that can give valuable guidance in designing compliance systems at the corporate level.

7.1.1.1 Implement Prescribed & Proscribed Behaviours

However, in the example above, the 'code of ethics' defines 'principles' and 'core values' but gives little attention to how these principles are to be applied in specific circumstances. By contrast, a set of 'codes of conduct' outline specific standards of conduct expected in a range of realistic circumstances, representing a particular organization's preferred or required interpretation of the core values or principles that are seen as important to its work. The implementation of these prescribed and proscribed behaviours will be sustained and preserved by the next key aspect of economic development and institutional reform.

7.1.2 Aspect 2: Strict Enforcement of Regulations

Acemoglu and Robinson (2012) argue in *Why Nations Fail*; the main difference between rich and poor countries is their man-made political and economic institutions, not their culture or geography. The book's compelling narrative shows that nations prosper when they enforce and uphold inclusive and progrowth institutions, and they fail when their institutions benefit the interests of a narrow elite instead of creating economic benefits and political power that are widely shared.

But too often, poorly run institutions and excessive regulation force workers and businesses into the shadow or underground economy where legal goods and services are produced but are deliberately concealed from the authorities to avoid unnecessary taxes, labour standards, or other confining legal requirements. IMF (Singh et al., 2012) research confirms that businesses faced with onerous regulation, inconsistent legal enforcement, and corruption have an incentive to hide their activities in the underground economy. We find that institutions are a more important determinant of the size of the underground economy than high tax rates, inflation, or income levels.

7.1.2.1 Enforce Mechanisms of Trust, Honesty and Cooperation

Douglass North (2008) believes that the movement from personal exchange to impersonal exchange is the most fundamental dilemma of economic development today. Personal exchange is a natural human tendency to interact directly within small groups, but in the contemporary world, specialization, division of labour, and the size of the market are the keys to the wealth of nations (Smith, 1776). This necessitates moving from personal to impersonal exchange and developing structures for exchanges over exchange and developing structures for exchanges over long periods of time with people you do not know personally. Impersonal exchange requires mechanisms for ensuring honesty and cooperation without familiarity, personal links, and complete information. From a game-theoretic perspective, in the world under personal exchange conditions, it pays to cooperate with the other players when you have repeated dealings with them, and there is small number of players. In this scenario, you also know a lot about the other players. When there are no more dealings (or one-off transactions), you will defect, or when the number of players increases to large numbers and you begin to be unfamiliar with the other players. It took the western world five or six centuries to gradually evolve institutions that made possible a world of impersonal exchange – the evolution of the current conventional economic system. The ability to conduct personal exchanges is part of our social psyche, but impersonal exchange requires that we fundamentally alter the way the game is played. In the modern world today, there is a political system that puts in place rules and mechanisms to enforce contracts across time, space, and jurisdictions. These institutions will likewise need to evolve to continually monitor, enforce, and adapt to the changing nature of our world and how we conduct economic transactions. In order to successfully do this, we are required to understand the structure of the existing economy and learn about the way local institutions work. Then you can modify the formal rules, informal norms of behaviour, and enforcement mechanisms to make them work more effectively.

7.1.3 Aspect 3: Install Institutional Nudges

Real people are fallible, but because real people make mistakes systematically, it is a very useful primer for behavioural economics to affect decisions by presenting choices that would allow people to make choices that are beneficial to themselves. The predictability of human irrationality (Ariely, 2008) is good news because awareness of our vulnerabilities is a starting point for improving our business, professional, personal, and institutional decision-making. According to a report called *MINDSCAPE – Influencing behaviour through public policy* written on behalf of the British Cabinet Office in 2009, research has found that as much as 80% of the factors influencing behaviour do not result from knowledge or awareness. Rather, it has to do with automatic and unconscious influences on our behaviour such as the impact of social norms, emotions, and incentives. Instead of trying to change people's minds, it argues that one should focus on the environment within which we make our decisions. During the last few years, nudging as a tool has gained popularity amongst policymakers, private organizations, and NGOs who want to influence people's behaviour. Besides the United Kingdom setting up the Behavioural Insights Team (BIT) in 2010, in June 2014, a European Nudging Network was launched during a conference in Copenhagen to provide concrete examples of how nudging can be used to promote sustainable behaviour.

However, not everybody will embrace the popularity of nudging strategies. Some point to the risk of governments implementing such tools as a cheap and soft alternative to other policy instruments. Others emphasize that the challenges ahead require radical changes in people's attitudes and values, and this cannot be achieved without making people aware of the actions required. For instance, there is an opposition between values that are related to people's pursuit of personal status, wealth, and success (self-enhancement) and values that are concerned with the well-being of others, such as equality and protecting the environment (self-transcendence). Several researchers have found that when engaging one set of values, this has a spillover effect on related values whereas those in opposition are weakened. For instance, people who are reminded of generosity have been found to be more likely to support proenvironmental policies than those reminded of financial success and status (Thøgersen, 1999; Spence et al., 2014). To achieve radical behavioural change, it is argued that we need to shift focus away from focusing on people's self-interest and instead try to actively engage values that are related to sustainability. In Islamic economics, the two motivations are balanced: one that drives our own interests (that profits and does not waste) and one that motivates the collective benefit for all. This should be pursued in tandem to draw contributions from all levels of society.

7.1.3.1 Encourage People to Do the Right Things

Because people do not always act rationally and according to their self-interest, this explains, for example, the infamous gap between attitudes and behaviour or between what people say and what people actually do. Targeting the conditions that shape people's automatic responses can therefore help people make decisions that are better for themselves, the society, and the environment. These tools can be used as institutional nudges to gently push or remind shareholders and stakeholders alike (of a society or any institution) to the right direction that benefits themselves and their community as a whole.

7.1.3.2 Overcome Cognitive Obstacles That Inhibit Action

The cognitive barriers related to decision-making were introduced in Chapter 3, and then, discussed more intimately in Chapter 4 are innate and pervasive roadblocks that prevent individuals from adopting beneficial and efficient choices and behaviours. Decades of research confirming these biases paint a bleak picture of the difficulty of overcoming hard-wired patterns. However, armed with the knowledge that people act in predictably irrational ways, we can structure choices in a way that optimally exploits our stubborn reliance on heuristics to gently nudge us towards better decisions. In particular, Richard Thaler and Cass Sunstein, the champions of such 'choice architecture', have identified several ingenious ways of seamlessly designing choice environments to avoid systematic pitfalls in decision-making (2008). There is great potential to design decision-making contexts in ways that lead to wiser choices, as Thaler and Sunstein (2008) have shown. Based on this choice construction, we propose some examples that can be utilized as tools to overcome the pitfalls of our decision biases.

The Power of Defaults

A simple intervention would be to make use of existing human tendencies. Notably, people have an exaggerated tendency to stick with a default option. An excellent example of the power of defaults was conducted by Eric Johnson and Daniel Goldstein in their investigation of organ donation behaviour (2003). Using the variation in timing of the shift in European Union countries from opt-in organ donation policies to opt-out policies that enrolled all citizens by default, the authors revealed a staggering difference caused simply by the established default. Countries with opt-in policies had donor consent rates of 4.25%–27.5%; countries with opt-out policies had effective consent rates of 85.9%–99.98% (Johnson and Goldstein, 2003).

Desirable Action

In the modern society, people are bombarded with messages that try to influence them in different ways, which we then unconsciously filter out 'unrelated' information and select what is relevant for us at that point. Generally, we are drawn to messages that are easy to understand, that correlates with our values and beliefs, and that are presented to us in an attractive way. Furthermore, we are significantly more likely to react to a message when given to us at the right time or framed as a 'call to action'. The recycling project example adopted by most modern societies (where different coloured bins are designated for different types of recyclable trash) illustrates the power of using a visual and easy to understand reminder of throwing the trash where it belongs. When collectively adopted in a particular community, the project generates desirable actions from those who would be reluctant to take action in the first place as they see their own actions having little impact to saving the environment. Collectively, however, it becomes more obvious and even more so when other communities (schools, offices, and malls), even in other countries, also adopt the same projects with the same colour-coded bins.

7.1.4 Aspect 4: Manage Perceptions and Reputation

As governments respond to the financial crisis and its reverberations in the real economy, a company's reputation has begun to matter more now than it has in decades. Most recognize the perception that some companies in certain sectors (particularly financial services) have violated their social contract with consumers, shareholders, regulators, and taxpayers. They also know that this perception seems to have spilled over to business more broadly. In a March 2009 McKinsey Quarterly survey of senior executives around the world, 85% and 72% of them, respectively, said that public trust in business and commitment to free markets had deteriorated.[3] The growing importance of web-based participatory media (like social media, blogs, and online news outlets allowing comments and views), the increasing significance of non-governmental organizations (NGOs) and other third parties, and declining trust in advertising have also altered the reputational environment. Together, these forces are promoting wider, faster scrutiny of companies and rendering traditional public-relation tools less effective in addressing reputational challenges. Aside from having a solid crisis management plan, now more than ever, it will be action – not spin – that builds strong reputations.

In the civil service institutions, civil servants and public officials are expected to maintain and strengthen the public's trust and confidence in government, by demonstrating the highest standards of professional competence, efficiency, and effectiveness; upholding the constitution and the laws; and seeking to advance the public good at all times. The detailed and quick scrutiny afforded by social media to the public can be a boon or bane to public officials.

7.1.4.1 Enhance Transparency and Openness of Practices

Openness and transparency are key ingredients to build accountability and trust, which are necessary for the functioning of democracies and market economies. Openness is one of the key values that guide the OECD vision for a stronger, cleaner, fairer world. A vast amount of academic and policy-support research has been conducted on integrity, transparency, and accountability and conversely corruption in the public sector (Ashour, 2004). The issue of ethical conduct of public employees received a great deal of focus from international, regional, and national organizations interested in promoting the performance of the public sector. A consensus has developed worldwide over the importance of reforming public sector institutions to strengthen integrity, transparency, and accountability and to prevent and combat corruption. Such reforms are crucial to protecting public resources, enhancing public sector performance, and strengthening the government's role in orchestrating development and providing basic services.

[3]See Economic Conditions Snapshot, March 2009: McKinsey Global Survey Results, mckinseyquarterly.com, March 2009.

From a corporate standpoint, leaders can create a culture of trust and openness by making sure they themselves engage in transparent business practices. Creating systems for high involvement in change efforts, openly discussing decision-making criteria, giving and receiving feedback, and ensuring organizational policies and procedures and applied fairly and equitably are all valuable strategies to increase transparency. On an individual basis, it is important for leaders to note that people want to know their values, beliefs, and what motivates their decisions and actions.

Also, transparency involves voluntary information declaration and dissemination. In the absence of information, people will make up their own version of the truth. This leads to gossip, rumors, and misinformation that results in people questioning leadership decisions and losing focus on the mission at hand. Leaders who share information about themselves and the organization build trust and credibility with their followers. When people are entrusted with all the necessary information to make intelligent business decisions, they are compelled to act responsibly, and a culture of accountability can be maintained.

7.1.4.2 Reinforce Self-Regulating Behaviours

Businesses use self-regulation to decrease risks to consumers, increase public trust, and combat negative public perceptions. It complements existing laws by imposing supplemental rules to govern the behaviour of firms. Industries have chosen self-regulation in response to both the absence of government regulation and the threat of excessive government regulation. For example, corporate social responsibility (CSR) programs are a great example of self-regulatory programs that form a means for the organization to engage the public or other organizations (charitable or otherwise) directly to accumulate social capital and fortify its reputation in the public eye or the consumer community.

In the governance arena, self-regulation is much sought after, as adding more regulations to comply to increases transaction costs and may suffocate smooth operations and future innovations. This, although a comprehensive review to improve the regulatory system is warranted. As noted in President Obama's executive order, policymakers should 'identify and use the best, most innovative, and least burdensome tools for achieving regulatory ends'. Clearly, not every public-policy problem should be solved with legislation or government action. Policymakers should remember that self-regulation is an important tool for governing rapidly changing businesses in the information economy. For example, multistakeholder agreements between the content industry, Internet service providers, and user-generated content sites have been used to help reduce online piracy. To combat privacy issues, government agencies and other government stakeholders would likely better serve consumers by working cooperatively with existing self-regulatory organizations (SROs) to create robust self-regulatory programs that foster innovation whilst protecting individual privacy.

From an individual standpoint, the self-regulatory rules specified in the metaframework and in the archetypal model (Mirakhor and Askari, 2010) are given so that humans can achieve the fullest potential individually and collectively. According to them, the degree of rule compliance determines the quality of the individual and collective progress. Rule compliance brings self-development, which, in turn, leads to the cognition of the oneness of humanity as a manifestation of the Oneness of its Creator. And where self-regulation has limits, the divine prescribed rules need to be implemented institutionally.

7.2 RULE-BASED VERSUS PRINCIPLE-BASED SYSTEMS

To design a well-functioning regime for behavioural development and reform, the desired behaviour needs to be defined within the context of the overall moral conditions present and management reform approaches. To begin, Ashour (2004) picked two conditions to illustrate what needs to be differentiated at different moral conditions, for example, high and low levels of corruption:

- *High levels of corruption* imply a greater need for rule-based management, with control and sanctions, than low levels of corruption. High-corruption situations imply low ethical standards and a high tolerance for wrongdoing. It is not advisable, when people are actively doing the wrong things to reform the system (at least for the short run) through moving into result-based management with the implied devolution of authority, discretion, and empowerment. 'Empowering ethically bankrupt people' (or institutions) 'simply leads to corruption more quickly'. The same notion applies to societies characterized by nepotism and political corruption or lacking in democratic accountability. The suitable reform strategy to improve ethics in such situations is compliance or rule-based, perhaps with the enforcement of firm and strong penalties associated with corrupt practices.
- *Low levels of corruption* imply the possibility of using integrity or principle-based management. Where public sector employees are

highly motivated to perform to the best of their abilities, integrity or value-based management is more likely to succeed. Where civil servants are unmotivated or trying to escape responsibility, either by staying passive (not necessarily engaging in corruption) or by actively engaging in wrongdoing, such an approach will likely fail. More typically, unethical business practice involves the tacit, if not explicit, cooperation of others and reflects the values, attitudes, beliefs, language, and behavioural patterns that define an organization's operating culture. Ethics, then, is as much an organizational as a personal issue. Managers who fail to provide proper leadership and to institute systems that facilitate ethical conduct share responsibility with those who conceive, execute, and knowingly benefit from corporate misdeeds. A principle-based system provides its agents with flexibility in the decision-making process, which is based on trust induced by the operating culture.

Islam is a rule-based religion, and the Qur'ān provides the foundational rules for its followers as it is directed to mankind. These rules were interpreted and put into practice by the Prophet Mohammad ﷺ in the first Muslim community in Medina. The Prophet Mohammad ﷺ developed the first Muslim community in Medina through the adherence to these rules that turned into laws, statutes, and regulations accepted and abided by the community. Under his guidance, the Muslim community flourished with justice as its hallmark. Muslims are asked to study the Qur'ān and the life of the Prophet Mohammad ﷺ to internalize the rules prescribed by Allåh (s.w.t.) and to follow them to develop just and flourishing communities (Fig. 7.1).

7.3 BEHAVIOURAL APPROACH APPLICATIONS AND FINDINGS

By seeking to understand how personal, social, and environmental factors shape human behaviour, behavioural research helps to reveal why individuals do not always act as one would expect or as they themselves intended to and sometimes not even in the way that might be best for their welfare. Years of experiments conducted by academics and practitioners have identified common behavioural biases many people face. This deeper understanding of some of the most commonly observed behavioural biases in emerging and developing markets also helps to identify and test new ways to improve economic behaviours and decision-making, often through relatively small changes in financial product design, localized implementation,

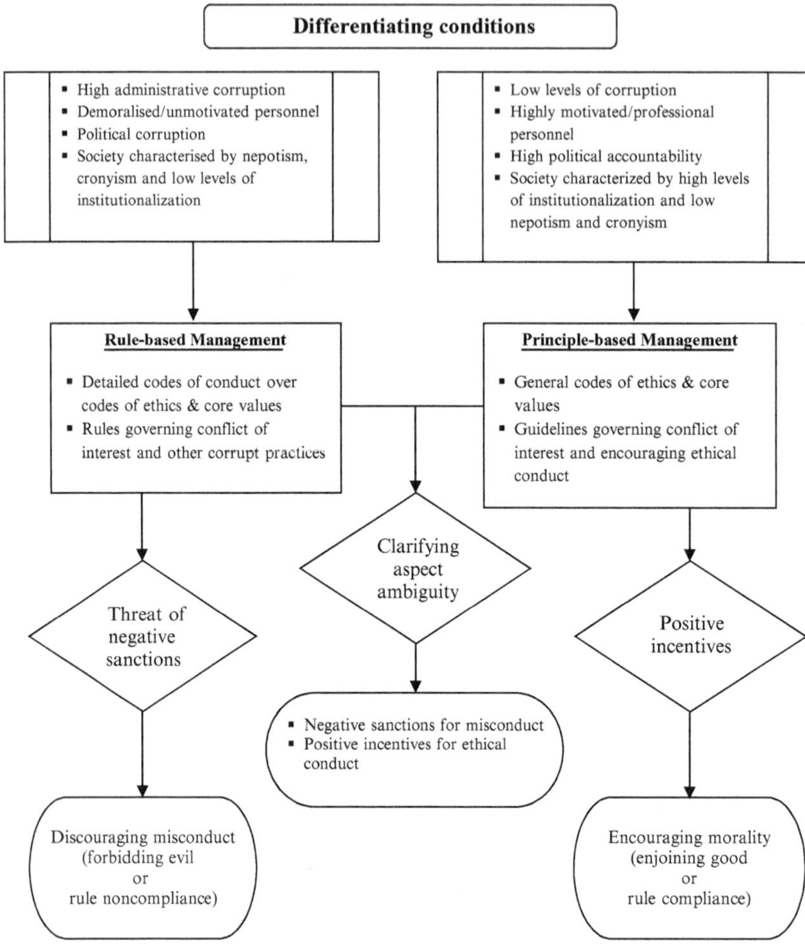

Fig. 7.1 Summary of the elements and conditions for the rule-based and principle-based systems.

or overarching regulations. Datta and Mullainathan (2012) demonstrate cases where a series of minor modifications of channel factors[4] had substantial impact on the effectiveness of economic and social development programs and interventions. The following sections highlight the actual implementation of programs and initiatives grounded in behavioural applications in six sectors.

[4]Bertrand et al. (2004) describe a framework focused on 'channel factors' that can facilitate some behaviours whilst blocking others.

7.3.1 Application I. Corruption

One of the most important barriers to development in poor countries is the lack of uniform and basic infrastructure, such as roads, bridges, power, and means of communication. Without these basic infrastructures, goods and people cannot be moved quickly and efficiently to allow for economic growth and prosperity. The resources for development may have been diverted to personal gains and other unintended ends, instead of being directed to where they were rightfully allocated for. This injustice is closely related to the different levels of corruption. Corruption often accompanies centralization of power, when leaders and public servants are not accountable to those they serve. Most directly, corruption inhibits development when leaders and government officials help themselves to money that would otherwise be used for development projects. In other cases, leaders reward political support by providing services to their followers. It sets an unhealthy precedent and creates inefficiencies and injustice. "The Messenger ﷺ cursed both the briber and the bribed person" (At-Tirmidzi Vol. 3: 1337, Ibn Majah Vol. 3.2313, and Sunan Abi Dawud 3580).

It is then important to understand how the decision to engage in corruption takes place in the mind of a public official. If people believe that the purpose of obtaining office is to provide one's family and friends with money, goods, favours, or appointments, then social networks can perpetuate the norm of corruption. Social networks can even serve as a source of punishment for public servants who violate that norm. In Uganda, for instance, reciprocal obligations of kinship and community loyalty may have contributed to a governance outcome in which public officials needed to use their position to benefit their network in order to be regarded as good people (Fjeldstad, 2005). Holders of public positions who did not use their influence to assist friends and relatives risked derision and disrespect (Fjeldstad et al., 2003). These types of social expectations can become internalized, as demonstrated in a study that found that when diplomatic immunity meant they had no legal obligation to pay for parking violations in New York City, diplomats from countries where corruption is high had significantly more unpaid fines than those from countries where corruption is low (Fisman and Miguel 2007). The finding that country of origin can predict corrupt actions has been replicated (Barr and Serra, 2010) and suggests that corruption is at least in part associated with social norms.

Where corruption is common, acting corruptly may become automatic thinking for officials. If so, an appropriate countermeasure might be to create novel situations to get them to think deliberatively about their behaviour and reassess their attitudes and mental frames about public service. When a non-governmental organization (NGO) called 5th Pillar created a zero-rupee note in India with the inscription 'I promise to neither accept nor give a bribe' for people to hand out when asked for bribes, one official was supposedly 'so stunned to receive the note that he handed back all the bribes he had solicited for providing electricity to a village' (Panth, 2011). Because people behave differently in private from how they behave when they are (or think they are) being observed, transforming opaque corrupt acts into public behaviour may exert social pressure on officials to uphold their positions as intended. Newspapers also can make corrupt behaviour public and empower citizens with information to monitor officials. Conversely, the persistent nature of long-held mental models makes it challenging to convince the public that governance reforms are real and taking place. Thus, anti-corruption campaigns may be more successful when their enforcement is highly conspicuous, especially when public enforcement action is taken against politically powerful individuals widely believed to be above the law (Rothstein, 2005).

Viewed through a social lens, changing a social norm about corruption constitutes a collective action problem rather than simply the repression of deviant behaviour (Mungiu-Pippidi, 2013). Establishing social action coalitions to unite and mobilize public and private actors with overlapping political interests is one promising strategy that has been pursued in Ghana and in Bangalore, India. Providing non-material incentives for participation, such as a shared sense of purpose, feelings of solidarity, and public prestige, may be particularly important in sustaining a broad coalition with varied interests (Johnston and Kpundeh, 2004). At the same time, fostering collective action is not purely a matter of incentivizing self-interested individuals. People can be intrinsically motivated to cooperate and to punish norm violators. In fact, as experimental findings show, "a social norm, especially where there is communication between parties, can work as well or nearly as well at generating cooperative behaviour as an externally imposed set of rules and system of monitoring and sanctioning" (Ostrom, 2000).

7.3.2 Application II. Poverty

At the Innovations for Poverty Action (IPA), President Dean Karlan and his team are developing deep local knowledge and expertise in specific sectors and using evidence and behavioural economics to fight poverty. Their research studies are filling evidence gaps that are important to policymakers who are engaged from the start and stay involved throughout the research and understand the importance of data-driven decision-making. Karlan and Appel (2011) tackled the poverty conundrum through randomized control trials (RCTs). Originally designed for the pharmaceutical industry to test the safety and effects of drugs, the pair has pioneered RCTs to test the claims that small, uncollateralized loans to the poor are a persuasive antidote to poverty. Karlan and Appel detailed how microloans have made a positive impact throughout the developing world in unexpected ways. Intended to spark entrepreneurship and, thereby, growth, it was the 'mundane side' of this small loan lending that is starting to make a difference amongst the poor. In particular, they highlight savings and the *ability to move money from place to place quickly and securely*, as the key to unlock the poverty conundrum, not innovation.

Likewise, Duflo and Banerjee (2011), economists and co-founders of the Abdul Latif Jameel Poverty Action Lab (J-PAL) at the Massachusetts Institute of Technology (MIT), journey into the incredibly multi-faceted and complex economic lives of the poor. Poverty, they hypothesize, may be more of a question of ending stereotypes and changing behaviours. Their behavioural approach focused on how decisions were made and how they can be improved. For example, in Bogotá, a conditional-cash transfer program paid mothers a monthly stipend if they took their children to school. Attendance during the school year was good but re-enrolment rates were low. A shift in the timing of the hand-out – withholding a part of the regular payment until just before the start of the school year – boosted enrolment sharply. Some small-scale policies turn out to be far from marginal. A program in Jamaica in the 1990s taught mothers of chronically malnourished toddlers how to play with them in such a way as to encourage greater verbal and physical skills – a behavioural tweak. Twenty years later, the average earnings of these children (amongst the most deprived in the country) were higher than those of children who had not been malnourished and far higher than malnourished children who were not part of the program. Paying attention to how the poor actually think would also imply big changes to financial inclusion policies, encouraging financial products that people want to buy (Duflo and Banerjee, 2011).

Conventional economic thinking assumes the poor will want to earn their way out of poverty. But poverty makes people feel powerless and blunts their aspirations, so they may not even try to improve their lot. When they do, they face obstacles everywhere. Furthermore, traditional development programs stress resources and markets. People are poor, the argument goes, because they lack resources: not just money but roads, clinics, schools and irrigation canals. The job of development is to provide those things. Resources also need to be allocated properly, and hence, prices have to be right. So a lot of development is about freeing prices and making markets more efficient. But the field of behavioural economics has shown that the poor, instead, lacks the institutional framework that, in the more affluent countries, improves decisions. Everywhere, people underestimate the benefits of education and save too little for their retirement. But educated and privileged children go to school by default; pension systems make retirement savings automatic. Poverty-stricken countries provide few such leg-up conditions for the poor to succeed.

7.3.3 Application III. Environmental/Resource Preservation

The economic activities of a society determine the natural resources allocation and the kinds of resources involved in these movements. The degree of environmental change, like the increase in waste production and careless disposal of pollutants, will inadvertently result in environmental damage. In agricultural communities, the contribution of economic activities to environment deterioration is small in comparison with what takes place in developed communities. In fact, problems of earth, water, and air pollution and other environmental crises become increasingly evident as societies developed. Hence, for emerging economic markets, prevention of damage and corruption before it occurs is better than the cure after. Another important juristic rule in Islamic law states, 'The averting of harm takes precedence over the acquisition of benefits'. Accordingly, all activities that aim at achieving good and securing benefits by way of satisfying human needs (providing services and developing agriculture, industry, and means of communication) should be carried out without causing significant environmental damage, injury, or pollution. It is therefore imperative that precautions be taken in the processes of strategizing, planning, and implementing such activities so that, as far as possible, they may not be accompanied by or result in any form of damage or corruption. The degree and strength of environment hazards depend on the degree of development and progress and on the complexity of the economic activities. Muslims derived economic principles from the Qur'ān and Sunnah that are designed for humans to cultivate the natural resources in the best way possible.

With regard to reviving abandoned lands, the Prophet (ﷺ) said "He who brings back a land to life becomes its owner". He also said "He who settles in a land, nobody has a right to it except him".[5] Islam urges the cultivation

[5]Abou Abdellah Ismail Al Boukhari, Matn Al Boukhari bi hashiyat Sanadi, Cairo, Library of the House of Arab Books Revival, First Volume, 2nd Part, Kitab al Ijara, p. 33.

of the land for the benefit of mankind. Islam makes sure the necessities of life are guaranteed before taking care of superfluous things. The necessities of life are summarized as follows: "Neither to suffer from thirst nor from the sun's heat" (Qur'ān 20:118–119).

The Prophet ﷺ even forbade that a person relieve himself in a water source or on a path or in a place of shade or in the burrow of a living creature (related by Abu Dawud). The values underlying these prohibitions should be understood as applicable to the pollution of critical resources and habitats in general. Waste products, exhaust fumes, and similar pollutants should be treated at their sources with the best feasible means of treatment, and care should be taken in their disposal to avoid adverse side effects that lead to great damage or injury. The juristic principle in this connection is "Damage shall not be eliminated by means of similar or greater damage".[6]

Awareness and concern about environmental degradation have grown around the world over the last few decades and are currently shared by people of different nations, cultures, religions, and social classes. However, the negative impacts of environmental degradation are disproportionately felt by the poor. Throughout the developing world, the poor often relies on natural resources to meet their basic needs through agricultural production and gathering resources essential for household maintenance, such as water, firewood, and wild plants for consumption and medicine. Thus, the depletion and contamination of water sources directly threaten the livelihoods of those who depend on them.

A randomized experiment design in Cobb County, Georgia, in 2007 compared information provision alone with information plus socially normative messages, including the ability to compare one's water usage with median rates for the county from the previous year (Ferraro and Price, 2013). Information on how to reduce water consumption had little effect on usage rates: a 1% reduction in the experimental group compared with the control. By adding messages conveying social norms and enabling social comparisons with median county water use in the previous year, water consumption is reduced by another 4.8%. Furthermore, socially normative messages appealed more strongly to high-use rather than low-use consumers with a 94.1% difference in the treatment effect between groups. Also, providing US households with information on their own and peers' home electricity usage induced electricity conservation, although only amongst

[6]Quoted in books of al-Ashbah wa 'n-Naza 'ir by Jalal ad-Din as-Suyuti and Zayn al-Abidin ibn Nujaym and in the Majalat al- Ahkam al-'Adliyah.

liberals (Costa and Kahn, 2013). Providing people with information on household appliances also helped them in buying more energy efficient machinery (Kallbekken et al., 2013).

Although most studies of recycling behaviours have been conducted with suburban or urban residents of developed nations, one particular study on recycling focused on a developing nation with a rural community in Hunan, China. Tang et al. (2011) sought to identify that factors are most important for increasing recycling from the following list:

a. Personal morals about waste and recycling
b. Others' attitudes towards recycling
c. Perceptions about others' attitudes towards their own behaviour
d. Knowledge of harms associated with not recycling
e. Ease of recycling
f. Belief in personal knowledge and capabilities for how to recycle
g. Perceived impact of recycling
h. Justifications for not taking action
i. Concern for the health and well-being of the community

It turned out that the individuals' beliefs in their knowledge and capabilities for how to recycle were second to their concern for the community. Interestingly, *I can do it* can be critical in determining whether people even try. In this case, positive self-assessments translated to active recycling, making that leap from believing in being able to do to actually doing it. Whilst knowledge gain and attitude change are often necessary conditions for behavioural adoption, other factors can interfere with the progression from proenvironmental knowledge and attitudes to action. These factors include perceptions as to whether others support the action (social norms), believe about the feasibility of completing the action, and obtain a favourable outcome and the presence (or absence) of opportunities to do so (Kollmuss and Agyeman, 2002).

7.3.4 Application IV. Financial Contracts and Risk-Sharing

Imperfect information about economic variables prevents lenders and borrowers, for instance, in a real estate transaction, from achieving the optimal benefit. Under the traditional financing arrangement, borrowers build little equity in the early years of a contract and, therefore, have little incentive to protect (i.e. not forfeit) the asset when faced with financial shortfalls. Lenders are also not insured for such borrower behaviour (i.e. foreclosure) and are faced with unexpected losses. These losses, cost of foreclosure and attenuated costs, negatively impact both the lender and the market. Under the risk-sharing model (of *musyarakah mutanaqisah* or diminishing partnership), the lender shares ownership of the property asset and buys insurance against future downturns by offering renegotiated mortgage installment rates; buyers accumulate greater equity sooner than interest-based conventional contracts. This makes the asset relatively more valuable, and therefore, the buyer is more likely to engage in positive behaviour to prevent forfeiture of the asset. This is an optimal risk allocation that is not achieved in the traditional real estate financing market. The optimal risk allocation agreement reduces ruthless behaviours and lessens the economic loss in the real estate market during periods of economic downturn and financial shortfalls. Such concept of risk sharing looks into the long-term effects of not only in the real estate industry but also towards its impact to the whole economy. As evident in Islamic banks, these financial institutions and investors must forfeit short-term speculative gratification for long-term stability. This is more congruent to the Islamic vision of healthy, resilient, and sustainable economy, where members of society consider the overall benefit to both individual and society *in lieu of* purely their own individual benefit.

7.3.5 Application V. Financial Products, Disclosure and Innovation

Behavioural experiments to test the possible impact of cognitive biases on decisions pertaining to investments in structured products reveal that, to varying degrees, behavioural biases affect investors (Ofir and Wiener, 2012). As a modern alternative for household investment, structured products contribute to the completeness of financial markets by enhancing alternatives open to investors. The structured products offer the investors a menu of investment alternatives from the traditional financial assets they know. In demonstrating the impact of these behavioural biases on investors, Ofir and Weiner's results support the idea of specific regulation for structured products to improve investor protection. The proposed regulation can vary and can be shaped in different forms as sale prohibition to unprofessional investors or as different levels of mandatory disclosure.

By focusing on common traits and patterns, behaviourally informed policies can subtly change discrete aspects of current market practices in ways that can change the behaviour of many market actors in similar ways, often at a very low overall cost. For example, simple wording changes to (the amount and process for redemption) make a rebate more salient in an offer mailed to customers of a UK insurance provider. This resulted in an increased uptake of the rebate offer by these customers (Adams and Hunt, 2013).

Believe it or not, many investors base their investments on trust. The idea that a complex and enormous economic institution such as a securities market might be based on a widespread belief in others' trustworthiness may come as surprising. The investors may not necessarily trust individual security professionals and corporate insiders to be honest and dependable, but they at least trust 'the system'. As a result, they are willing to buy trillions of dollars of securities even when not quite sure what they are buying or from whom they are buying. Of course, experienced lawmakers and businesspeople, as well as experienced con artists such as Madoff, are well aware that trust is a potent force in explaining investor behaviour.

We have discussed in earlier chapters that much experimental evidence regarding attention shows that people also make decisions based on heuristics, or shortcuts, instead of considering all available information. Further, people pay attention to some kinds of information more than others. The implication for investment advisors is that the most important, decision-relevant information needs to be up front and clearly presented in a salient manner. The evidence on limited computational ability implies that investors will have difficulty in making optimal choices when information requires complex processing, such as aggregating risks across investments or time (Lipe, 1998). The implication for investment advisors is that information should be processed and presented in a format that simplifies optimal choices. For example, individual investments could be aggregated into portfolios instead of presented separately (Hirshleifer and Teoh, 2003). Horizon specific return projections could be made instead of presenting annual return information (Klos et al., 2005). An advisor could ask for the investor's preferences across efficient portfolio choices instead of expecting investors to build efficient portfolios by themselves (Ibbotson et al., 2007). These observations suggest, for example, that appropriately designed and communicated lifetime funds may improve investor choices.

To make financial advice as effective as possible in helping investors with the asset allocation problem, it should incorporate theoretically relevant information (e.g. average asset returns, variances, and correlations) and consideration for how investors use information in making decisions and how information can be best packaged to meet the needs, preferences, and biases of investors (McDonald and Rietz, 2010). Whilst experimental economics and behavioural finance provide some insights, much research still remains to be done in this area to complement quantitative research and innovation.

7.3.6 Application VI. Management and Corporate Responsibility

In most companies, only one or a few people make decisions involving millions (even billions) of dollars. Thus, their biases can have a direct impact on corporate behaviour that may not be susceptible to arbitrage corrections. Therefore, behavioural finance is likely to be just as, if not more, important to corporate finance than it is to investments and markets. Shefrin (2007) states that "Like agency costs, behavioural phenomena also cause managers to take actions that are detrimental to the interests of shareholders". Knowledgeable managers can avoid these mistakes in financing, capital budgeting, dividend policy, corporate governance, initial public offerings, mergers, and acquisition decisions to add value to the firm.

A growing literature in financial economics focuses on managers' personality traits such as optimism and overconfidence that are two well-documented biases in the psychology literature on judgment under uncertainty (Stein, 1996; Baker et al., 2007; Hackbarth, 2008). Decision makers who are excessively optimistic and overconfident tend to predict favourable future events as more likely than they actually are and also tend to believe that they have more precise knowledge about future events than they actually have. Optimistic managers also tend to overestimate the firm's expected earnings (value), and overconfident managers tend to underestimate the riskiness of the firm's expected earnings (value).

In principle, a firm's decision to invest in a new project should be made according to whether the project increases the wealth of the firm's shareholders. For example, the net present value (NPV) rule specifies an objective process by which firms can assess the value that new capital investments are expected to create. Because the estimation of a project's future cash flows and the rate at which they should be discounted is still a relatively subjective process, the behavioural traits of managers still affect this process. In fact, research shows that professionals from many fields exhibit overconfidence in their judgments and their ability to control risk, including investment bankers (Stael von Holstein, 1972), engineers (Kidd, 1970), entrepreneurs (Cooper et al., 1988), lawyers (Wagenaar and Keren, 1986), negotiators (Neale and Bazerman, 1990), and managers (Russo and Schoemaker, 1992).

Milgram (1974) suggests that human nature includes reflexive loyalty to authority, wherein people recast themselves as agents rather than autonomous decision makers. By this virtue, subordinates and boards tend to support CEOs advancing risky strategies; a behaviourally grounded agency problem of excessive loyalty imposes economic costs. Its moral overtone lets people behave in overtly unethical ways yet justifies their behaviour in terms of morally charged concepts like loyalty, trust, and duty; this subservience is tenacious. Thus, managers and directors justify acquiescence to corporate fraud as loyalty, trust, and duty to a powerful CEO. Governance reforms might involve distant authorities, dissenting peers, and rival authorities that reinitiate subjects' rational reasoning.

7.4 SOME POINTS TO CONSIDER

Understanding human decision-making is at the foundation of this approach, in which policy is designed to modify the choice architecture of individuals. In other words, interventions are designed to modify the context in which a decision takes place without changing the constraints faced and thus retaining freedom of choice. This is the philosophy of 'libertarian paternalism' – by not affecting the options available in the choice set, it can be deemed to be libertarian, whilst it is paternalistic in the sense of trying to induce 'better' choices (Thaler and Sunstein, 2008). It leverages the heuristics and biases that behavioural scholars have identified in their critiques of rational choice.

As much as good intentions follow these policy recommendations, there are views that seem to look at behavioural interventions as making assumption that real world thinking and behaviours are irrational and mistaken. Some may view behavioural intervention as a practice of sly manipulation, based on the idea that the affected party cannot know what is going on. This may be particular more so when government interventions are involved and may not be so much of private enterprises. Consumers are used to (or even expect) enterprise to nudge them to their products through advertising or marketing, but citizens of democracies are not used to governments trying to change their behaviour without being noticed. Like all policy or proposals involving human beings, there is no magic solution. Any form of policy intervention will impose a criterion against someone's will (it will always be the case) and any true democracy requires the following:

a. Transparency from the political system in terms of the values selected in deciding and designing an intervention

b. At least an evidence-based justification of choice

Overt and explicit coercion by 'nudgers' is arguably better than covert manipulation by those designing environmental and contextual cues. It is clear from Islam's scaffolding that the legitimacy of regulators and governments (rulers) is earned by their being even more compliant to the spirit and higher objectives of the Sharī'ah than required of individual Muslims.

One suggestion would be to replace the strategies involved (in cases where interventions have been viewed as manipulation) with a slightly different and 'better' approach – self-knowledge. Policymakers who assume people are constantly making mistakes must strive to correct 'errors' by subtly rearranging choices, but policymakers who do not assume people make mistakes can instead orient their efforts to bringing people's attention to their own mental processes. Once aware of these mental processes, people can then do what they will. It may be a subtle but important difference. The first approach nudges people towards a prechosen goal; the second informs people about the workings of their own minds, so they can better achieve whatever goals they desire.

Following Fischhoff and Eggers (2013), we imagine the ideal policy supporting behavioural research as comprising three steps:

- *Normative analysis*. Identify, using consolidated theory and evidence, the possible outcomes of choices X and decision makers' values to weight them.
- *Empirical analysis*. Predict, using behavioural experiments, the choices X that consumers would actually make, under the conditions created by possible policies.
- *Prescriptive analysis*. Characterize the gap between the normative idea and the descriptive reality, with each policy option.

This would improve the quality of the outputs, educate policy clients, and better manage expectations and inform decisions through experimental behavioural studies.

CHAPTER 8
Conclusion

Know thyself.

Oracle of Delphi

Knowing yourself is the beginning of all wisdom.

Aristotle

This is true knowledge, to seek the Self as the true end of wisdom always.

Bagavad Gita

Knowing others is intelligence; knowing yourself is true wisdom.
Mastering others is strength; mastering yourself is true power.

Lao Tzu

He who knows himself, knows his Lord.

Prophet Muhammad ﷺ

8.1 SUMMARY OF FINDINGS AND CONTRIBUTION

First and foremost, we would like to point out that the work in this research is new and hence termed experimental,[1] which requires it to be viewed from an exploratory approach. In many published papers in the United States, the sample size varies and, although somewhat larger, was mostly only limited to students (i.e. effectively restricting age to 20s only, a particular income group, and a particular education level), and this seems to be one of the major criticisms. Our sample, though small, was a more accurate snapshot of society – ranging from 20s to 50s, various income groups, and educational backgrounds.

In our data, we find that the best overall performers in adherence to the rules extracted from the Qur'ān and Sunnah were the Muslims – and that generally, the primed Muslim performed the same as the unprimed Muslim.

[1]Behavioural economics is often interchangeably termed as experimental economics.

Belief and Rule Compliance
https://doi.org/10.1016/B978-0-12-813809-0.00008-4

The primed Muslim performed better for the tests on contract and Golden Rule, whilst the unprimed Muslim performed better for the tests on property rights and trust. However, we find no evidence that Islamic identity salience affects the adherence to capstone rule, cooperation, and reciprocity as both primed and unprimed segments in the Muslim groups in Singapore and Malaysia performed the same.

Amongst the non-Muslim group, we find that religious identity salience causes increased adherence to capstone rule, property rights, Golden Rule, and trust with negative effects on the rules of cooperation, contract, and reciprocity.

Interestingly, where we have expected positive effects of religious saliency in both groups, we noted significant negative effects from triggering the religious identity in both of them in rules of cooperation and reciprocity. This may indicate a reactionary behaviour towards their religious identity. For example, a poorer performance by both primed groups of Muslims and non-Muslims in cooperation and reciprocity may indicate the perceived mistrust towards their religious identity and the reactionary[2] poorer performance in turn by them in those tests. The negative effect of primes in both groups for the respective tests may have triggered an adversarial view of others and that their game partners were *outside* of their social network (including shared values) based on their religious identity.

We conclude with advice on prudence in interpreting our findings. First, when an effect of religious identity salience is not distinctively obvious, we should not necessarily rule out the effect's existence. It is possible that we did not have sufficient statistical power due to sample size (budget constraints) to detect the effect or that a much stronger priming method would have produced a detectable effect. It is also possible that the strength of our religious identity-salience priming varies by religious group (since we have lumped non-Islamic religions under non-Muslim and used one universal priming instrument for them), making us more likely to find null effects in some games than others. Hence, our positive and negative findings deserve greater attention than our null findings.

Second, whilst a key advantage of identity-salience priming is that they can be assigned randomly, exogenously making religious identity salient is different from instilling values from different religious traditions. According

[2]This behaviour can also be due to a skewed understanding of their own religion that has formed into their religious identity that is perceived as distrusting towards other ethnicities or religions. Another possibility is the reactionary responses towards perceived biases in public policies or perceived social stratifications.

to self-categorization theory, identity-salience effects identify the marginal directional effect of religious identity norms. Thus, religious identity primes provide information regarding one channel – identity norms – through which religion might affect behaviour. But regardless of the mechanisms responsible for our identity-salience effects, religious identity will be salient outside the laboratory some of the time to members of a particular religious consciousness, so religious salient primes allow us to measure how behaviour is likely to be affected by identity affiliation heightened through such primes. Therefore, we believe that religious identity saliencies through priming instruments – interpreted appropriately and cautiously – are useful tools in understanding those effects of identity triggered by faith affiliation in beneficial decision-making.

Lastly, the identity formulation through individual experiences, upbringing, cultural conditioning, and external expected rules of behaviours by those of society are also governed by rules that are enforced by the economic, legal, and political institutions of a country where one resides. The effective understanding of how behavioural interventions can be applied to fully develop these institutions in countries, especially Islamic countries, could produce immense improvements through much needed reforms that are more in the spirit of the *Sharī'ah*. Effective governance through bridging policy and practice is established by specific institutions with mechanisms for rule-based enforcement through the intervention of administrative bodies mandated with specific functions of supervision and control.

In addition, it has to be acknowledged that there are some challenges to a rule-based order that need to be continually surmounted. The first is the problem of legitimacy. For a system based on rules to have effect, these rules must be visibly observed by their principal and most powerful advocates. There exist possibilities for the elite groups or interest groups to influence the rule setting. This can also lead to collusion between members of the elite, policymakers, and government officials that could undermine the interests of marginalized sections of the communities. The second problem, which is tied to the question of legitimacy, is one of the equity, in that a rule-based order must work to the advantage of the entire population and not just the majority or specific minority group, no matter what the justification. The third problem is one of the complacencies. The longevity of the current ruling system may have led to the assumption that it was in some way the natural order of things, requiring only occasional repair and defense against particular opposition or disruption. All these three problems are interconnected and must be resolved. Governing rules need to be revised to ensure that they remain relevant and that they need to be applied as consistently and extensively as possible. A modernization effort should reflect a reforming agenda intended to tackle the problems of the current 2010s and future landscapes.

8.2 LIMITATIONS OF STUDY

This study is limited by three general constraints. First, the research did not cover extensively all of the nine extracted rules of behaviours according to the Qur'ān and Sunnah (see Section 2.4). The benefit in meeting and consulting matters that affect people is fairly obvious (hence, the test for rule of consultation was omitted), but additional games could be played to quantify the contribution of asymmetric information in Islamic salient decision-making. This, however, is constrained by cost and time to acquire further funding and to run the experimental games outside of the months of Ramadan and Syawal, which may have positive-biased effects on behaviours of Islamic salient test subjects. Also, due to the high cost of the administration and actual cash involved in the games, the sample size had to be severely limited in our study to work within the means of the approved budget. Not only a larger sample size would have been ideal, but also it would have required more financial resources. Alternatively, a study could be employed to empirically investigate into a methodology to accurately extrapolate reliable data and statistics from small sample sizes (also with higher predictive power) so as to reduce costs for such experiments and relief sources of funds for more variations of such behavioural experiments for research.

8.3 DIRECTIONS FOR FUTURE RESEARCH

We would like to point out that this research is a ground-level experimental research that lays the foundation to investigating behaviours relevant to economics and finance, in general and in particular Islamic economics and finance. It forms a basis for subsequent research when it is better resourced, specifically better funded. A wider sample size would definitely be more conclusively convincing. Future follow-up research could focus on specific areas like those described in Section 7.4 as behavioural applications. The broad areas of impact in terms of behavioural interventions would make them worth exploring in the future. This could include research on the importance of nudges and Islamic principles in uncertainty.

As research and development progress, the two most obvious areas that will likely be the mainstay of research for the next 50 years are big data and online gaming (Klein et al., 2013; Stafford and Dewar, 2014). As technologies advance in data mining and modelling, so that researchers can interrogate large data sets more efficiently and effectively, so too will the scope for tracking and predicting choice behaviour, beliefs, preferences, judgments, and even emotions, across vast groups of people (Boyd and Crawford, 2012; Wolfe, 2013). Not only will it be possible to track choice behaviour over large populations, but also crucially more efficient data mining of large data sets will in turn require ever more sophisticated models to explain the causal mechanisms for explaining dynamic choice behaviour, which will provide insights at the micro- and macroeconomic level.

Similarly, massively multiplayer online games and serious gaming initiatives provide a means of examining cognitive and social behaviour across wide networks (Stafford and Dewar, 2014). It is already becoming a valuable research methodology for setting up large-scale social experiments and behavioural experiments cheaply to collect more detailed data on a variety of social behaviours (cooperation, coordination, competition, trust, and punishment) and interactions between groups (organizational behaviour and team dynamics). The limits at the moment are simply down to not knowing how to exploit the methodology or the large data sets generated, because this requires significant advances in modelling techniques. This will most certainly change as analytical and computational challenges are surmounted.

Finally, there are potentially significant benefits from policies and practices that facilitate subtle implementation and help coordinate behavioural interventions. Whilst these policy measures and practices may be already in place in some countries, it is necessary to examine whether these existing measures targeted towards the strengthening of prescribed rules can be further enhanced in other areas to complete the development of the Islamic economy according to the Qur'ān and Sunnah.

8.4 CONCLUDING REMARKS

Although a relatively young field, behavioural economics and finance seems to be growing exponentially. This growth is not surprising given that behavioural finance has the potential to explain not only how people make financial decisions and how markets function but also how to improve them. In behavioural finance, four key areas – emotions, framing, heuristics, and market forces – characterize the field. These areas are integrated into the review and application of investments, corporations, markets, regulations, and education.

In the encompassing realm of economics, behavioural experiments on rule compliance help to bridge the expected behaviours of human beings, regardless of religiosity, to the prescribed behaviours of divine revelation.

> *'Recite to them [O Muħammad!] the news of him whom We had given our signs, but he abandoned them and the devil pursued him so that he became one of the deviants; if We had willed, We would have exalted him through those signs, but he gravitated down to the earth and followed his own desires.'*
>
> ***(Qur'ān 7:175–176)***

In the verse above, when 'man gravitates down to the earth', the Qur'ān deems his conscience has become dull, and he cannot effectively listen to the voice of his true, higher nature "[as though] these people are being called from a distant place" (Qur'ān 41:44). To draw near to God is to obey Him, and to be rule-compliant is to comply with His rules at every decision point in our lives. For example, one is regarded as patient when one displays patience. But as soon as one demonstrates impatience, he is no longer deemed patient. Where we have demonstrated a virtue in the past, it does not necessarily mean that virtue remains with us constantly. Hence, one becomes *muttaqin* only when one is fully rule-compliant all the time. Here, the person's consciousness radically leaps from *fitri* consciousness (*iman*) to Allåh consciousness (*taqwa*) where he has obtained *al-ihsan* and behaves accordingly as he knows Allåh (s.w.t.) sees him all the time although he may not see Him. The idea here is of constancy and consistency for our adherence to Allåh's laws that fluctuate through the course of a day and through time as it is in the nature of man to tire, to forget, to be overcome by emotions, to be influenced by his social surroundings, and to be attracted to material wealth and power.

> *Verily, man was created impatient, irritable when evil touches him and niggardly when good touches him. Except for those devoted to prayer those who remain constant in their prayers.*
>
> ***(Qur'ān 70:19–23)***
>
> *And those who believe in the Day of Recompense.*
> *And those who are fearful of the punishment of their Lord -*
>
> ***(Qur'ān 70:26–27)***
>
> *And those who are faithful to their trusts and their covenant,*
> *And those who are upright in their testimonies*
> *And those who keep guard on their prayer*
> *Those shall be in gardens, honoured.*
>
> ***(Qur'ān 70:32–35)***

Man's cognitive faculties are great, but his faculty of the moral sense and sense of responsibility are subjected to choice and decision-making that are in turn subjected to their own emotions and other factors that can be outside of their control. Hence, an individual's blessings (leaps in spiritual consciousness and worldly economic gains) are conditional upon making the right choices despite these obstacles. Compliance to such rules of behaviour may not only improve economies and the well-being of a society but also help us live well and achieve our highest potential as human beings. The right behavioural interventions within a rule-based system in the right manner may be able to reduce cognitive errors and psychological biases that affect beneficial choices and decisions. Behavioural policy interventions may also be able to expose people to innovative solutions to social dilemmas, improve ways of thinking, and develop role models that expand mental concepts and frames, thereby overcoming stereotypes, improving trust, encouraging collective action, and increasing risk-sharing transactions.

Annex

ANNEX 1A: SAMPLE SIZE AND RATIOS OF BACKGROUND SPREAD

Sample size	Singapore	Malaysia	Total	Ratio
Sample subtotal	**30**	**40**	**70**	**100%**
Muslim	**12**	**20**	**32**	**46%**
Non-Muslim	**18**	**20**	**38**	**54%**
Atheist	1	0	1	
Buddhist	6	10	16	
Catholic	3	1	4	
Christian (non-Catholic)	1	3	4	
Free-thinker	5	3	8	
Hindu	1	3	4	
Taoist	1	0	1	
Age	**30**	**40**	**70**	**100%**
20s	10	18	28	40%
30s	10	16	26	37%
40s	9	6	15	21%
50s	1	0	1	1%
Gender	**30**	**40**	**70**	**100%**
Male	17	20	37	53%
Female	13	20	33	47%
Education	**30**	**40**	**70**	**100%**
Tertiary	19	38	57	81%
Nontertiary	11	2	13	19%
Income	**30**	**40**	**70**	**100%**
< S$/RM24k per annum	6	14	20	29%
S$/RM24k–36k per annum	14	13	27	39%
S$/RM36k–48k per annum	6	10	16	23%
> S$/RM72k per annum	4	3	7	10%

ANNEX 1B: SAMPLE SIZE AND RATIOS OF MUSLIM VERSUS NON-MUSLIM AND PRIMED VERSUS UNPRIMED GROUPINGS

Sample size	Singapore	Malaysia	Total
Sample subtotal	**30**	**40**	**70**
Muslim	12	20	**32**
Non-Muslim	18	20	**38**
Primed	**18**	**20**	**38**
Muslim	7	9	16
Non-Muslim	11	11	22
Unprimed	**12**	**20**	**32**
Muslim	5	11	16
Non-Muslim	7	9	16

Ratios (%)	Singapore	Malaysia	Total
Sample subtotal	**100%**	**100%**	**100%**
Muslim	40%	50%	46%
Non-Muslim	60%	50%	54%
Primed	**60%**	**50%**	**54%**
Muslim	23%	23%	23%
Non-Muslim	37%	28%	31%
Unprimed	**40%**	**50%**	**46%**
Muslim	17%	28%	23%
Non-Muslim	23%	23%	23%

ANNEX 2: CRITICAL BEHAVIOUR THRESHOLDS ON SAMPLE SPLITS BASED ON WEF'S GLOBAL COMPETITIVENESS INDEX 2015–16

Critical behavioural parameter	Malaysia (scale 0–7) (rank of 144 countries)	Singapore (scale 0–7) (rank of 144 countries)
Property rights	5.4 (27/144)	6.2 (3/144)
Ethics and corruption	4.8 (26/144)	6.3 (1/144)
Public trust in politicians	4.8 (14/144)	6.3 (1/144)
Undue influence (judicial/favouritism)	4.8 (25/144)	5.5 (10/144)
Wastefulness of government spending	4.9 (8/144)	5.9 (3/144)
Ethical behaviour of firms	5.2 (23/144)	6.1 (4/144)
Corporate accountability	5.5 (10/144)	5.9 (4/144)
Tertiary education enrollment rate (gross %)	37.2% (69/144)	82.7% (9/144)
Quality of education	5.4 (13/144).	6.1 (1/144)
Cooperation in labour-employer relations	5.5 (11/144)	6.0 (3/144)
Trustworthiness and confidence (financial/legal)	5.1 (21/144)	5.9 (4/144)

ANNEX 3: PRIMING INSTRUMENT

Instructions

Unscramble the following groups of words to make a four-word phrase or sentence by dropping the irrelevant word.

For example, high winds the flies plane → the plane flies high

Islam-Specific Priming Instrument (for Priming Muslims)

1. At the park on sat she bench
2. You be upon peace conflict
3. The self-interest pursuit of in busy
4. Good and evil forbid then enjoin
5. Pictures deleted some glee she
6. Others is to fasting prescribed you
7. Is option not failure an succeed
8. Theft an charity is obligation
9. Is the warm water take
10. Of mothers under paradise feet is the love

God-Related Priming Sentences (for Priming Non-Muslims)

1. Theft an charity is obligation
2. Dessert divine was fork the
3. Appreciated presence was imagine her
4. More paper it once do
5. Send I over it mailed
6. Evil thanks give God to
7. Yesterday it finished track he
8. Sacred was book refer the
9. Reveal the future simple prophets
10. Prepared somewhat I was retired

ANNEX 4: GAME SCRIPTS

Instructions to Game Masters:

1. Always use neutral terms only to avoid any bias.
2. Do not give examples that are one-sided. For example, do not say you can choose like if you like it. You must say, you can choose like if you like it or don't choose if you don't like it.
3. Follow the notes for each game, whether players can or cannot discuss.
4. Record player's ID number accurately. Failing to do so will result in data inaccuracy.
5. Please note the answers in your answer sheet and record the answers in the player's score cards. There is no room for mistakes.
6. Please note other observations on your answer sheet, for example, whether players discuss or not, changes their minds, etc.
7. Please ensure amounts given to players are correct, both at the start of each game and at the end of each game.
8. Players are to sign for the amounts received for each game, and Game Master must tally their balance on the answer sheet.

Introduction by Game Masters:

Good morning/afternoon, my name is ....

Thank you for coming today to take part in our research study. We are about to play a few games together with different Game Masters.

At the end of each game, please proceed to the waiting area to be invited to play the next game.

At the waiting area, do not discuss the game you have played so as not to influence the other players who have yet to play the game.

Each set of games has different instructions. Please follow the instructions for each game.

You should also have a score card (check that each player has a score card).

At the end of each game, I will record information on your score card. Please keep the score card with you at all times and submit this to us at the end of the games.

Some of the games involve money. Whatever money that is not taken away from you at the end of the game is yours to keep. You will have to sign for the amount that you take away from each game.

Please keep the money from each game separately and do not use money from the previous game for the next game.

During the game sessions, there will be observers to ensure the Game Masters are doing the right thing.

There may be photography or recording for our reference or research purposes only. None of these materials will be published without your permission.

Let's begin.

Game 4.1. Game Master Shareen (yellow room)

Materials:	Condition board Two envelopes Each player: four S$2 bills and two S$1 coins Game Master: nine S$2 bills and two S$1 coins

Game Master: Gives out money and envelope to the players.

Here is S$10 and an envelope. In the first game, imagine both of you are a pair of rowers in a boat trying to get to an island 100 m away. One of you is paddling on the right side, and one of you is paddling on the left side. You need to decide how much effort you want to put in to row across to the island.

This game is played with cash to indicate your effort of rowing. Put the choice of the amount inside the envelope when you have decided.

There are no right or wrong answers or choices; you will only be revealing a preference:

S$10 represents maximum rowing effort.

S$5 represents medium rowing effort.

S$2 represents low rowing effort.

A matching bonus is paid out to both players if your efforts match:

S$10 is paid for matching maximum effort.

S$5 is paid for matching medium effort.

S$2 is paid for low effort.

No payout is made if efforts do not match.

You have 1 min to decide. Please place your choice in the envelope.

Note: If players ask if they can discuss, the answer is yes.

Game ends:

Check the amounts in the envelop and give out bonus accordingly.

Record response in your score card and player's score card.

Game 4.2. Game Master Liyi (green room)

Materials:	Two condition boards Two envelopes Each player: one red card and one black card Game Master: four S$5 bills

Game Master: Gives out cards and envelope to the players.

Here are two cards and an envelope. In the next game, imagine both of you are a pair of suspects apprehended by the police and are being interrogated in separate rooms. You use the cards to indicate your choice. Put the choice inside the envelope when you have decided. There are no right or wrong answers or choices; you will only be revealing a preference:

i. Confess, and if your partner does not confess, then you will get a reduced sentence (2 years), and your partner will get the maximum charge of the crime – an imprisonment of 5 years.

ii. If both of you confess, then both will be convicted of the robbery. (Sentence will be reduced – 2 years only – because of guilty plea.)

iii. If neither confesses, then no conviction can be made, so the police will have to release you.

iv. Both of you are offered the same deal.

Use a red card to confess and use a black card to not confess.

A red card gets you S$5, and a black card gets you nothing, but your partner gets S$10.

You have 1 min to decide. Please place your choice in the envelope.

Note: Ask each player to face their back to each other. If players ask, there is no discussion allowed.

Game ends:

Check the amounts in the envelop and give out bonus accordingly.

Record response in your score card and player's score card.

Game 4.3. Game Master Goh (server room)

Materials:	One condition board Player one: 10 S$2 bills (offerer) Player two: no money Game Master: no money

Game Master: Give out money to the player on the right.

Here is S$20. In the next game (indicate to player on the right), imagine you are the offerer, and (indicate to player on the left) imagine you are the responder. I want you, the offerer (indicate to player on the right), to make an offer to the responder (indicate player on the left). There are no right or wrong answers or choices; you will only be revealing a preference:

If the responder is happy with the offer, he/she can accept it. And you get to keep your respective portions of the money.

If the responder rejects the offer, you both lose what you have.

Say to the offerer, 'You have 1 min to decide how much to offer'.

After offer has been made, say to the responder, 'Do you accept or reject?'
If the offer is rejected, ask why did you reject the offer?
What amount would you accept?
Note: If players ask if they can discuss, the answer is no.
Game ends:
Check the amounts in the envelop and take away money accordingly.
Record response in your score card and player's score card.

Game 4.4. Game Master Avril (focus group room)

Materials:	One condition board Two envelopes Each player: two S$10 bills Game Master: no money

Game Master: Gives out money and envelope to the players.

Here is S$20. In the next game (indicate to player on the left), you will be cutting a cake, and (indicate to the player on the right) you will be choosing a piece of cake.

For the chooser:

When you have chosen the piece of cake and are satisfied that the cake has been cut fairly, reward the cutter with S$10.

For the cutter:

If you are satisfied with the choice of the chooser, reward the chooser accordingly.

There are no right or wrong answers or choices; you will only be revealing a preference.

Note: If players ask if they can discuss, the answer is no.

Game ends:

Record responses in your score card and player's score card.

Game 4.5. Game Master Avril (focus group room)

Materials:	One condition board Every two new players gets two S$1 coins Game Master: 30 S$1 coins

Game Master: Gives out money to the players.

In this game, there is a blackout in the street of a row of houses. Everybody is given S$2.

It takes only one person to call the Electric Company to turn the power back on and costs S$1 to make that call. That is, to indicate that you want to make the call, you put up S$1.

If at least one person volunteers to call the Electric Company, everyone earns S$2 each.

If there are no volunteers in the group, each participant earns nothing.

You have 2 min to respond.

There are no right or wrong answers or choices; you will only be revealing a preference.

Note: If players ask if they can discuss, the answer is yes.

Game ends:

Record responses in your score card and player's score card. Mark X if the player volunteers; mark O if player did not volunteer. Distribute bonus and indicate for the next pair to come in.

Game 4.6. Game Master Beng Teck (CATI room)

Materials:	One condition board Two envelopes Player one: four S$10 bills (investor) Player two: no money Game Master: eight S$10 bills

Game Master: Gives out money and envelope to the player.

Here is S$40. In the next game (indicate to player on the left), you are the investor. You decide how much money you want to give to (indicate to player on the right) the trustee as an investment.

The moderator decides if the investment makes a profit or not.

The trustee then decides what to do next with the investment.

There are no right or wrong answers or choices; you will only be revealing a preference.

When the amount has been given to the trustee, say 'Your investment has tripled' and give him the corresponding amount.

Then, ask the trustee what he/she wants to do next.

Note: If players ask if they can discuss, the answer is no.

Game ends:

Record responses in your score card and player's score card.

Final steps:

Direct players back to the waiting area and then to the CATI room for the postgame questionnaire.

ANNEX 5: POSTEXPERIMENT QUESTIONNAIRE

Participant particulars	
Personal information	
Player code:	
Date of birth:	Mother tongue:
Current address:	
City/state:	Postal code:
Gender:	Nationality:
Race:	Religion:
Age (as of 1 Jan 2015):	Hometown (indicate urban or rural):
Highest education:	Course of study:
Current occupation:	Previous occupation:
Marital status:	No. of children:
Annual income:	Household annual income:
Family information	
Father's occupation:	Mother's occupation:
Father's last drawn salary:	Mother's last drawn salary:
No. of siblings: Brothers: Sisters:	Rank (e.g. eldest, youngest, second of four, etc.):
Other information	
How many hours per week do you spend your free time with the following: Parents: Siblings: Spouse: Relatives: Friends: Co-workers: Neighbours:	
Who do you discuss important matters with?	
Do you consider yourself a practising believer of your faith?	

On average, how many minutes do you set aside in a day for worship?
On average, how many hours do you spend in a day on the internet? (e-mail, search engines, social media, etc.) On average, how many hours do you spend in a day on your mobile phone? (including surfing for information, social media, WhatsApp, Snapchat, and Skype communications) What do you use your mobile phone most for?
On average, how many hours do you spend in a day on just social media? Rank your level of interest on stories that visit most on social media (1 being most and 5 least): Cute and funny: Inspiring anecdotes, clips, and quotes: Light entertainment news: Political events and news: Religion and morality:
On a scale of 1 to 5 (lowest to highest), how important are morality and ethics (e.g. compassion, empathy, fairness, honesty, justice, reciprocity, and trust) in everyday human interactions to you? Rate them according to these settings below: Economic interactions (any agreements involving monetary or good exchange): Online interactions (blogs, forums, social media platforms, WhatsApp, etc.): Personal interactions (one-on-one): Social interactions (in an informal group setting):
What aspect of your identity is most important to you? (e.g. gender, profession, nationality, ethnicity, personal trait, activity group, political orientation, and socio-economic class)
For official use
I confirm that the information provided on this form is accurate, and I authorize the researchers to verify the information provided, including those pertaining to my education, income, and employment history.

Signature of Applicant	Date

ANNEX 6: OTHER POSSIBLE ADHERENTS TO PRESCRIBE BEHAVIOURS (SINGAPORE)

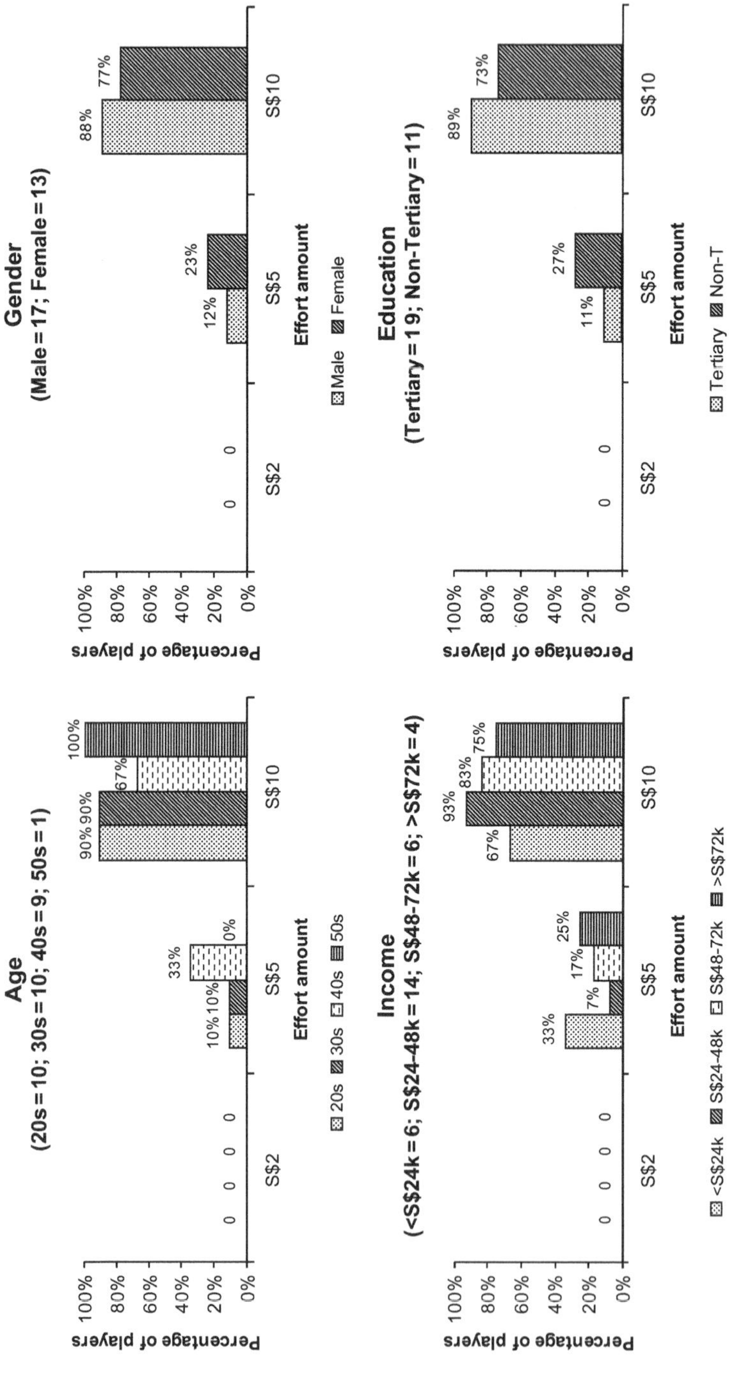

Game 6.1: Rowing game (rule of enjoin good and forbid evil)

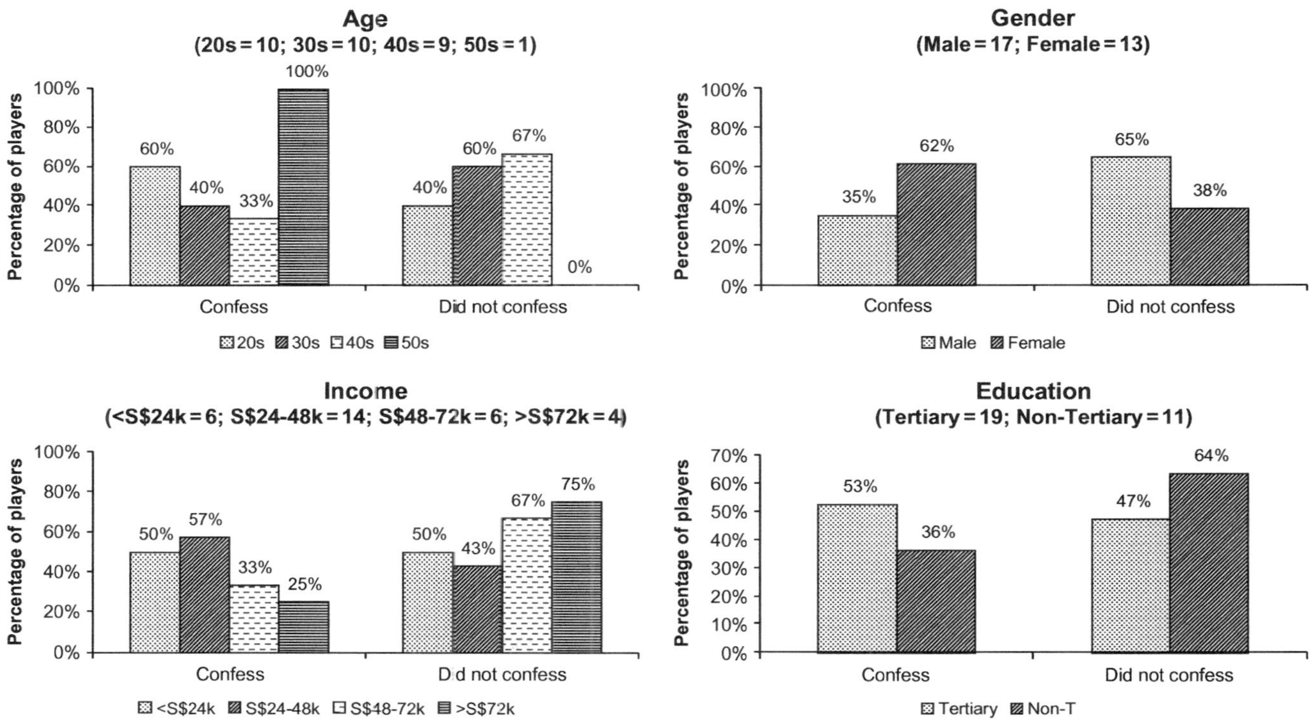

Game 6.2: Prisoner's dilemma (rule of cooperation)

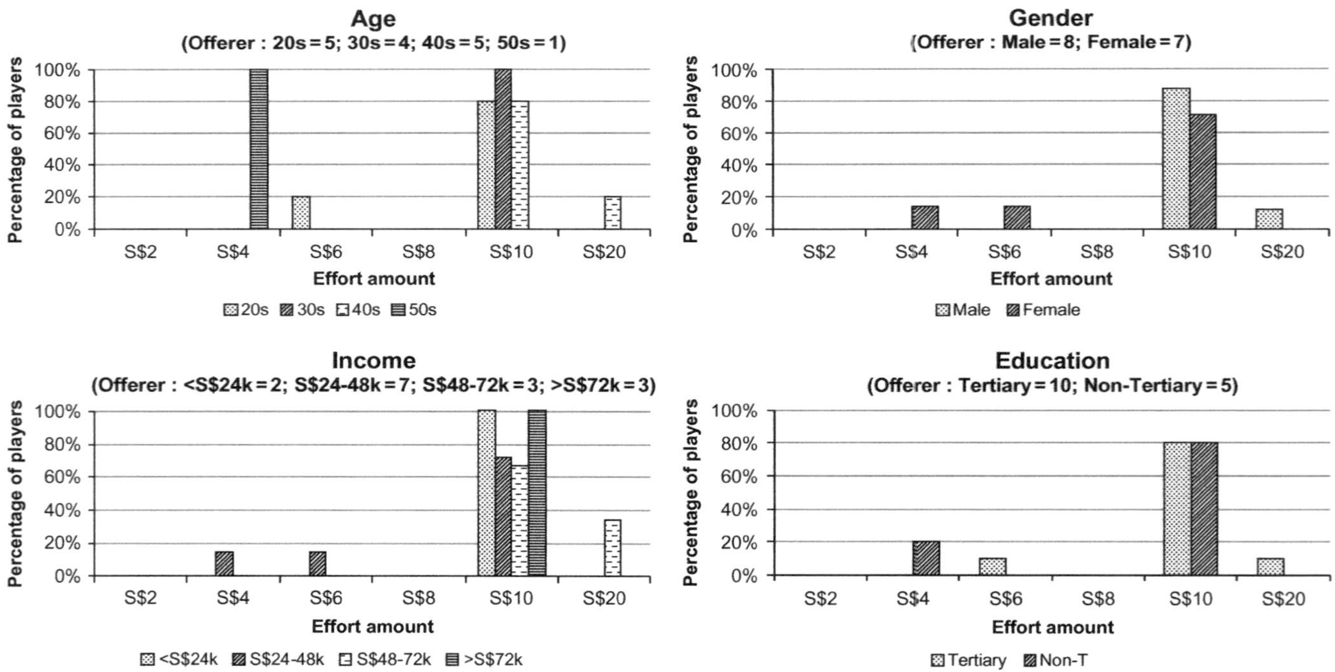

Game 6.3: Ultimatum game (rule of contract)

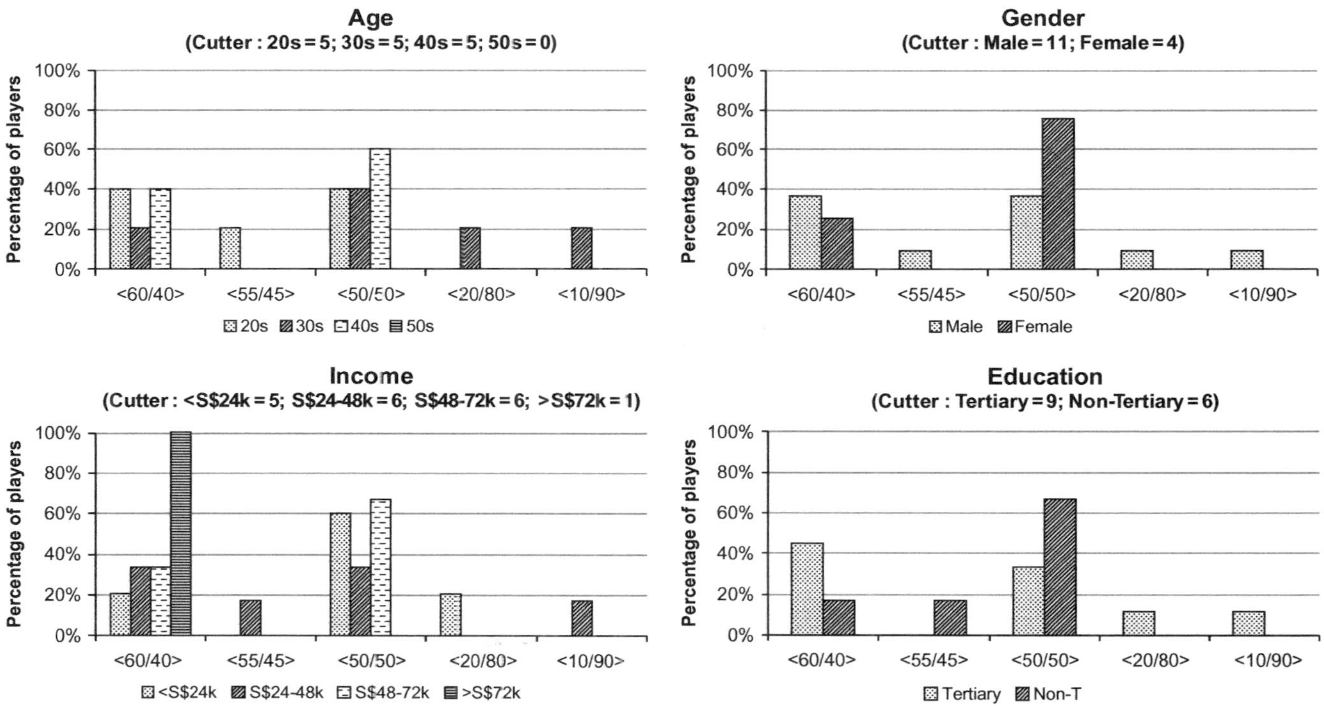

Game 6.4: Cake-cutting game (rule of property rights)

(Continued)

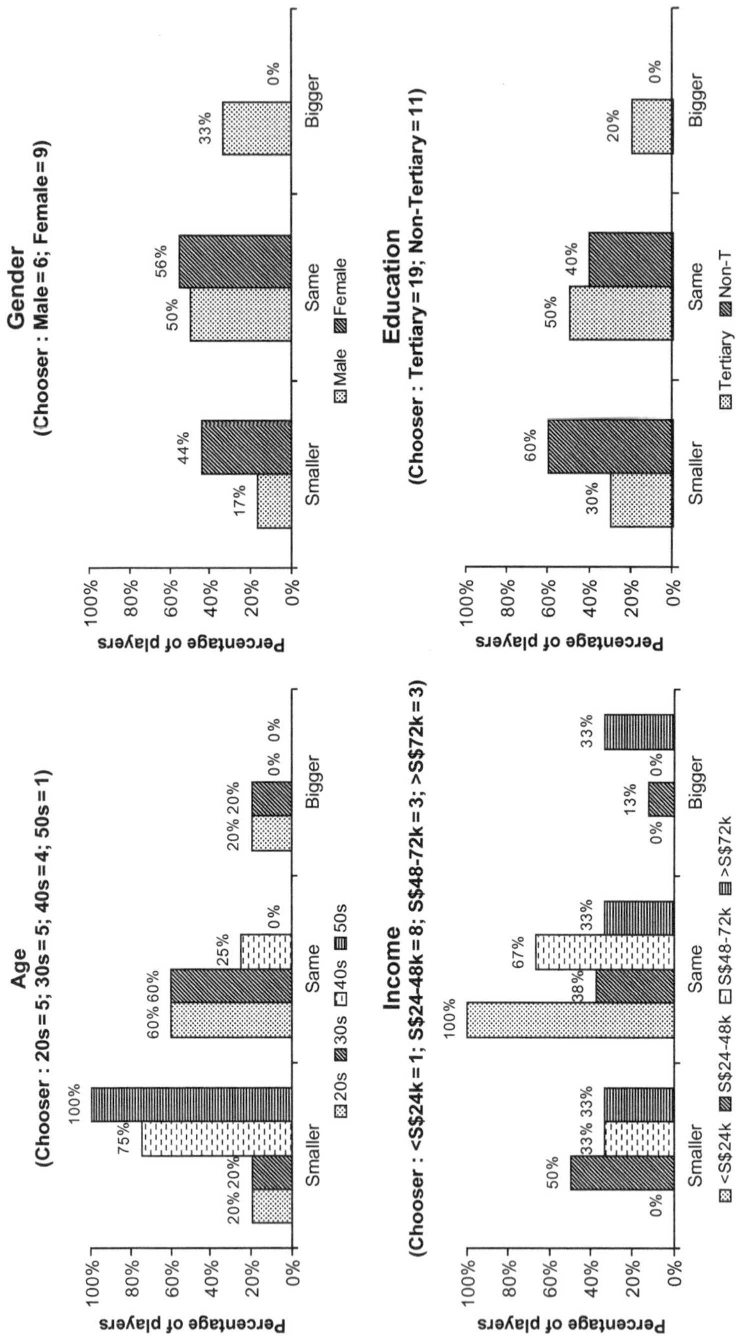

Game 6.4, Cont'd

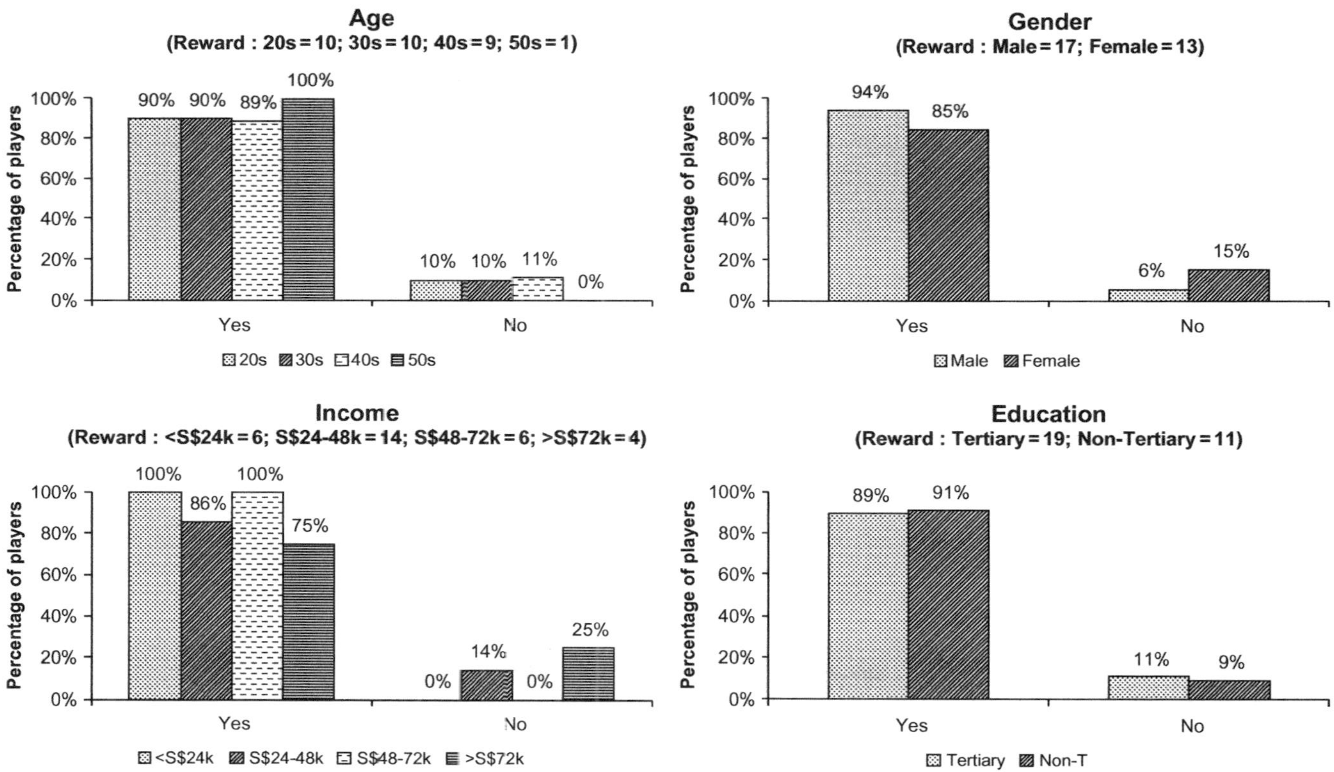

Game 6.4, Cont'd

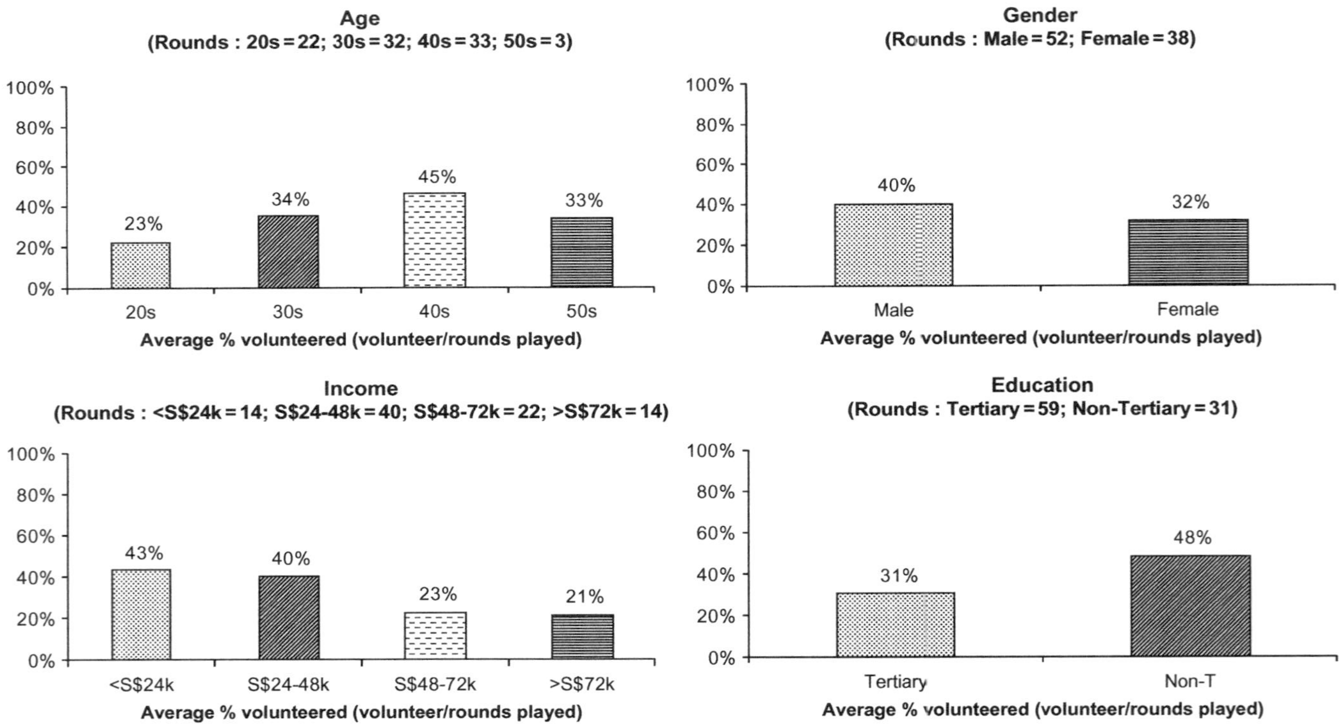

Game 6.5: Volunteer's dilemma (golden rule)

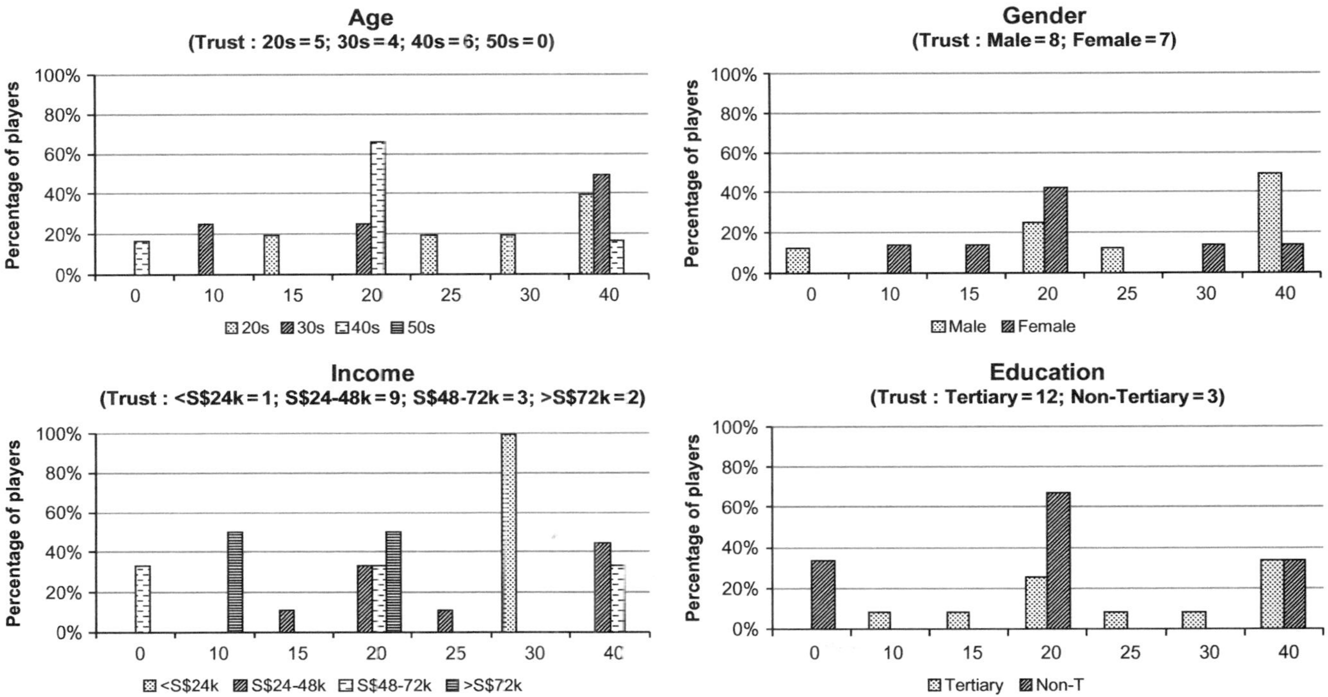

Game 6.6: Trust game (rule of trust and reciprocity)

(Continued)

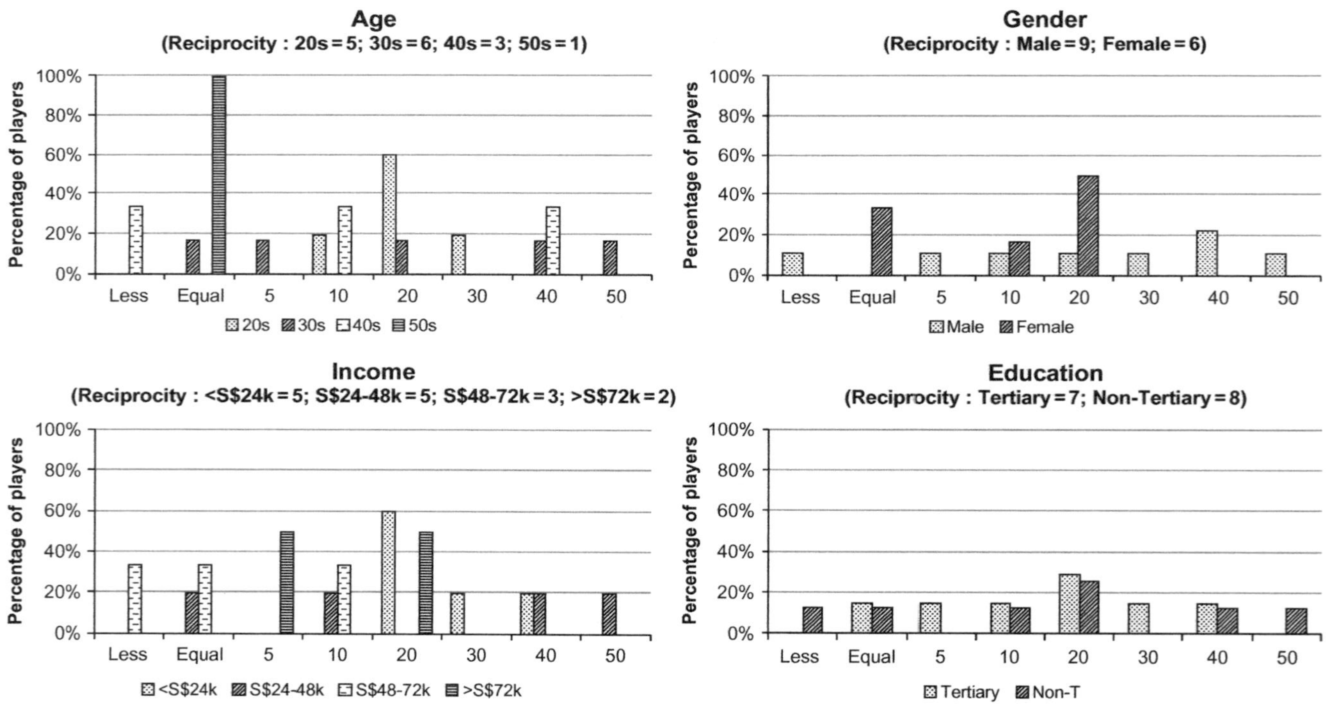

Game 6.6, Cont'd

ANNEX 7: OTHER POSSIBLE ADHERENTS TO PRESCRIBE BEHAVIOURS (MALAYSIA)

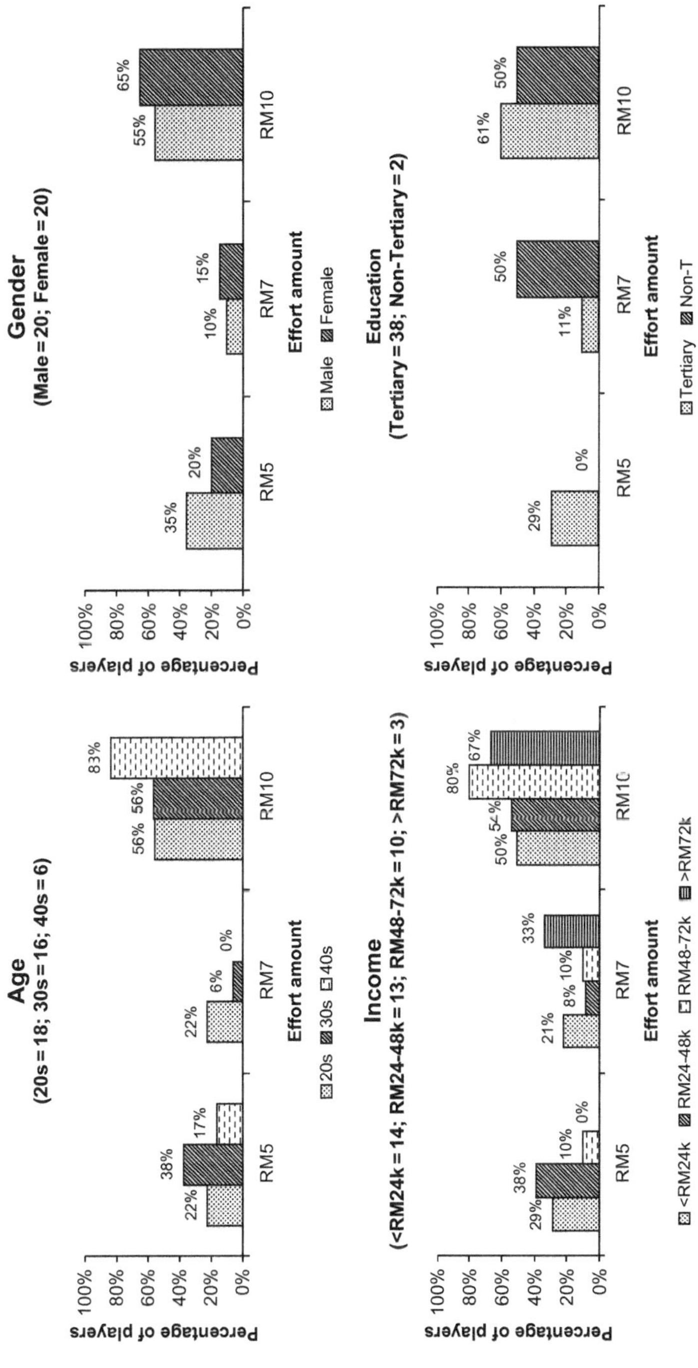

Game 7.1: Rowing game (rule of enjoin good and forbid evil)

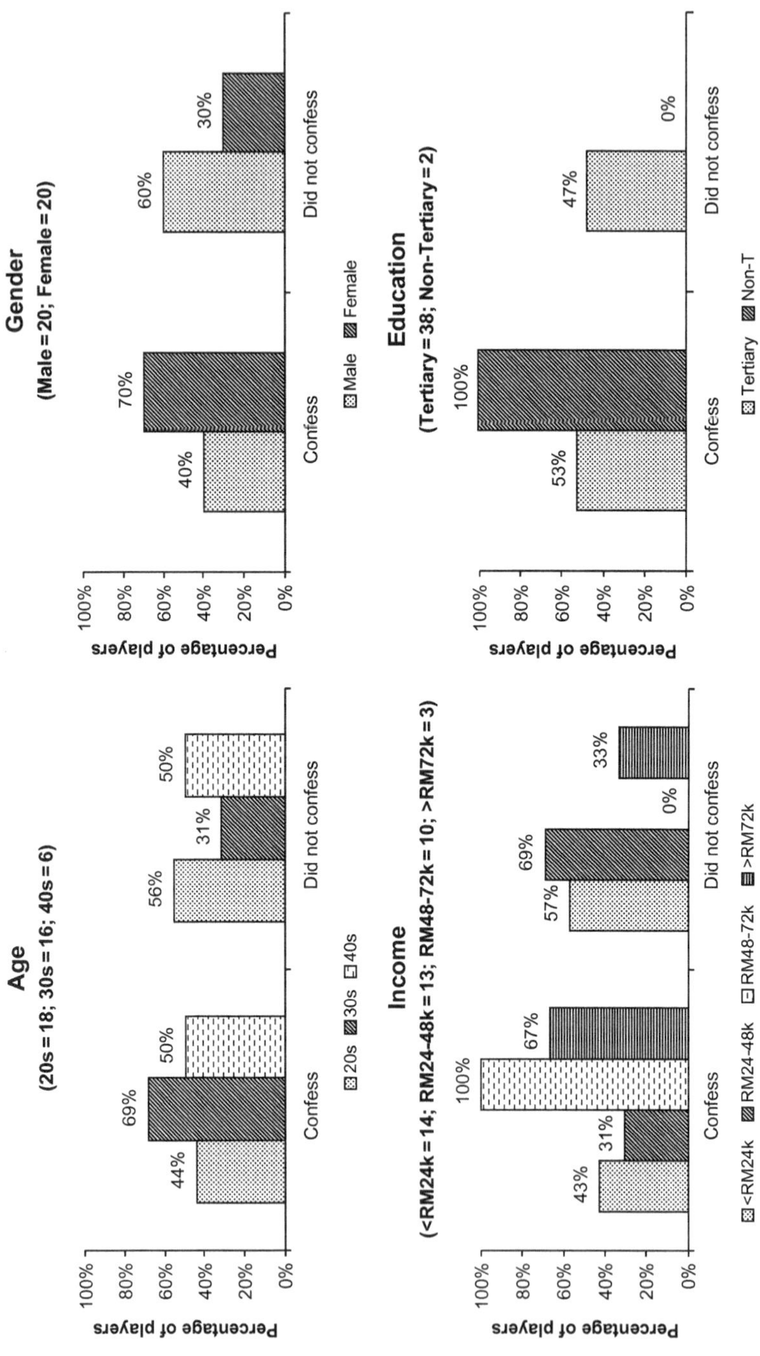

Game 7.2: Prisoner's dilemma (rule of cooperation)

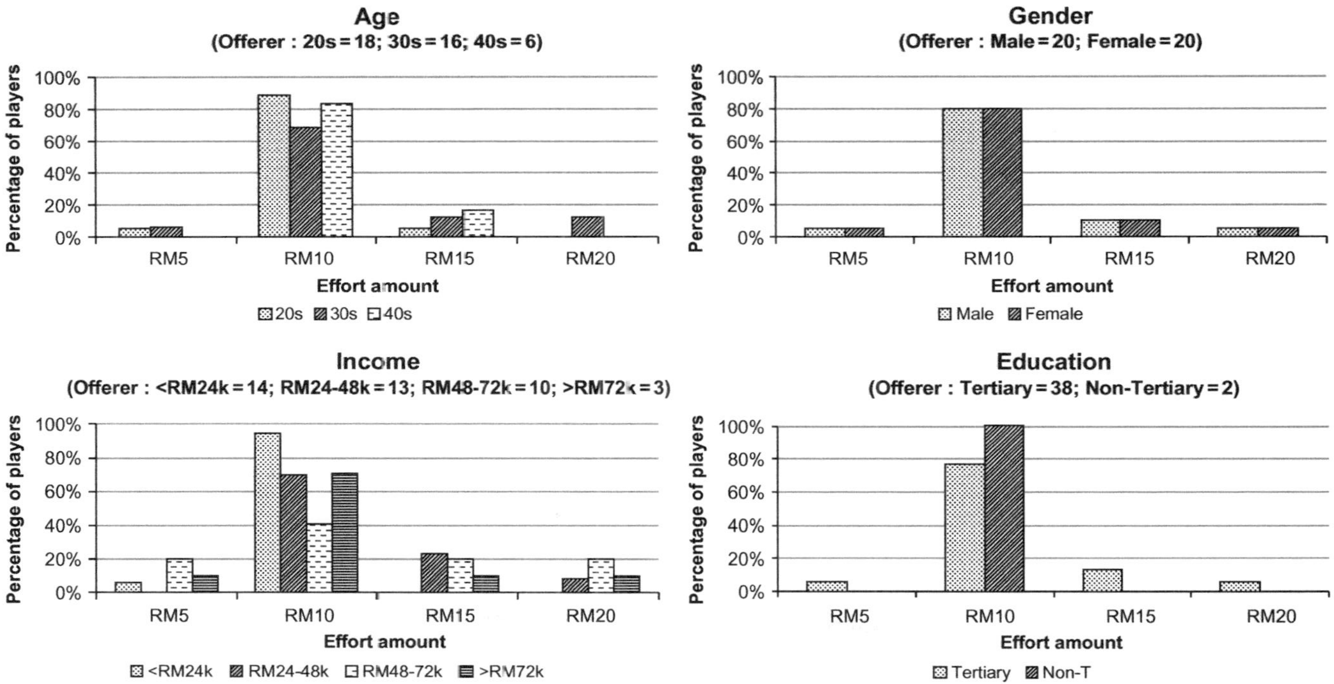

Game 7.3: Ultimatum game (rule of contract)

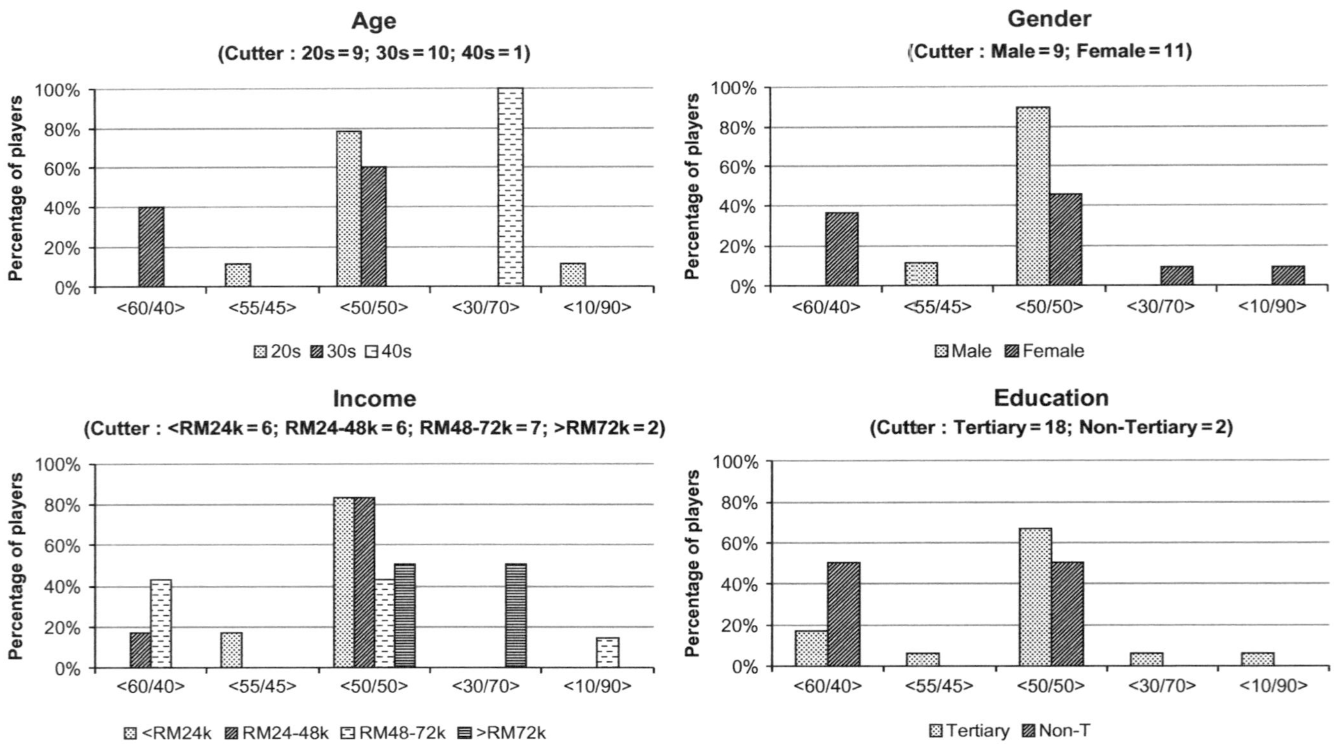

Game 7.4: Cake-cutting game (rule of property rights)

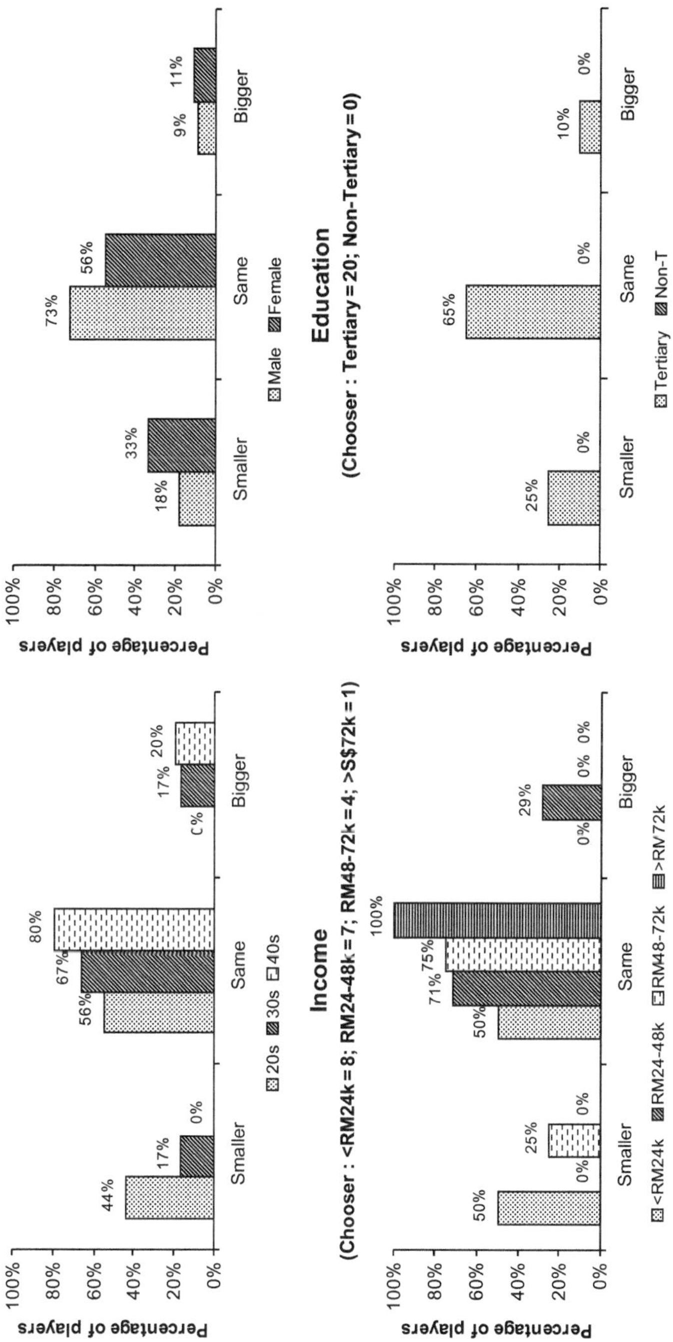

Game 7.4, Cont'd

(Continued)

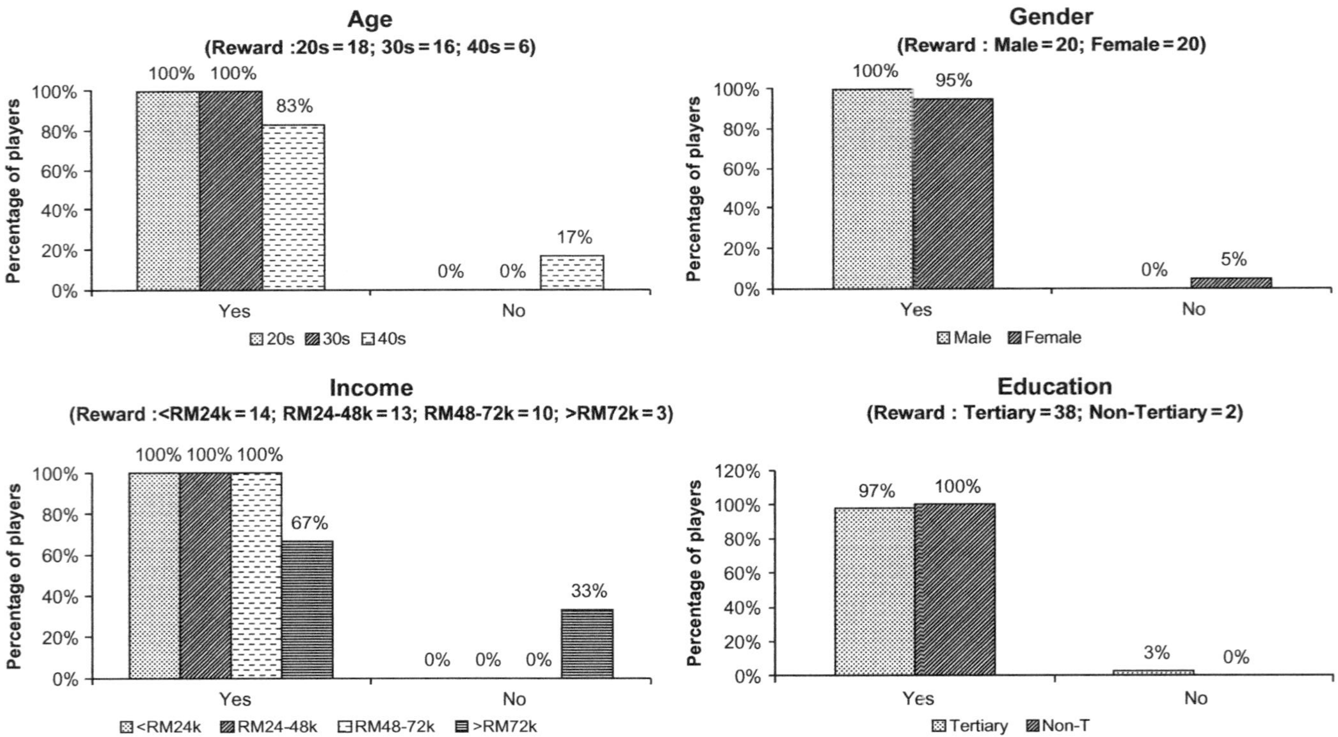

Game 7.4, Cont'd

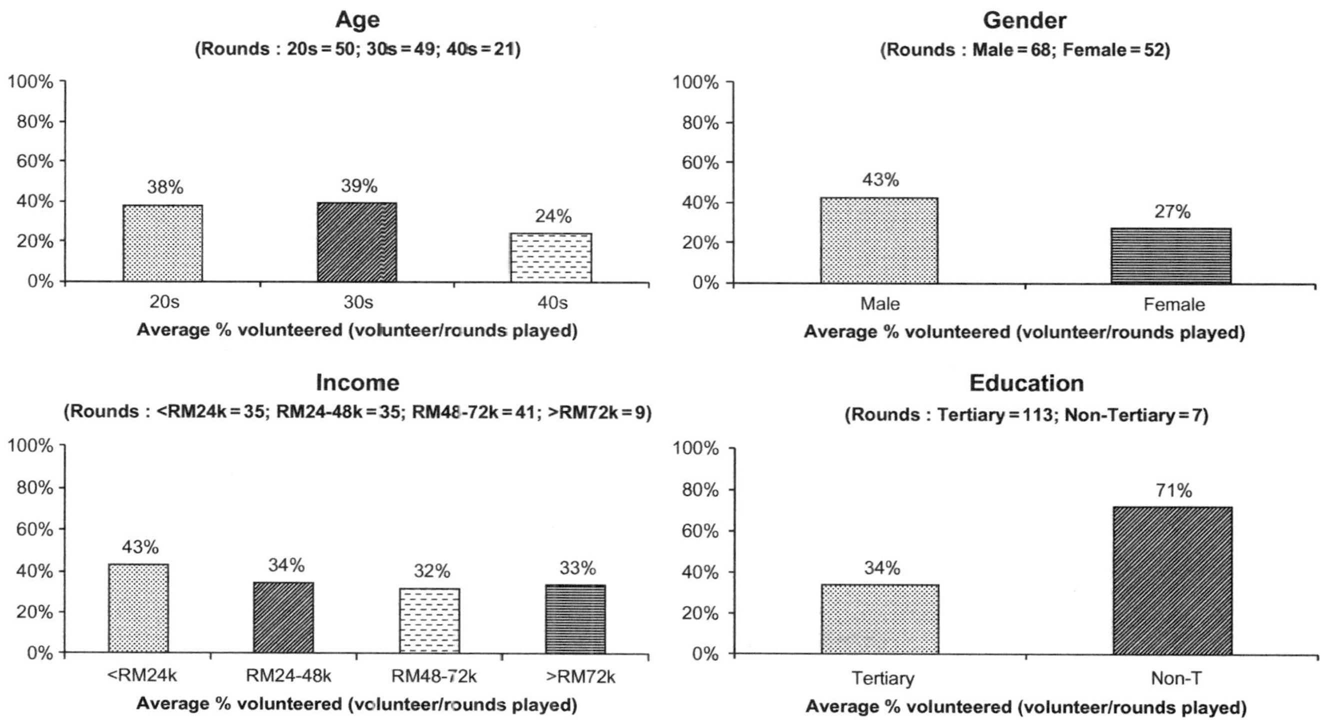

Game 7.5: Volunteer's dilemma (golden rule)

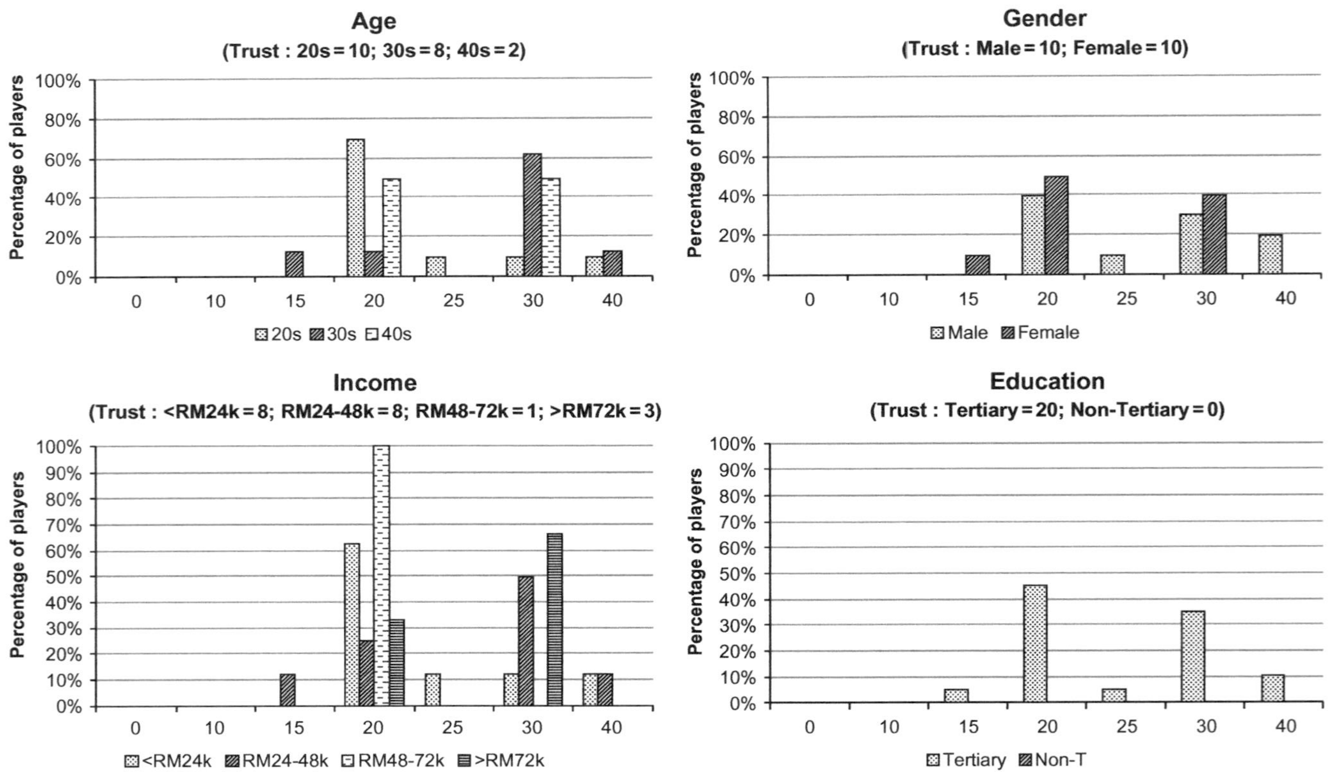

Game 7.6: Trust game (rule of trust and reciprocity)

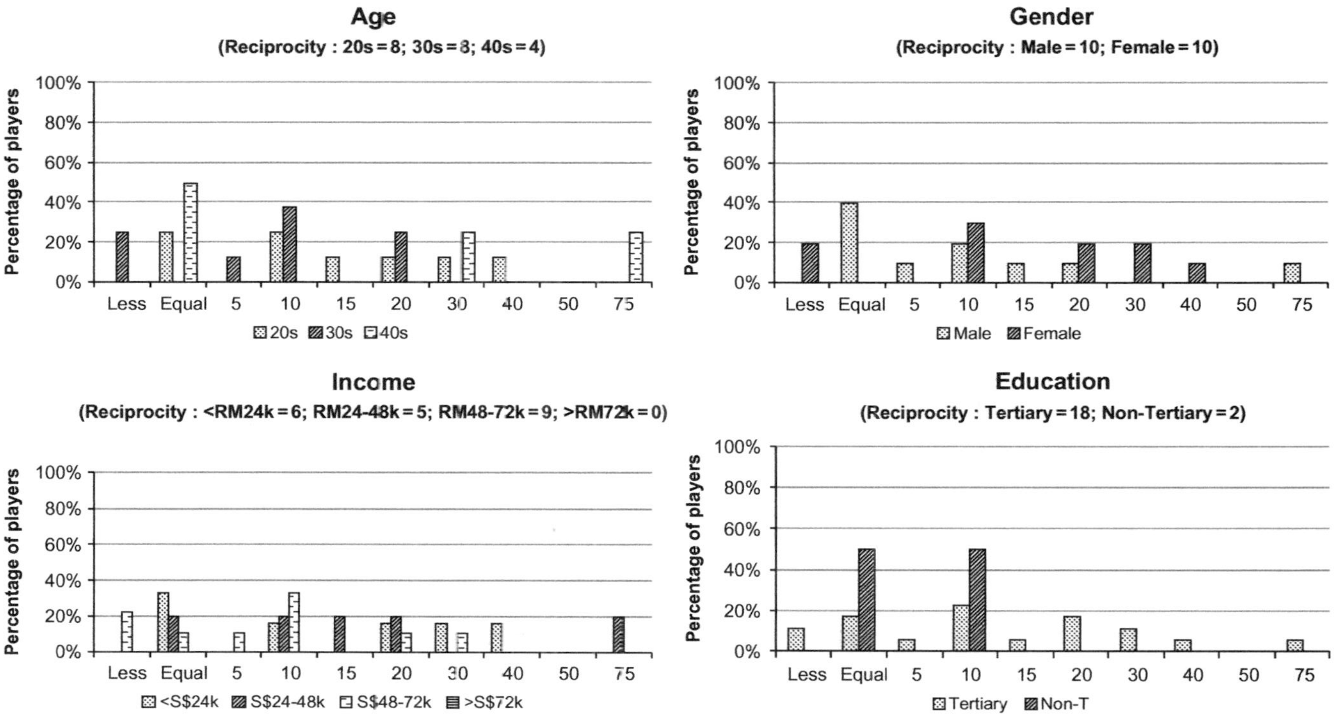

Game 7.6, Cont'd

ANNEX 8: OTHER STATISTICAL DATA

Descriptive statistics

	Mean	Std Dev	*N*
Rule compliance	1.6866	0.43332	349
Religion	0.460	0.499	349
Priming	0.540	0.499	349

Pearson corelation

	Rule compliance	Religion	Priming
Rule compliance	1.000	−0.003	0.008
Religion	−0.003	1.000	−0.088
Priming	0.008	−0.088	1.000
Significance (1-tailed)			
Rule compliance		0.477	0.439
Religion	0.477		0.050
Priming	0.439	0.050	

ANOVA[a]

Model	Sum of squares	*df*	Mean square	*F*	Sig
Regression	0.005	2	0.002	0.013	0.987[b]
Residual	65.338	346	0.189		
Total	65.343	348			

[a] Dependent variable: rule compliance.
[b] Predictors: (constant), priming, religion.

Collinearity diagnostics[a]

			Variance proportions		
Model	Eigenvalue	Condition index	(Constant)	Religion	Priming
Regression	2.252	1.000	0.050	0.070	0.060
Residual	0.548	2.027	0.000	0.560	0.360
Total	0.199	3.360	0.940	0.370	0.580

[a] Dependent variable: rule compliance.

Residuals statistics[a]

Model	Minimum	Maximum	Mean	Std dev	*N*
Predicted Value	1.6817	1.6907	1.6866	0.00372	349
Residual	−0.69074	0.31833	0.0000	0.43331	349
Std predicted value	−1.322	1.119	0.000	1.000	349
Std residual	−1.590	0.733	0.000	0.997	349

[a] Dependent variable: rule compliance.

REFERENCES

Abreu, D., Brunnermeier, M., 2003. Bubbles and crashes. Econometrica 71, 173–204.

Acemoglu, D., Robinson, J., 2005. Institutions as a fundamental cause of long-run growth. In: Aghion, P., Durlauf, S. (Eds.), Handbook of Economic Growth. North Holland, Amsterdam.

Acemoglu, D., Robinson, J., 2012. Why Nations Fail: The Origins of Power, Prosperity, and Poverty. Crown Publishers, New York.

Adams, P., Hunt, P., 2013. Encouraging Consumers to Claim Redress: Evidence From a Field Trial. Occasional Paper No. 2, Financial Conduct Authority, London.

Aggarwal, R., 2014. Animal spirits in financial economics: a review of deviations from economic rationality. Int. Rev. Financ. Anal. 32, 179–187.

Aghion, P., Algan, Y., Cahuc, P., Shleifer, A., 2010. Regulation and distrust. Q. J. Econ. 125 (3), 1015–1049.

Ahmad, K., 1981. In: Ahmad, K. (Ed.), Economic Development in an Islamic Framework in Studies in Islamic Economics. The Islamic Foundation, Leicester.

Akerlof, G.A., 1970. The market for "Lemons": quality uncertainty and the market mechanism. Q. J. Econ. 84, 488–500.

Akerlof, G.A., 1991. Procrastination and obedience. Am. Econ. Rev. Pap. Proc. 81 (2), 1–19.

Akerlof, G., Kranton, R., 2000. Economics and identity. Q. J. Econ. 115 (3), 715–733.

Akerlof, G., Shiller, R., 2010. Animal Spirits: How Human Psychology Drives the Economy, and Why It Matters for Global Capitalism. Princeton University Press, Princeton.

Al-Allaf, M., 2003. Mirror of Realization: God Is a Percept—The Universe Is a Concept. IIC Classic Series, St Louis.

Al-Ghazāli, 1937–1938. Muḥammad ibn Muḥammad. *Iḥyāʾ ʿul ūm al-dīn*. 1356–1357. Lajnat Nashr al-Thaqāfa al-Islāmiyya, Cairo. 16 vols.

Alvard, M.S., 2004. Introduction. Socioeconomic aspects of human behavioral ecology. Res. Econ. Anthropol. 23, 1–15 (Special Issue).

Anderson, C., 1982. Inoculation and counter-explanation: debiasing techniques in the perseverance of social theories. Soc. Cogn. 1 (2), 126–139.

Andreoni, J., 1988. Why free ride? Strategies and learning in public goods experiments. J. Public Econ. 37, 291–304.

Argandona, A., 2012. Three Ethical Dimensions of the Financial Crises. IESE Working Paper WP-944.

Ariely, D., 2008. Predictably Irrational: The Hidden Forces That Shape Our Decisions. HarperCollins, London.

Arrow, K., 1975. Gifts and exchanges. In: Phelps, E.S. (Ed.), Altruism, Morality and Economic Theory. Russel Sage Foundation, New York.

Arrow, K., Debreu, G., 1954. Existence of an equilibrium for a competitive economy. Econometrica 22 (3), 265–290.

Ashour, A.S., 2004. Integrity, Transparency and Accountability in Public Sector Human Resources Management. UN DESA DPADM. RAB/01/006.

Axelrod, R., 1984. The Evolution of Cooperation. Basic Books, New York.

Baker, K., Nofsinger, J. (Eds.), 2010. Behavioural Finance: Investors, Corporations, and Markets. John Wiley & Sons, Inc., Hoboken, NJ.

Baker, M., Ruback, R.S., Wurgler, J., 2007. Behavioral corporate finance: a survey. In: Espen Eckbo, B. (Ed.), Handbook of Corporate Finance: Empirical Corporate Finance. vol. 1. Elsevier, Amsterdam, pp. 145–168.

Ballard, K., Knutson, B., 2009. Dissociable neural representations of future reward magnitude and delay during temporal discounting. NeuroImage 45 (1), 143–150.
Banz, R.W., 1981. The relationship between returns and market value of common stocks. J. Financ. Econ. 9 (1), 3–18.
Barbanel, J., Taylor, A., 1995. Preference relations and measures in the context of fair division. Proc. Am. Math. Soc. 123 (7), 2061. https://doi.org/10.1090/S0002-9939-1995-1233964-5.
Barberis, N.C., Thaler, R.H., 2003. A survey of behavioral finance. In: Constantinides, G., Harris, M., Stulz, R. (Eds.), Handbook of the Economics of Finance. North-Holland, Amsterdam, pp. 1052–1121.
Barr, A., Serra, D., 2010. Corruption and culture: an experimental analysis. J. Public Econ. 94 (11), 862–869.
Battalio, R., Samuelson, L., Van Huyck, J., 2001. Optimization incentives and coordination failure in laboratory stag hunt games. Econometrica 69, 749–764.
Baumeister, R., Vohs, K., 2003. Willpower, choice and self-control. In: Loewenstein, G., Read, D., Baumeister, R. (Eds.), Time and Decision: Economic and Psychological Perspectives on Intertemporal Choice. Russell Sage Foundation, New York, pp. 201–216.
Bayley, D.H., 1966. The effects of corruption in a developing nation. Polit. Res. Q. 19 (4), 719–732.
Bayrak, T., 1997. Interpretation of ibn Arabi's Divine Governance of the Human Kingdom. Fons Vitae, Louisville.
Beck, A., 2008. The evolution of the cognitive model of depression and its neurobiological correlates. Am. J. Psychiatr. 165, 969–977.
Benjamin, D., Choi, J., Strickland, J., 2010. Social identity and preferences. Am. Econ. Rev. 100 (4), 1913–1928.
Berg, J., Dickhaut, J., McCabe, K., 1995. Trust, reciprocity, and social history. Games Econ. Behav. 10, 122–142.
Berger, P., 1999. The Desecularization of the World: Resurgent Religion and World Politics. Ethics and Public Policy Center; Eermans Publishing, Grand Rapids, MI.
Bernoulli, D., 1738. Specimen Theoriae Novae de Mensura Sortis. Commentarii Academiae Scientiarum Imperialis Petropolitanea V, 175–192. (Translated and republished as "Exposition of a New Theory on the Measurement of Risk," 1954, Econometrica 22, 23–36.).
Bertrand, M., Mullainathan, S., Shafir, E., 2004. A behavioural-economics view of poverty. Am. Econ. Rev. 94 (2), 419–423.
Beshears, J., Choi, J.J., Laibson, D., Madrian, B.C., 2008. How are preferences revealed? J. Public Econ. 92, 1787–1794.
Bion, W., 1952. Group dynamics: a re-review. Int. J. Psychoanal. 33, 235–247.
Binmore, K., 1994. Game Theory and the Social Contract. MIT Press, Cambridge, MA.
BIT (Behavioural Insights Team), 2012. Applying Behavioural Insights to Reduce Fraud, Error and Debt. Cabinet Office, Behavioural Insights Team, London.
Bloom, P., 2013. Just Babies: The Origins of Good and Evil. The Crown Publishing Group, New York.
Bolton, G., 1991. A comparative model of bargaining: theory and evidence. Am. Econ. Rev. 81, 1096–1136.
Boudet, A.M.M., Petesch, P., Turk, C., Thumala, A., 2013. On Norms and Agency: Conversations about Gender Equality with Women and Men in 20 Countries. Directions in Development Series. World Bank, Washington, DC.
Bourgeois-Gironde, S., Corcos, A., 2011. Discriminating strategic reciprocity and acquired trust in the repeated trust-game. Econ. Bull. 31 (1), 177–188.
Boscheck, R., 2002. Market Drive and Governance: Reexamining the Rules for Economic & Commercial Contest. Routledge, New York.

Bowles, S., Gintis, H., 2004. The evolution of cooperation in heterogeneous populations. Theor. Popul. Biol. 65, 17–28.
Boyd, D., Crawford, K., 2012. Critical questions for big data: provocations for a cultural, technological, and scholarly phenomenon. Inf. Commun. Soc. 15, 662–679. https://doi.org/10.1080/1369118X.2012.678878.
Boyd, R., Richerson, P., 1992. Punishment allows the evolution of cooperation (or anything else) in sizable groups. Ethol. Sociobiol. 13, 171–195.
Brams, S., Taylor, A., 1995. An envy-free cake division protocol. The American Monthly 102 (1), 9–18.
Brams, S., Jones, M., Klamler, C., 2006. Better Ways To Cut a Cake. Stony Brook Center for Game Theory, Stony Brook, NY.
Brennan, T., Lo, A., 2011. The origin of behavior. Q. J. Finance 1, 55–108.
Brown, C., Dinc, S., 2011. Too many to fail? Evidence of regulatory forbearance when the banking sector is weak. Rev. Financ. Stud. 24, 1378–1405.
Brulhart, 2012. Does the trust game measure trust? Econ. Lett. 115 (1), 20–23.
Brunnermeier, M., Nagel, S., 2004. Hedge funds and the technology bubble. J. Financ. 59 (5), 2013–2040.
Brunnermeier, M., Pedersen, L., 2009. Market liquidity and funding liquidity. Rev. Financ. Stud. 22 (6), 2201–2238.
Burckhardt, T., 2000. Universal Man by Abd Al-Karim Al-Jili. Carvan Press, Lahore.
Burger, N., Charness, G., Lynham, J., 2008. Three Field Experiments on Procrastination and Willpower. Mimeo, Rand Corporation, USA.
Burger, N., Charness, G., Lynham, J., 2011. Field and online experiments on self-control. J. Econ. Behav. Organ. 77 (3), 393–404.
Burnell, S.J., Evans, L., Yao, S., 1999. The ultimatum game: optimal strategies without fairness. Games Econ. Behav. 26, 221–252.
Camerer, C.F., 2003. Behavioural Game Theory: Experiments in Strategic Interaction. Princeton University Press, Princeton.
Camerer, C.F., Johnson, E., 1991. The process-performance paradox in expert judgment: how can experts know so much and predict so badly? In: Anders Ericsson, K., Smith, J. (Eds.), Toward A General Theory of Expertise. Cambridge University Press, Cambridge.
Camerer, C.F., Loewenstein, G., 2004. Behavioural economics: past, present, future. In: Camerer, C.F., Loewenstein, G., Rabin, M. (Eds.), Advances in Behavioural Economics. Russell Sage, New York, pp. 3–51.
Camerer, C.F., Thaler, R., 1995. Anomalies: ultimatums, dictators and manners. J. Econ. Perspect. 9, 209–219.
Cameron, L., Shah, M., 2012. Risk-taking Behavior in the Wake of Natural Disasters. IZA Discussion Paper 6756.
Capraro, V., 2013. A model of human cooperation in social dilemmas. PLoS ONE 8 (8), e72427. https://doi.org/10.1371/journal.pone.0072427.
Chadhuri, A., Gangadheran, L., 2002. An experimental analysis of trust and trustworthiness. South. Econ. J. 73, 959–985.
Carr, P., Steele, C., 2010. Stereotype threat affects financial decision making. Psychol. Sci. 21, 1411–1416.
Cesarini, D., Dawes, C.T., Fowler, J.H., Johannesson, M., Lichtenstein, P., Wallace, B., 2008. Heritability of cooperative behavior in the trust game. Proc. National Acad. Sci. 105 (10), 3721–3726.
Chapra, M.U., 1985. Towards a Just Monetary System. The Islamic Foundation, Leicester.
Choi, J., Laibson, D., Metrick, A., 2004. For better or for worse: default effects and 401(k) savings behaviour. In: Bodie, Z., Shoven, J., Wise, D. (Eds.), Perspectives in the Economics of Aging. NBER, pp. 81–126.
Chomsky, N., 1980. Rules and Representations. Columbia University Press, New York.

Christakis, N., Fowler, J., 2010. Connected—The Amazing Power of Social Networks and How They Shape Our Lives. Harper Press, London.
Clarke, R., 1997. Situational Crime Prevention—Successful Case Studies, second ed. Harrow and Heston, New York.
Coase, R., 1960. The problem of social cost. J. Law Econ. 3 (1), 1–44.
Coates, J.M., Herbert, J., 2008. Endogenous steroids and financial risk taking on a London trading floor. Proc. Natl. Acad. Sci. U. S. A. 105, 6167–6172.
Cochrane, J., 2011. Presidential address: discount rates. J. Financ. 66 (4), 1047–1108.
Cohn, A., Maréchal, M.A., Noll, T., 2013. Bad Boys: The Effect of Criminal Identity on Dishonesty. Working Paper 132, University of Zurich, Zurich.
Cohn, A., Engelmann, J., Fehr, E., Maréchal, M.A., 2014. Evidence for countercyclical risk aversion: an experiment with financial professionals. Am. Econ. Rev. 105 (2), 860–885.
Cooper, M.J., Gulen, H., Schill, M., 2008. Asset growth and the cross-section of stock returns. J. Financ. 63 (4), 1609–1651.
Cooper, M.J., McConnell, J., Ovtchinnikov, A., 2006. The other January effect. J. Financ. Econ. 82 (2), 315–341.
Cooper, A.C., Woo, C.Y., Dunkelberg, W.C., 1988. Entrepreneurs' perceived chances for success. J. Bus. Ventur. 3 (2), 97–108.
Costa, D.L., Kahn, E., 2013. Energy conservation "Nudges" and environmentalist ideology: evidence from a randomized residential electricity field experiment. J. Eur. Econ. Assoc. 11 (3), 680–702.
Costa-Gomes, M.A., Weizsäcker, G., 2008. Stated beliefs and play in normal form games. Rev. Econ. Stud. 75, 729–762.
Coval, J., Stafford, E., 2007. Asset fire sales (and purchases) in equity markets. J. Financ. Econ. 86 (2), 479–512.
Credit Suisse Global Investor Report, 2011. Expert know-how for Credit Suisse investment clients. Global Investor 1.11, May.
d'Aspremont, C., Gérard-Varet, L.A., 1998. Collective choice mechanisms and individual incentives. In: Schmidt, C. (Ed.), Game Theory and Economic Analysis. Routledge, London and New York.
Darley, J.M., Latané, B., 1968. Bystander intervention in emergencies: diffusion of responsibility. J. Pers. Soc. Psychol. 8, 377–383.
Dasgupta, P., 1988. Trust as a commodity. In: Gambetta, D. (Ed.), Trust: Making and Breaking Cooperative Relations. Basil Blackwell, Oxford.
Davis, D.D., Holt, C.A., 1993. Experimental Economics. Princeton University Press, Princeton, NJ.
Datta, S., Mullainathan, S., 2012. Behavioural Design: A New Approach to Development Policy. CGD Policy Paper 016 Center for Global Development, Washington, DC.
Davis, A., 2005. Media effects and the active elite audience: a study of communications in the London stock exchange. Eur. J. Commun. 20 (3), 303–326.
Davis, K., Fisher, A., Kingsbury, B., Merry, S.E., 2012. Governance by Indicators: Global Power through Classification and Rankings. vol. 1. Oxford University Press, Oxford.
de Larosière Group, 2009. The High-Level Group of Financial Supervision in the EU. European Commission, Brussels.
De Becker, G., 1997. The Gift of Fear: Survival Signals That Protect Us From Violence. Little Brown and Co, Boston.
De Long, J., Shleifer, A., Summers, L., Waldmann, R., 1990. Noise trader risk in financial markets. J. Polit. Econ. 98, 703–738.
De Martino, B., O'Doherty, J., Ray, D., Bossaerts, P., Camerer, C., 2013. In the mind of the market: theory of mind biases value computation during financial bubbles. Neuron 79, 1222–1231.
Deaves, R., Luders, E., Luo, G., 2009. An experimental test of the impact of overconfidence and gender on trading activity. Rev. Financ. 13, 555–575.

DeBondt, W., Thaler, R., 1990. Do security analysts overreact? Am. Econ. Rev. 80 (2), 52–77.
Department of Statistics, Malaysia, 2014. https://www.dosm.gov.my/v1/index.php.
Detemple, J., Murthy, S., 1994. Intertemporal asset pricing with heterogeneous beliefs. J. Econ. Theory 62, 294–320.
Devetaga, G., Warglien, M., 2008. Playing the wrong game: an experimental analysis of relational complexity and strategic misrepresentation. Games Econ. Behav. 62 (2), 364382.
Diekmann, A., 1986. Volunteer's dilemma: a social trap without a dominant strategy and some empirical results. In: Diekmann, A., Mitter, P. (Eds.), Paradoxical Effects of Social Behaviour: Essays in Honour of Anatol Rapoport. Physica-Verlag, Heidelberg, pp. 187–197.
Diekmann, A., 1993. Cooperation in asymmetric volunteer's dilemma game: theory and experimental evidence. Int. J. Game Theory 22, 75–85.
Disner, S., Beevers, C., Haigh, E., Beck, A., 2011. Neural mechanisms of the cognitive model of depression. Nat. Rev. Neurosci. 12, 467–477.
Döbeli, B., Vanini, P., 2010. Stated and revealed investment decisions concerning retail structured products. J. Bank. Financ. 34, 1400–1411.
Duflo, E., Banerjee, A., 2011. Poor Economics: A Radical Rethinking of the Way to Fight Global Poverty. Public Affairs, USA, Perseus Books Group, UK.
Easley, D., Kleinberg, J., 2010. Networks, Crowds, and Markets: Reasoning about a Highly Connected World. Cambridge University Press, New York.
Easterwood, J., Nutt, S., 1999. Inefficiency in analysts' earnings forecasts: systematic misreaction or systematic optimism. J. Financ. 54 (5), 1777–1797.
Eckel, C., El-Gamal, M., Wilson, R., 2009. Risk loving after the storm: a Bayesian-Network study of Hurricane Katrina evacuees. J. Econ. Behav. Organ. 69 (2), 110–124.
Edison, H.J., Warnock, F., 2008. Cross-border listings, capital controls, and equity flows to emerging markets. J. Int. Money Financ. 27 (6), 1013–1027.
Edmans, A., Garcia, D., Norli, Ø., 2007. Sports sentiment and stock returns. J. Financ. 62 (4), 1967–1998.
Eggertsson, T., 1990. Economic Behaviour and Institutions. Cambridge University Press, Cambridge.
Einhorn, H., 1972. Expert measurement and mechanical combination. Organ. Behav. Hum. Perform. 7, 86–106.
Erbaş, S.N., Mirakhor, A., 2013. In: Iqbal, Z., Mirakhor, A. (Eds.), The Foundational Islamic Market Principles, Knightian Uncertainty and Economic Justice: An Institutional-Behavioural Assessment, Economic Development and Islamic Finance. World Bank, Washington, DC, pp. 93–129.
Erta, K., Hunt, S., Iscenko, Z., Brambley, W., 2013. Applying Behavioural Economics at the Financial Conduct Authority. FCA Occasional Paper 1.
Fama, E., 1965. The behavior of stock market prices. J. Bus. 38, 34–105.
Fama, E., French, K., 1992. The cross-section of expected stock return. J. Financ. 47, 427–465.
Fehr, E., Fischbacher, U., Gachter, S., 2002. Strong reciprocity, human cooperation, and the enforcement of social norms. Hum. Nat. 13 (1), 1–26.
Fehr, E., Schmidt, K.M., 1999. A theory of fairness, competition, and cooperation. Q. J. Econ. 114, 817–868.
Feltovich, N., Iwasaki, A., Oda, S.H., 2012. Payoff levels, loss avoidance, and equilibrium selection in the stag hunt: an experimental study. Econ. Enq. 50 (4), 932–952. https://doi.org/10.1111/j.1465-7295.2011.00406.x.
Ferraro, P.J., Price, M.K., 2013. Using non-pecuniary strategies to influence behaviour: evidence from a large scale field experiment. Rev. Econ. Stat. 95 (1), 64–73.
Fischhoff, B., Eggers, S., 2013. Questions of competence: the duty to inform and the limits to choice. In: Shafir, E. (Ed.), The Behavioural Foundations of Public Policy. Princeton University Press, Princeton, NJ, pp. 217–230.

Fischhoff, B., Beyth-Marom, R., 1983. Hypothesis evaluation from a Bayesian perspective. Psychol. Rev. 90 (3), 239.
Fisher, F.M., 1989. Games economists play: a noncooperative view. RAND J. Econ. 20 (1), 113–124.
Fisman, R., Miguel, E., 2007. Corruption, norms, and legal enforcement: evidence from diplomatic parking tickets. J. Polit. Econ. 115 (6), 1020–1048.
Fjeldstad, O.-H., 2005. Corruption in Tax Administration: Lessons from Institutional Reforms in Uganda. Working Paper 2005: 10. Chr. Michelsen Institute, Bergen.
Fjeldstad, O.-H., Kolstad, I., Lange, S., 2003. Autonomy, Incentives and Patronage: A Study of Corruption in the Tanzania and Uganda Revenue Authorities. CMI Report 2003:9, Chr. Michelsen Institute, Bergen.
Folbre, N., 2006. Measuring care: gender, empowerment, and the care economy. J. Human Develop. 7 (2), 183–199.
Foley, R., 1995. The adaptive legacy of human evolution: a search for the environment of evolutionary adaptedness. Evol. Anthropol. 41, 94–203.
Forsythe, R., Horowitz, J.L., Savin, N.E., Sefton, M., 1994. Fairness in simple bargaining experiments. Games Econ. Behav. 6, 347–369.
Frank, R.H., 1988. Passions Within Reason: The Strategic Role of the Emotions. Norton, New York.
Frank, M., Bishop Tiller, S., 2005. When it Comes to Investing, Gender a Strong Influence on Behavior. Hindsight 2 Insight, Merrill Lynch Investment Managers (MLIM) Survey.
Franzen, A., 1995. Group size and one shot collective action. Ration. Soc. 7, 183–200.
Freese, J., 2009. Preferences. In: Hedström, P., Bearman, P. (Eds.), The Oxford Handbook of Analytical Sociology. Oxford University Press, Oxford, pp. 94–114.
French, K., 1980. Stock returns and the weekend effect. J. Financ. Econ. 8 (1), 55–69.
Freud, S., 1921. Group Psychology and the Analysis of the Ego. Standard Edition 18, Hogarth Press, London, pp. 65–144.
Freud, S., 1911. Formulations Regarding the Principles of Mental Functioning. Standard Edition 12 Hogarth Press, London, pp. 212–226.
Friedman, M., 1970. Essays in Positive Economics: Part I – The Methodology of Positive Economics. University of Chicago Press (1953), Chicago, pp. 3–43.
Friedman, D., Cassar, A., 1984. Economics Lab: An Intensive Course in Experimental Economics. Routledge, New York.
Friedman, D., Cassar, A., 2004. Economics Lab: An Intensive Course in Experimental Economics. Routledge, London.
Froot, K.A., Dabora, E., 1999. How are stock prices affected by the location of trade. J. Financ. Econ. 53, 189–216.
Frydman, C., Barberis, N., Camerer, C., Bossaerts, P., Rangel, A., 2014. Using neural data to test a theory of investor behaviour: an application to realization utility. J. Financ. 69 (2), 907–946.
Frydman, R., Goldberg, M.D., 2007. Imperfect Knowledge Economics: Exchange Rates and Risk. Princeton University Press, Princeton, NJ.
Gale, J., Binmore, K., Samuelson, L., 1995. Learning to be imperfect: the ultimatum game. Games Econ. Behav. 8 (1), 56–90.
Gambling, T., Karim, R.A.A., 1991. Business and Accounting Ethics in Islam. Mansell, London.
Garoupa, N., 2003. Behavioural economic analysis of crime: a critical review. Eur. J. Law Econ. 15, 5–15.
Geanakoplos, J., 2003. In: Liquidity, default, and crashes: endogenous contracts in general equilibrium. Advances in Economics and Econometrics Theory and Applications, Eighth World Conference. vol. 2. Econometric Society Monographs, pp. 170–205.
Geanakoplos, J., 2010. The leverage cycle. NBER Macroecon. Annu. 24, 1–65.

Geary, D., 2005. The Origin of Mind: Evolution of Brain, Cognition and General Intelligence. American Psychological Association, Washington, DC.
Gensler, H., 2013. Ethics and the Golden Rule. Routledge Press, New York.
Gigerenzer, G., 2004. Fast and frugal heuristics: the tools of bounded rationality. In: Koehler, D.J., Harvey, N. (Eds.), Blackwell Handbook of Judgment and Decision-making. Blackwell, Malden, MA, pp. 62–88.
Gilovich, T., Griffin, D., Kahneman, D. (Eds.), 2002. Heuristics and Biases: The Psychology of Intuitive Judgment. Cambridge University Press, New York and Cambridge.
Glaeser, E., Laibson, D., Scheinkman, J., Soutter, C., 1999. What is Social Capital? The Determinants of Trust and Trustworthiness. NBER Working Paper no. 7216.
Glaser, M., Langer, T., Reynders, J., Weber, M., 2007. Framing effects in stock market forecasts: the difference between asking for prices and asking for returns. Rev. Financ. 11 (2), 325–357.
Gottlieb, J., 2014. Why Women Participate Less in Civic Activity: Evidence from Mali. Unpublished paper. http://mgape.files.wordpress.com/2013/06/gottlieb_civic-behaviour.pdf.
Greycourt & Co. Inc, 2008. The Financial Crisis and the Collapse of Ethical Behaviour. White Paper No. 44.
Greif, A., 1994. Cultural beliefs and the organization of society: a historical and theoretical reflection on collectivist and individualist societies. J. Polit. Econ. 102 (5), 912–950.
Grinstein, A., Wathieu, L., 2012. Happily (Mal)adjusted: cosmopolitan identity and expatriate adjustment. Int. J. Res. Mark. 29, 337–345.
Griffin, J., Harris, J., Topaloglu, S., 2003. The dynamics of institutional and individual trading. J. Financ. 58 (6), 2285–2320.
Guala, F., Mittone, L., 2010. How history and convention create norms: an experimental study. J. Econ. Psychol. 31, 349–356.
Gunningham, N., Rees, J., 1997. Industry self-regulation: an institutional perspective. Law Policy 19 (4), 363–414.
Hackbarth, D., 2008. Managerial traits and capital structure decisions. J. Financ. Quant. Anal. 43 (4), 843–882.
Haidt, J., 2012. The Righteous Mind: Why Good People are Divided by Politics and Religion. Random House, New York.
Hammond, K., 1996. Human Judgment and Social Policy. Irreducible Uncertainty, Inevitable Error, Unavoidable Injustice. Oxford University Press, New York.
Hardin, R., 1991. Trusting persons, trusting institutions. In: Zeckhauser, R.J. (Ed.), Strategy and Choice. MIT Press, Cambridge, MA.
Haruvy, E., 2002. Identification and testing of modes in beliefs. J. Math. Psychol. 46 (1), 88–109.
Heaton, J., 2002. Managerial optimism and corporate finance. Financ. Manag. 31 (2), 33–45.
Helbling, D., 2013. Economics 2.0: The Natural Step Towards a Self-Regulating, Participatory Market Society. Institute for New Economic Thinking (INET), New York.
Henrich, J., McCabe, K., 1998. Behavioural foundations of reciprocity: experimental economics and evolutionary psychology. Econ. Inq. 36, 335–352.
Henrich, J., Shachat, K., Smith, V., 1994. Preferences, property rights, and anonymity in bargaining games. Games Econ. Behav. 7, 346–380.
Henrich, J., Boyd, R., Bowles, S., Camerer, C., Fehr, E., Gintis, H. (Eds.), 2004. Foundations of Human Sociality: Economic Experiments and Ethnographic Evidence from Fifteen Small-Scale Societies. Oxford University Press.
Hilary, G., Menzly, L., 2006. Does past success lead analysts to become overconfident? Manag. Sci. 52 (4), 489–500.
Hirshleifer, D., Shumway, T., 2003. Good day sunshine: stock returns and the weather. J. Financ. 58 (3), 1009–1032.

Hirshleifer, D., Teoh, S.H., 2003. Limited attention, information disclosure, and financial reporting. J. Account. Econ. 36 (1–3), 337–386.
Hobbes, T., 1991. In: Tuck, R. (Ed.), Leviathan [65]. Cambridge University Press, Cambridge.
Hodgson, G.M., 1999. Evolution and Institutions: On Evolutionary Economics and the Evolution of Economics. E. Elgar Publishing, Northampton, MA.
Hoff, K., Pandey, P., 2006. Discrimination, social identity, and durable inequalities. Am. Econ. Rev. 96 (2), 206–211.
Hoff, K., Stiglitz, J.E., 2010. Equilibrium fictions: a cognitive approach to societal rigidity. Am. Econ. Rev. 100 (2), 141–146.
Hofstede, G., 2001. Culture's Consequences: Comparing Values, Behaviours, Institutions, and Organizations Across Nations, second ed. Sage Publications, Thousand Oaks, CA.
Hogarth, R., 2005. Deciding analytically or trusting your intuition? The advantages and disadvantages of analytic and intuitive thought. In: Betsch, T., Haberstroh, S. (Eds.), The Routines of Decision Making. Lawrence Erlbaum Associates, Inc., Mahwah, NJ, pp. 67–82.
Holt, C., Capra, M., 2000. Classroom Games: Prisoner's Dilemma. Unpublished. Partially funded by National Science Foundation (SBR-9617784 and SBR-9818683).
Horn, J., Lovallo, D., Viguerie, S., 2006. Learning to let go: making better exit decisions. McKinsey Quarterly, 2, 64.
Huang, W., et al., 2011. Agency costs, top executives' overconfidence and investment-cash flow sensitivity: evidence from listed companies in China. Pac. Basin Financ. J. 19, 261–277.
Hume, D., 1978/1739–40. In: Selby-Bigge, L.A. (Ed.), A Treatise of Human Nature, second ed. rev Peter Nidditch. Clarendon Press, Oxford.
Huizinga, H., Laeven, L., 2010. Bank Valuation and Regulatory Forbearance During a Financial Crisis. European Banking Center Discussion Paper No. 2009–17.
Ibbotson, R., Mileversusky, M., Chen, P., Zhu, K., 2007. Lifetime Financial Advice: Human Capital, Asset Allocation, and Insurance. vol. 1. The Research Foundation of CFA Institute, USA, pp.1–95.
Ibn Khaldun, 1981. Kitab al-'ibar (The Book of Examples', trans. J.F.P. Hopkins). In: Levtzion, N., Hopkins, J.F.P. (Eds.), Corpus of early Arabic Sources for West African History. Cambridge University Press.
Ivković, Z., Weisbenner, S., 2007. Information diffusion effects in individual investors' common stock purchases: covet thy neighbors' investment choices. Rev. Financ. Stud. 20, 1327–1357.
Iqbal, Z., Mirakhor, A., 2011. An Introduction to Islamic Finance: Theory and Practice, second ed. Wiley, Singapore.
Izutsu, T., 2004. Ethico-Religious Concepts in the Qur´an. Islamic Book Trust, Kuala Lumpur.
Janis, I., 1982. Groupthink, second ed. Houghton Mifflin, Boston, MA.
Johnson, E.J., Goldstein, D.G., 2003. Do defaults save lives? Science 302, 1338–1339.
Johnston, M., Kpundeh, S.J., 2004. Building a Clean Machine: Anti-Corruption Coalitions and Sustainable Reform. vol. 3466. World Bank, Washington, DC.
Kahneman, D., 2011. Thinking, Fast and Slow. Farrar, Straus and Giroux, New York.
Kahneman, D., 2003. Maps of bounded rationality: psychology for behavioural economics. Am. Econ. Rev. 93 (5), 1449–1475.
Kahneman, D., Tversky, A., 2000. Choices, Values, and Frames. Cambridge University Press and Russell Sage Foundation, Cambridge.
Kahneman, D., Tversky, A., 1979. Prospect theory: an analysis of decision under risk. Econometrica 47 (2), 263–291.
Kahneman, D., Knetsch, J.L., Thaler, R.H., 1986. Fairness and the assumptions of economics. J. Bus. 59, 285–300.

Kallbekken, S., Sælen, H., Hermansen, E.A.T., 2013. Bridging the energy efficiency gap: a field experiment on lifetime energy costs and household appliances. J. Consum. Policy 36 (1), 1–16.

Kamstra, M.J., Kramer, L.A., Levi, M.D., 2003. Winter blues: a SAD stock market cycle. Am. Econ. Rev. 93 (1), 324–343.

Karlan, D., Appel, J., 2011. More Than Good Intentions: How a New Economics is Helping to Solve Global Poverty. Penguin Group, New York.

Kaznatcheev, A., 2015. A short history of iterated prisoner's dilemma tournaments. Theory, Evolution, and Games Group. Retrieved June 8.

Keen, S., 2011. Debunking Economics—Revised, Expanded and Integrated Edition: The Naked Emperor Dethroned? Zed Books, London and New York.

Kent, D., Hirshleifer, D., Subrahmanyam, A., 1998. Investor psychology and security market under- and over-reactions. J. Financ. 53, 1839–1885.

Keynes, J.M., 1932. The End of Laissez-Faire, in Essays in Persuasion. Harcourt, Brace & Co, New York.

Keynes, J.M., 1936. The General Theory of Interest, Employment and Money. Macmillan Cambridge University Press.

Kidd, J.B., 1970. The utilization of subjective probabilities in production planning. Acta Psychol. 34, 338–347.

Kirchgaessner, S., Farrell, G., 2008. Fuld breaks silence on Lehman collapse. Financial Times. October 7.

Klein, M., 1935. A contribution to the psychogenesis of manic-depressive states. Int. J. Psychoanal. 16, 145–174.

Klein, R.A., et al., 2013. Investigating Variation in Replicability: The "Many Labs" Replication Project. 14 June, https://openscienceframework.org/project/WX7Ck.

Klos, A., Weber, E.U., Weber, M., 2005. Investment decisions and time horizon: risk perception and risk behavior in repeated gambles. Manag. Sci. 51 (12), 1777–1790.

Knack, S., Keefer, P., 1997. Does social capital have an economic payoff? A cross-country investigation. Q. J. Econ. 112 (4), 1251–1288.

Knight, F., 1921. Risk, Uncertainty and Profit. Beard Books, Washington, DC. 2002.

Kollmuss, A., Agyeman, J., 2002. Mind the gap: why do people act environmentally and what are the barriers to pro-environmental behaviour? Environ. Educ. Res. 8 (3), 239–260.

Kuhnen, C., Knutson, B., 2005. The neural basis of financial risk taking. Neuron 47, 763–770.

Kumar, S., 2002. Does participation in common pool resource management help the poor? A social cost-benefit analysis of joint forest management in Jharkhand, India. World Dev. 30 (5), 763–782.

Kurz, M., 1996. Rational beliefs and endogenous uncertainty. Economic Theory 8, 383–397.

Kurz, M., 1994. On the structure and diversity of rational beliefs. Economic Theory 4, 877–900.

Laibson, D., 1997. Golden eggs and hyperbolic discounting. Q. J. Econ. 7/2 (2), 443–477.

LaPorta, R., Lopez-de-Silanes, F., Shleifer, A., Vishny, R., 1997. Trust in large organizations. Am. Econ. Rev. Pap. Proc. 87, 333–338.

Larrick, R., 2004. Debiasing. In: Koehler, D., Harvey, N. (Eds.), Blackwell Handbook of Judgment and Decision Making. Blackwell, Malden, MA.

Larrick, R.P., Soll, J.B., 2008. The MPG illusion. Science 320, 1593–1594.

Larson, D., Shevchenko, A., 2010. Status seekers: Chinese and Russian responses to U.S. primacy. Int. Secur. 34 (4), 63–95.

Leon, A.K., Pfeifer, C., 2013. Religious Activity, Risk Taking Preferences, and Financial Behaviour: Empirical Evidence from German Survey Data. University of Lüneburg Working Paper Series in Economics No. 269.

Levin, J., Milgrom, P., 2004. Consumer Theory, first ed. [ebook] Stanford. Available at https://web.stanford.edu/~jdlevin/Econ%20202/Consumer%20Theory.pdf.

Loewenstein, G. (Ed.), 2007. Exotic Preferences: Behavioural Economics and Human Motivation. Oxford University Press, New York.

Lord, C., Lepper, M., Preston, E., 1984. Considering the opposite: a corrective strategy for social judgment. J. Pers. Soc. Psychol. 47, 1231–1243.

Lin, Y., Hu, S., Chen, M., 2005. Managerial optimism and corporate investment: some corporate evidence from Taiwan. Pac. Basin Financ. J. 13, 523–546.

Lipe, M.G., 1998. Individual investors' risk judgments and investment decisions: the impact of accounting and market data. Acc. Organ. Soc. 23, 625–640.

Lipschitz, D., Rasmusson, A., Southwick, S., 1998. Childhood posttraumatic stress disorder: a review of neurobiologic sequelae. Psychiatr. Ann. 28, 452–457.

Lo, A.W., 2011. Fear, greed, and financial crises: a cognitive neurosciences perspective (October 13). Available at SSRN: https://ssrn.com/abstract=1943325 or https://doi.org/10.2139/ssrn.1943325.

Locke, J., 1975. In: Nidditch, P. (Ed.), An Essay Concerning the Human Understanding. Clarendon Press, Oxford. First published 1689.

Loughran, T., Ritter, J., 1995. The new issues puzzle. J. Financ. 50 (1), 23–51.

Lunn, P., 2014. Regulatory Policy and Behavioural Economics. 9th meeting of the Regulatory Policy Committe, 12-13 November 2013, The OECD Conference Centre, Paris. OECD.

Lydon, G., 2008. On Trans-Saharan Trails Islamic Law, Trade Networks, and Cross-Cultural Exchange in Nineteenth-Century Western Africa. Cambridge University Press, Cambridge.

Madrian, B., Shea, D., 2001. The power of suggestion: inertia in 401(k) participation and savings behaviour. Q. J. Econ. 116 (4), 1149–1187.

Magzan, M., 2012. Mental models for leadership effectiveness: building future different than the past. J. Eng. Manag. Comp. 2 (2), 57–63.

Mantel, S.P., Tatikonda, M., Liao, Y., 2006. A behavioural study of supply manager decision-making: factors influencing make versus. Buy evaluation. J. Oper. Manag. 24 (6), 822–838.

Markowitz, H.M., 1952. Portfolio Selection. J. Financ. 7, 77–91.

Marschak, T., Nelson, R., 1962. Flexibility, uncertainty, and economic theory. Metroeconomica 14, 42–58.

Masini, A., Menichetti, E., 2012. Investment decisions in the renewable energy sector: an analysis of non-financial drivers. Technol. Forecast. Soc. Chang. 80, 510–524.

Matthey, A., 2010. The influence of primes on reference states. Games 1 (1), 34–52.

Mawet, S., Pereira, O., Petit, C., 2010. In: Nikova, S., Batina, L. (Eds.), Equitable cake cutting without mediator. 5th Benelux Workshop on Information and System Security.

McCleary, R.M., Barro, R.J., 2006. Religion and economy. J. Econ. Perspect. 20 (2), 49–72.

McConnell, J., Xu, W., 2008. Equity returns at the turn of the month. Financ. Anal. J. 64 (2), 49–64.

McDonald, R., Rietz, T., 2010. Implications From Experimental Behavioral Finance for Improving Portfolio Selection. TIAA-CREF Institute. Trends and Issues, Dec 2010.

Mercier, H., Sperber, D., 2011. Why do humans reason? Arguments for an argumentative theory. Behav. Brain Sci. 34 (2), 57–74.

Merton, R.C., 1969. Lifetime portfolio selection under uncertainty: the continuous time case. Rev. Econ. Stat. 51, 247–257.

Milgram, S., 1974. Obedience to Authority. Harper & Row, New York.

Miller, P., 2007. Swarm Theory, National Geographic. July, 126–147.

Mirakhor, A., 2009. Islamic economics and finance: an institutional perspective. IIUM J. Econ. Manag. 17 (1), 31–72.

Mirakhor, A., Askari, H., 2010. Islam and the Path to Human and Economic Development. Palgrave Macmillan, New York.

Mobarak, A.M., Rosenzweig, M., 2013. Informal risk sharing, index insurance, and risk taking in developing countries. Am. Econ. Rev. 103 (3), 375–380.

Moulin, H., 2003. Fair Division and Collective Welfare. MIT Press, Cambridge, MA, USA.

Mungiu-Pippidi, A., 2013. Becoming Denmark: historical designs of corruption control. Soc. Res. 80 (4), 1259–1286.
Neale, M.A., Bazerman, M.H., 1990. Cognition and Rationality in Negotiation. The Free Press, New York.
Nickerson, R., 1998. Confirmation bias: a ubiquitous phenomenon in many guises. Rev. Gen. Psychol. 2 (2), 175.
Norenzayan, A., 2013. Big Gods: How Religion Transformed Cooperation and Conflict. Princeton University Press, Princeton.
North, D.C., 2008. The Foundations of New Institutional Economics. Presentation at the Center for International Private Enterprise (CIPE), Washington, DC.
North, D.C., 1990. Institutions, Institutional Change and Economic Performance. Cambridge University Press, Cambridge.
Nowak, M., 2011. Super Cooperators. Canongate Books Ltd, London.
Nyarko, Y., Schotter, A., 2002. An experimental study of belief learning using elicited beliefs. Econometrica 70 (3), 971–1005.
O'Donoghue, T., Rabin, M., 1999. Doing it now or later. Am. Econ. Rev. 89, 103–124.
Odean, T., 1998a. Volume, volatility, price and profit when all traders are above average. J. Financ. 53, 1887–1934.
Odean, T., 1998b. Are investors reluctant to realize their losses? J. Financ. 53, 1775–1798.
Orbell, J., Dawes, R., van de Kragt, A., 1988. Explaining discussion-induced cooperation. J. Pers. Soc. Psychol. 54, 811–819.
Ofek, E., Richardson, M., 2003. DotCom mania: the rise and fall of internet stock prices. J. Financ. 58, 1113–1137.
Ofir, M., Wiener, Z., 2012. Investment in Financial Structured Products from Rational and Behavioural Choice Perspectives. Working paper. Available at SSRN http://ssrn.com/abstract=2193282.
Ostrom, E., 2000. Collective action and the evolution of social norms. J. Econ. Perspect. 14 (3), 137–158.
Ozdenoren, E., Salant, S.W., Silverman, D., 2012. Willpower and the optimal control of visceral urges. J. Eur. Econ. Assoc. 10 (2), 342–368.
Page, L., Savage, D., Torgler, B., 2012. Variation in Risk Seeking Behavior in a Natural Experiment on Large Losses Induced by a Natural Disaster. CESifo working paper series 3878.
Palfrey, T., Wang, S., 2009. On eliciting beliefs in strategic games. J. Econ. Behav. Organ. 71, 98–109.
Panayotou, T., 1993. Green Market: The Economics of Sustainable Development. Institute for Contemporary Studies, San Francisco, CA.
Panth, S., 2011. Changing Norms Is Key to Fighting Everyday Corruption. CommGAP Discussion Papers, Communication for Governance and Accountability Program World Bank, Washington, DC.
Pearce, D.W., Warford, J.J., 1993. World Without End: Economics, Environment and Sustainable Development. Oxford University Press, New York, NY.
Peterson, R., 2010. Neuroeconomics and neurofinance. In: Kent Baker, H., Nofsinger, J.R. (Eds.), Behavioural Finance: Investors, Corporations, and Markets. John Wiley & Sons, Inc, Hoboken, Canada.
Phelps, E.S., Pollak, R.A., 1968. On second-best national saving and game-equilibrium growth. Rev. Econ. Stud. 35, 185–199.
Pigou, A.C., 1920. The Economics of Welfare. Macmillan, London.
Poundstone, W., 1993. Prisoner's Dilemma: John von Neumann, Game Theory, and the Puzzle of the Bomb. Anchor Books, New York.
Rabin, M., Schrag, J.L., 1999. First impressions matter: a model of confirmatory bias. Q. J. Econ. 114 (1), 37–82.

Ramadorai, T., 2010. Institutional investors. In: Baker, K., Nofsinger, J. (Eds.), Behavioural Finance: Investors, Corporations, and Markets. John Wiley & Sons, Inc., Hoboken, NJ.
Rasmusen, E., 2006. Games and Information: An Introduction to Game Theory, fourth ed. Basil Blackwell Publishers, Oxford.
Read, R., Taleb, N., 2014. Religion, heuristics, and intergenerational risk management. Econ. J. Watch 11 (2), 219–226.
Reed, A., Forehand, M., Puntoni, S., Warlop, L., 2012. Identity-based consumer behaviour. Int. J. Res. Mark. 29, 310–321.
Rehman, S.S., Askari, H., 2010. How Islamic are Islamic countries? Glob. Econ. J. 10 (2), Art. 2. http://islamicity-index.org/wp/wp-content/uploads/2015/11/how-islamic-are-islamic-countries.pdf.
Rehman, S., Askari, H., 2013. The economic development of OIC countries: a survey. In: Iqbal, Z., Mirakhor, A., Uyanik, T. (Eds.), Islamic Finance and Economic Development. World Bank, Washington, DC. April 2013.
Rehman, S., Askari, H., 2010. How Islamic are Islamic countries? An Islamicity Index. Glob. Econ. J. 10 (2).
Reinganum, M., 1983. The anomalous stock market behaviour of small firms in January: empirical tests for tax-loss selling effects. J. Financ. Econ. 12 (1), 89–104.
Reinhart, C.M., Rogoff, K.S., 2011. From financial crash to debt crisis. Am. Econ. Rev. 101 (5), 1676–1706.
Ritter, J., 1991. The long-run performance of initial public offerings. J. Financ. 46 (1), 3–27.
Robbins, L., 1935. An Essay on the Nature and Significance of Economic Science. Macmillan, London.
Roca, C., Draief, M., Helbing, D., 2012. Coordination and competitive innovation spreading in social networks. In: Helbing, D. (Ed.), Social Self-Organization. Springer.
Roskos-Ewoldsen, D.R., Roskos-Ewoldsen, B., Dillman Carpentier, F., 2009. Media priming: an updated synthesis. In: Bryant, J., Oliver, M.B. (Eds.), Media Effects: Advances in Theory and Research. third ed, pp. 74–93.
Roth, A.E., Prasnikar, V., Okuno-Fujiwara, M., Zamir, S., 1991. Bargaining and market behaviour in Jerusalem, Ljubljana, Pittsburgh, and Tokyo: an experimental study. Am. Econ. Rev. 81, 1068–1095.
Rothstein, B. (Ed.), 2005. Social Traps and the Problem of Trust. Cambridge University Press, Cambridge.
Russo, J.E., Schoemaker, P.J.H., 1992. Managing overconfidence. Sloan Manag. Rev. 33 (2), 7–17.
Sadr, S.K., 2016. The Economic System of the Early Islamic Period: Institutions and Policies. Palgrave Macmillan, New York, NY.
Sahih International, The Holy Qur'ān: Translation and Commentary. https://quran.com/.
Sanfey, A.G., Rilling, J.K., Aronson, J.A., Nystrom, L.E., Cohen, J.D., 2003. The neural basis of economic decision-making in the Ultimatum Game. Science 300 (2003), 1755–1758.
Schelling, T.C., 1960. The Strategy of Conflict. Harvard University Press, Cambridge, MA.
Scheinkman, J., Xiong, W., 2003. Overconfidence and speculative bubbles. J. Polit. Econ. 111, 1183–1219.
Schoon, N., Nuri, J., 2012. Comparative Financial Systems in Judaism, Christianity and Islam: The Case of Interest. Working Paper, University of Surrey, Guildford.
Schotter, A., Weiss, A., Zapater, I., 1996. Fairness and survival in ultimatum and dictatorship games. J. Econ. Behav. Organ. 31, 37–56.
Schmid, A., 2004. Conflict and Cooperation: Institutional and Behavioural Economics. Blackwell Publishing, Malden, MA.
Selten, R., 2001. What is bounded rationality? In: Gigerenzer, G., Selten, R. (Eds.), Bounded Rationality: The Adaptive Toolbox. MIT Press, Cambridge, pp. 13–36.

Shariff, A., Norenzayan, A., 2007. God is watching you: priming god concepts increases prosocial behaviour in an anonymous economic game. Psychol. Sci. 18, 803–809.

Shefrin, 2007. Behavioral Corporate Finance. McGraw-Hill, New York.

Shefrin, H., Statman, M., 2000. Behavioural portfolio theory. J. Financ. Quant. Anal. 35, 127–152.

Shefrin, H., Statman, M., 1985. The disposition to sell winners too early and ride losers too long: theory and evidence. J. Financ. 40, 777–790.

Shiller, R.J., 2000. Irrational Exuberance. Princeton University Press, Princeton, NJ.

Shiller, R.J., 1981. Do stock prices move too much to be justified by subsequent changes in dividends? Am. Econ. Rev. 71 (3), 421–436.

Shiller, R.J., Pound, J., 1989. Survey evidence on the diffusion of interest and information among investors. J. Econ. Behav. Organ. 12 (1), 47–66.

Shin, H.S., Williamson, T., 1996. How much common belief is necessary for convention? Games Econ. Behav. 13, 252–268.

Shin, S.H., Hanna, S.D., 2014. Racial/ethnic difference in risky assets ownership after the financial crisis. Acad. Finan. Serv., https://academyfinancial.org/resources/Documents/Proceedings/2013/G4_Shin_Hanna.pdf.

Shirley, M., 2005. Institutions and development. In: Menard, C., Shirley, M. (Eds.), Handbook of New Institutional Economics. Kluwer Academic Publishers, Dordrecht.

Shleifer, A., 2000. Inefficient Markets: An Introduction to Behavioural Finance. Oxford University Press, New York.

Simon, H.A., 1955. A behavioral model of rational choice. Q. J. Econ. 69 (1), 99–118, compiled in, and quoted from, Simon (1957: 241–260).

Simon, H., 1976. From substantive to procedural rationality. In: Latsis, S.J. (Ed.), Method and Appraisal in Economics. Cambridge University Press, Cambridge, pp. 129–148.

Singh, A., Jain-Chandra, S., Mohommad, A., 2012. Out of the shadows. IMF Financ. Dev. 49 (2), 42–45.

Skyrms, B., 2001. The Stag Hunt. Pacific Division of the American Philosophical Association, San Diego, CA.

Slovic, P., Finucane, M., Peters, E., MacGregor, D., 2002. The affect heuristic. In: Gilovich, T., Griffin, D., Kahneman, D. (Eds.), Heuristics and Biases: The Psychology of Intuitive Judgment. Cambridge University Press, New York and Cambridge, England, pp. 397–420.

Slovic, P., Fischhoff, B., 1977. On the psychology of experimental surprises. J. Exp. Psychol. Hum. Percept. Perform. 3 (4), 544–551.

Smith, A., 1776. An Inquiry into the Nature and Causes of the Wealth of Nations, 1. 1st ed. W. Strahan, London.

Smith, V.L., 2000. Bargaining and Market Behaviour: Essays in Experimental Economics. Cambridge University Press, New York.

Spence, A., Leygue, C., Bedwell, B., O'Malley, C., 2014. Engaging with energy reduction: does a climate change frame have the potential for achieving broader sustainable behaviour? J. Environ. Psychol. 38, 17–28.

Stael von Holstein, C.-A.S., 1972. Probabilistic forecasting: an experiment related to the stock market. Organ. Behav. Hum. Perform. 8 (1), 139–158.

Stafford, T., Dewar, M., 2014. Tracing the trajectory of skill learning with a very large sample of online game players. Psychol. Sci. 25, 511–518.

Stanovich, K.E., West, R.F., 2000. Individual differences in reasoning: implications for the rationality debate. Behav. Brain Sci. 23 (5), 645–665.

Steenkamp, J., de Jong, M.G., 2012. A global investigation into the constellation of consumer attitudes toward global and local products. J. Mark. 74, 18–40.

Stein, J.C., 1996. Rational capital budgeting in an irrational world. J. Bus. 69 (4), 429–455.

Sugden, R., 1986. The Economics of Rights, Co-operation, and Welfare. Blackwell, Oxford.

Surowiecki, J., 2004. The Wisdom of Crowds: Why the Many Are Smarter than the Few and How Collective Wisdom Shapes Business, Economics, Societies, and Nations. Doubleday, New York.

Taffler, R., Tuckett, D., 2010. Emotional finance: the role of the unconscious in financial decisions. In: Baker, K., Nofsinger, J. (Eds.), Behavioural Finance: Investors, Corporations, and Markets. John Wiley & Sons, Inc., Hoboken, NJ.

Takooshian, H., 2014. Not just a bystander: the 1964 Kitty Genovese Tragedy: what have we learned? Psychology Today. March 24, 2014.

Tang, Z., Chen, X., Luo, J., 2011. Determining socio-psychological drivers for rural household recycling behaviour in developing countries: a case study from Wugan, Hunan, China. Environ. Behav. 43 (6), 848–877.

Tetlock, P.C., 2007. Giving content to investor sentiment: the role of media in the stock market. J. Financ. 62 (3), 1139–1168.

Thaler, R.H., 1992. The Winner's Curse: Paradoxes and Anomalies of Economic Life. Princeton University Press, Princeton, NJ.

Thaler, R., Sunstein, C., 2008. Nudge: Improving Decisions about Health, Wealth and Happiness. Yale University Press, New Haven, CT.

Thøgersen, J., 1999. Spillover processes in the development of a sustainable consumption pattern. J. Econ. Psychol. 20, 53–81.

Tomasello, M., 2014. A Natural History of Human Thinking. Harvard University Press, Cambridge, MA.

Tietenberg, T., 1994. Environmental Economics and Policy. Harper Collins College, New York.

Tuckett, D., 2009. Addressing the Psychology of Financial Markets. Economics Discussion Papers 2009-37. Available from: http://www.economics-ejournal.org/economics/discussionpapers/2009-37.

Tuckett, D., Taffler, R., 2008. Phantastic objects and the financial market's sense of reality: a psychoanalytic contribution to the understanding of stock market instability. Int. J. Psychoanal. 89 (2), 389–412.

Tversky, A., Kahneman, D., 1981. The framing of decisions and the psychology of choice. Science 211 (4481), 453–458.

Tyszka, T., Zielonka, P., 2002. Expert judgments: financial analysts versus. weather forecasters. J. Psychol. Finan. Markets 3, 152–160.

Van Huyck, J., Battalio, R., Bei, R., 1990. Tacit coordination games, strategic uncertainty, and coordination failure. Am. Econ. Rev. 80, 234–248.

Von Neumann, J., Morgenstern, O., 1953. Theory of Games and Economic Behaviour. Princeton University Press, Princeton, NJ.

Wade-Benzoni, K., Tenbrunsel, A., Bazerman, M., 1996. Egocentric interpretations of fairness in asymmetric, environmental social dilemmas: explaining harvesting behaviour and the role of communication. Organ. Behav. Hum. Decis. Process. 67 (2), 111–126.

Wagenaar, W.A., Keren, G.B., 1986. Does the expert know? The reliability of predictions and confidence ratings of experts. In: Hollnagel, E., Mancini, G., Woods, D.D. (Eds.), Intelligent Decision Support in Process Environments. Springer, Berlin, pp. 87–107.

Wason, P., 1960. On the failure to eliminate hypotheses in a conceptual task. Q. J. Exp. Psychol. 12 (3), 129–140.

Wetherick, N.E., 1962. Eliminative and enumerative behaviour in a conceptual task. Q. J. Exp. Psychol. 14 (4), 246–249.

Wicker, B., Keysers, C., Plailly, J., Royet, J.-P., Gallese, V., Rizzolatti, G., 2003. Both of us disgusted in my insula: the common neural basis of seeing and feeling disgust. Neuron 40, 655–664.

Willer, R., 2009. Groups reward individual sacrifice: the status solution to the collective action problem. Am. Sociol. Rev. 74 (1), 23–43.

Williamson, O., 1989. Transaction cost economics. In: Schmanlensee, R., Willig, R. (Eds.), Handbook of Industrial Organization, vol. 1. Elsevier Science, Amsterdam, pp. 136–182.
Williamson, O.E., 1998. Transaction cost economics: how it works, where it is headed. De Economist 146 (January), 23–58.
Williamson, O.E., 2000. The new institutional economics: taking stock, looking ahead. J. Econ. Lit. 38 (3), 595–613.
Wheeler, S.C., Petty, R.E., 2001. The effects of stereotype activation on behaviour: a review of possible mechanisms. Psychol. Bull. 127 (6), 797–826.
Wolfe, P.J., 2013. Making sense of big data. Proc. Natl. Acad. Sci. U. S. A. 110, 18031–18032.
World Bank, 2015. World Development Report 2015: Mind, Society, and Behaviour. World Bank, Washington, DC.
Wright, P., He, G., Shapira, N.A., Goodman, W.K., Liu, Y., 2004. Disgust and the insula: fMRI responses to pictures of mutilation and contamination. Neuroreport 15 (15), 2347–2351.
Yearbook of Statistics Singapore, 2015. Department of Statistics, Ministry of Trade & Industry, Republic of Singapore, ISSN 0583-3655. http://istmat.info/files/uploads/50355/yearbook_of_statistics_singapore_2015.pdf.
Zimbardo, P., 2014. Dr. Philip Zimbardo on the Bystander Effect and the Murder of Kitty Genovese. Bystander Revolution. www.bystanderrevolution.org. Retrieved 18 June 2015.

INDEX

Note: Page numbers followed by *f* indicate figures, *t* indicate tables and *b* indicate boxes.

Kolibri 360 GmbH
Ferdinand-Jühlke-Straße 7
99095 Erfurt, Deutschland
produktsicherheit@kolibri360.de